ALSO BY ABDUL WADUD KARIM AMRULLAH

Dari Subuh Hingga Malam
(From Dawn Until Dusk)

# SUMATRAN WARRIOR

## MIGHTY MAN OF LOVE AND COURAGE

Abdul Wadud Karim Amrullah

WESTBOW
PRESS®
A DIVISION OF THOMAS NELSON
& ZONDERVAN

Scripture taken from the Holy Bible, NEW INTERNATIONAL VERSION®. Copyright © 1973, 1978, 1984 by Biblica, Inc. All rights reserved worldwide. Used by permission. NEW INTERNATIONAL VERSION® and NIV® are registered trademarks of Biblica, Inc. Use of either trademark for the offering of goods or services requires the prior written consent of Biblica US, Inc.

Scripture taken from the *Amplified Bible*, copyright © 1954, 1958, 1962, 1964, 1965, 1987 by The Lockman Foundation. Used by permission.

All Scripture quotations in this publications are from The Message. Copyright © by Eugene H. Peterson 1993, 1994, 1995, 1996, 2000, 2001, 2002. Used by permission of NavPress Publishing Group.

WestBow Press books may be ordered through booksellers or by contacting:

WestBow Press
A Division of Thomas Nelson & Zondervan
1663 Liberty Drive
Bloomington, IN 47403
www.westbowpress.com
1 (866) 928-1240

ISBN: 978-1-5127-3182-8 (sc)
ISBN: 978-1-5127-3183-5 (hc)
ISBN: 978-1-5127-3181-1 (e)

Library of Congress Control Number: 2016902718

Print information available on the last page.

WestBow Press rev. date: 5/16/2016

My deepest gratitude goes to all my family and friends in Indonesia and the United States, who have given in prayer, the editing process, additional technical help, and financial support, to ensure publication of this book. My profound thank you for your time and giving with this project, and making it become reality for God's glory.

~~~~~~~~~~

I dedicate this book to all the faithful co-workers and supporters of my vision for the Minangkabau people of West Sumatra, Indonesia of whom I will forever be a part. God brought us together for this purpose and season. Your hard work, courage and faithfulness is counted beyond this world.

*To: Rehana, Sutan and Siti;*
*Tyson, Jerry, Ariani, and Anaya*

*My real purpose for writing this autobiography is not only as a testimony or witness of my life experiences, but especially to tell you about God's greatness. I openly share my story especially as a dedication to all of you as my children and grandchildren, to know and appreciate as well, the richness and greatness of your Minangkabau heritage. I hope you enjoy reading my words and will always remember that I love you and pray that God will continually bless your own life journeys.*
*To me you are a "greatest blessing" in life.*
*Remember always, my favorite verses of Jeremiah 29:11-13.*

*With all my love,*
*Daddy*

*"BABO"*

# CONTENTS

## SECTION FOUR: 1981 – 1991

## SECTION FIVE: 1991 – 2011

# FOREWORD

As I was speaking to a large audience, one man's face kept catching my attention amidst the sea of faces. It was hard to take my eyes off him, because his face was so bright. Then I saw his smile. It was contagious. His family lovingly surrounded him. You could tell they were proud of their father. His name was Willy Amrull – Abdul Wadud Karim Amrullah.

After the service, I approached him and said, "Something is up with you. You're glowing!" I later found out from his family that he too felt a strong connection with me. The moment felt as if I had met my long lost brother, or father. I like to think for him, I may have been like a younger brother he ran with during the Indonesian Revolution. I was someone who understood some of his heart for the world, his dreams for a church without walls, his yearning for the world to know the love of Isa Almasih that he grew to love.

I had already met his wife and children. If he was like them, it would be an easy relationship. His wife Vera, strong, steadfast, compassionate, courageous and maternal in her presence, carries herself like royalty. Both of them have an authority filled with confidence but with such love, grace, tenderness and hope. It is unusual. As I have gotten to know the family, they all have a spirit like their parents.

Behind Willy's gentle face, I saw a strong man. I learned over the years that the most influential people are not necessarily loud. The quiet ones that are not seen, the ones who know how to move in and out of light and shadows, the ones who can be silent yet stir revolution, are few and live among us unnoticed. Willy Amrull (a.k.a. Abdul Wadud Karim Amrullah) was one of these soft-spoken giants. He was a Sumatran Warrior but armed with a different type of weapon from his earlier days of the Indonesian Revolution.

His life was about waiting on God. Being able to hold back power is harder than just unleashing it. Willy embodied this type of life. Willy would take jobs that some consider beneath them, but Willy was on a quest where he dared to explore the unknown. He would do anything to find life. His journey overseas to countries around the world was part of his journey to taste a life that he yearned for and later found in *Isa Almasih*, Jesus the Messiah. That is why I think Isa became his pure obsession because nothing and no one filled his thirst for adventure and freedom like the Isa that met him personally. He chose Isa because nothing could bring as much inner joy and contentment, yet lead him into the adventure and fun that his soul naturally craved for since being a young boy in Indonesia.

I still remember a Saturday evening a few months after the moment I saw Willy glowing in church. I discovered that he had fallen ill. I did not know for sure if he was going to recover or if this battle would be his last. For some reason I felt an urgency to go see him immediately. So I gathered some little snacks that I thought he'd like, candy and some fruit.

I walked in to see him at his home where he was already in hospice care. His children told me he was not expected to live much longer. He was in the winter of his life here on earth. As I looked at him, his physical strength was failing, but he was still a man on fire. The glow remained. Looking back, it was probably because with each passing day the visitation of God was getting more evident to him, more real. Songs filled the room. Memories must have flooded his mind bringing joy and hope for the future he knew was bright for his family and his home country of Indonesia. He was a father wanting to pass on his spiritual inheritance.

He took my hand and smiled with the infectious smile that could light up a city. Tears filling his eyes and mine, we shared a few words, scriptures, songs, and prayed together. I will never forget that night. It would not be until I read this book, which is in your hand, that I grew to know Willy's entire story. He was a broken man who had been thrust in the furnace of criticism, ridicule, institutional attack, marginalization, abuse, homelessness, wandering, misunderstanding by those near and far, and even among the former Muslim followers of Isa Almasih – Jesus Christ.

Willy loved Indonesia so much that he held back sharing his whole story till after he died, because he wanted to show respect to his Muslim Minangkabau family members. He did not want to embarrass them or bringing any shame to them. Even in lieu of the relentless requests for him to share his story widely, he knew there would be a day the unveiling of his journey would have the greatest impact. Today is that day!

While reading Willy's life story, I felt I could read between the lines. It was as if I was having a cup of tea with him, and he was openly sharing his life with me. Even during his pauses, I knew what his silence meant. I could feel his heart as I read each word. Reading this book changed me and you will be as well.

I got a taste of his love and respect for Indonesia, Muslims, and the Minangkabau people. His love for Isa Almasih, his Savior, drove him to places, people, pain, and pleasure few on earth will ever experience. I am sure his heart desire was that all would know this Isa Almasih whom he had encountered later in life. His personal relationship would bring him supernatural joy, life, love and freedom like no other.

As you read this book, you will catch Willy's passion and heart. If you do, Willy Amrull – Abdul Wadud Karim Amrullah – will live on through you. You will receive this mantle of the Sumatran Warrior armed with the greatest weapon on the planet – LOVE.

Willy, I thank you for your willingness to share your adventure. Thank you for sharing the glory and the suffering, the beauty and the brokenness. Few have more impact on earth after their death than when they lived. You are one of those chosen ones, beloved of God. You are one of the children of the King. Your children and others are carrying what you prayed for and dreamed about most. Your dream lives on!

I am looking forward to seeing your smile again someday soon.

Your brother,
Dave Gibbons

Lead Pastor
NEWSONG CHURCH Santa Ana, California, USA

# INTRODUCTION

**Abdul Wadud Karim Amrullah** was born in the village of Sungai Batang, Maninjau, West Sumatra, in Indonesia on June 7, 1927 as the youngest son of seven children. He spent his childhood in his native region of West Sumatra. His education began in 1934 in a Dutch colonial government school. Abdul Wadud later transferred to a school, which also focused more deeply on Islamic studies. His father, Dr. Haji Abdul Karim Amrullah, was a renowned and popular Islamic cleric, a reformist, and much-respected leader of the Gerakan Kaum Muda – Youth Movement (a movement for Islamic reform in Minangkabau).

Abdul Wadud followed his father, when the Dutch colonial government exiled him to Sukabumi, West Java in 1941. He attended Sekolah Taman Siswa there, the school where he developed strong national pride for his country. The Japanese occupation of Indonesia ended the exile of his father in 1942, allowing them to move to Jakarta. Abdul Wadud continued his education there at Taman Siswa School by day and helped teach the Quran during evenings. Due to political conditions at that time, the educational system could not complete his insatiable desire for learning.

As turmoil continued in Indonesia, 18-year-old Abdul Wadud joined the API – Angkatan Pemuda Indonesia (Youth Movement of Indonesia), and soon became group leader of an API Division. Under Abdul Wadud's leadership, this division's main task was to prevent the Netherlands/NICA soldiers from entering villages and suburbs of Jakarta.

After fighting in the Indonesian Revolution, Abdul Wadud's desire to seek experience abroad, made him willing to start by working onboard ship as a laundry man. In early 1949, Abdul Wadud left Indonesia and worked on ships with lines to major cities in countries around the world including the United States. At the end of 1950, he and several friends left their ship while in San Francisco, immediately finding temporary work in California farm fields. In 1952, Abdul Wadud accepted a position at the Indonesian Supply Mission in New York. He later transferred to the Indonesian Consulate in San Francisco, where he functioned as Public Relations Information Officer for almost twenty years.

While living in the United States, Abdul Wadud took on the name *"Willy Amrull,"* the name by which the majority of friends in the US knew him. In 1962, Willy Amrull founded the IMI–Ikatan Masyarakat Indonesia (Indonesian Community Center) which he led with activities for people of Indonesian heritage in America.

In 1977, he returned to Indonesia with his wife and children with intention that they be a "good Muslim family." After being a devout Muslim for fifty-four years, Abdul Wadud made the decision to begin his life as a follower of Christ in 1981 while living on the island of Bali. Baptized in Jakarta, February of 1983, he, his wife and their three children, returned that same year to the United States. In 1983, Abdul Wadud entered Talbot Theological Seminary followed by Fuller Theological Seminary, both in California. He was ordained in 1989.

Realizing God wanted Him to reach out to a church "without walls," he knew that he must obey, by returning to Indonesia and his beloved West Sumatra. His work among his own Minangkabau people began in 1995. For the last three decades of his life, Abdul Wadud faithfully served God in both Indonesia and the United States.

SUMATRAN WARRIOR: *Mighty Man of Love and Courage*, describes the singular journey of Abdul Wadud Karim Amrullah. This journey brought Pastor "Willy Amrull" ultimately to the most beautiful peak of his lifetime, the full commitment of serving his Master with joy, love and courageous faith.

Wardhani Soedjono

Author
Jakarta, Indonesia

# AUTHOR'S MESSAGE

In 2007, I took my last trip to West Sumatra, Indonesia, while in declining health. At that time, I had such a sense of happiness, joy and delight seeing abundant growth in the maturing faith of the Spiritual children, *anak-anak Rohani* I had left there a few years earlier. Witnessing what God had done for them encouraged me.

I knew after this particular trip that I would not be traveling so far again to see my beautiful *Ranah Minang,* land of the Minangkabau, where I was born. Through these circumstances, I realized that time had finally arrived for me to tell my story and write this book.

I thank God that this memoir was first published in Indonesia under the title DARI SUBUH HINGGA MALAM, (From Dawn Until Dusk). Suggestions to write this book came a long time ago, but I disregarded offers to publish because of issues I felt would develop if I shared my story prematurely. I believed it might become an obstacle for people who did not understand my purpose. It is my hope for readers to have wisdom and tolerance from deep within as I openly share my life's journey. It is my desire to give God all the glory through the recounts from birth until advanced age, as a legacy of faith for future generations. I thank all the friends in Indonesia and the US, who supported me, have prayed, assisted and provided me advice as this writing project developed.

With support of my beloved wife Vera, this book was completed. I feel blessed to have such a faithful wife who helped me gather and organize information for my writing of the manuscripts (Indonesian and English). I am grateful and endlessly proud of Vera. How thankful I am to God for giving me the best "helpmate."

I am also grateful to my children and grandchildren. Through past years, they have experienced the adventures and challenges of life with me, in America as well as Indonesia. Without the trust and love of my family for me, none of this would have been possible. I am aware of their gift and that we have overcome much with God's love.

I have learned that even when our lives seem chaotic or out of control, all power remains in God's hand, and nothing can hinder Him. For me that was experiencing the Shadow of the Almighty, which I have felt through the years.

Finally, I wish every reader *selamat membaca*, happy reading. May you enjoy our time together as you walk with me through every page of this memoir. In addition, may God richly bless your own journey today and with every tomorrow!

Abdul Wadud Karim Amrullah – Willy Amrull
California, USA –

# SOLDIER FOR THE CROSS

"You have your orders – I send you to battle.
You are a soldier,
and I would not promise a soldier ease.
I promise you difficulty, but with it, resources and
purpose and joy.
Go to where men die of thirst
a stone's throw from pure water…
go back as my water-bearer.

Quote from ~ "Edge of Eternity" by Randy Alcorn
(From: "In Light of Eternity" PERSPECTIVES
on HEAVEN by Randy Alcorn)

# SECTION ONE

*1935 – 1949*

# 1

# DAWN OF BEGINNINGS

"Run, Wadud, run, *lakeh-lah pulang;* darkness is falling!" As I hastily dart forward, the terrifying voice shouts within me. Perspiration oozes down my face, neck, and back. I run as fast as my small feet can take me moving down the narrow village road. "Hurry; go home quick, *lakeh-lah pulang,* before it is too late!"

Glancing upward every few moments, I can see the sky frightfully spewing its fiery glow over the waters of *Danau Maninjau,* the lake of my West Sumatra village. Casting ever-changing hues of red, swirling oranges, and glaring yellows over my lakeside village of *Sungai Batang,* it seems like the great vault of heaven has suddenly opened and is crashing down upon the earth. I am running toward home as fast as I can, thinking my life depends on it!

A red and yellow sky in my child-like thinking is like the flames of *Neraka,* Hades-blazing fires, which I had heard about during afternoon Muslim religious classes. In my mind, the end of the world is coming. I fear that if I am not home on time, I might not find *Amak,* my mother, there! Besides, if this really is the end of the world, I need to be safe at home and near my mother's presence. It is there I know I am safe, secure, and loved by her.

With the closing of this day, the flaming colors in the sky rapidly change. Nighttime is quickly falling upon my *kampuang,* my village of Sungai Batang where I was born. The year is 1935; I am a young boy, seven years old.

"Beyond all roads of adventures and oceans of experiences,
life travels to its ultimate destiny.
Along the way it brings hope and purpose,
planned by God long ago."
Abdul Wadud Karim Amrullah

(From: Personal Journal)

In late October of 1948, amid the city's bustle and vehicle fumes, my friend Ahmad and I climb onto a bus that takes us through Jakarta streets busy with early morning traffic. With the sun already brightly shining and the tropical heat rising, we maneuver ourselves onboard the rickety old bus.

Together with countless others both seated and standing, we pass by horse-drawn *delman*, cart-like carriages, and three-wheeled *becaks*, most also carrying passengers. The bus strategically manages to weave through the chaos of automobiles, countless bicycles, and pedestrians precariously attempting to cross the busy streets.

Earlier that day, Ahmad had encouraged me to come along with him. He finally received news that he could take the required physical exam for a job on one of the large Dutch ships docked at Tanjung Priok Harbor. For that day's examination, ten men were expected. We arrive early at the harbor. Ahmad immediately walks toward the group of men already gathered and joins them in waiting for that day's roll call. A short distance away, I see a place for me to pass the time. I turn and cross toward it. After climbing atop a large wooden spool of coiled rope, I sit myself down along the waterfront edge.

I feel ocean breezes gently come my way, delivering balmy scents. Coming to our Indonesian shores from faraway places, these currents caress and awaken senses within me that deeply touch the core of my being. Sitting there, my mind races, bringing waves of questions I desperately need answered.

A wandering restlessness is set in motion within my soul. I only recently returned from fighting and the battlefield. Three years ago, at age eighteen, along with many of my friends, I too had passionately offered myself to the call of being part of Indonesia's revolution. Even now as I sit here, the struggle for independence and the duress in people's lives constantly remains. The battle of unceasing turmoil and the fight for freedom incessantly surround me. I wonder about the uncertainties of my own future and what lies ahead for me in Indonesia.

Silently I cry to Allah, "God, what are you going to do with me now? What are you going to do with the country I have fought for?" Frustration and restlessness continue building within me. With my gaze still out toward the ocean, I somewhat rebelliously express to Allah, "I am tired of praying and trying to perfectly follow your commands! What are you going to do with my life, God?"

The longing to see the world has been within me since the earlier days of my childhood in Sungai Batang, West Sumatra. Those days, however, seem far away with no return.

A commotion nearby suddenly interrupts my thoughts. It is the frantic voice of the shipping company's *mandor darat,* the shore agent. In desperation, he is calling out a name of one more person registered on the physical exam list.

The shore agent's voice becomes louder and shrill in pitch, as he approaches the water's edge where I am sitting. Having promised the shipping company a full roster of names, he knows he must do his job well in order to keep it. Thus, the shore agent's voice is rapidly rising along with his distress.

Realizing the situation, my reaction is swift. I jump down from where I am sitting and hurry toward the man. I respond to his calling, asking him if I could possibly take the missing man's place. While looking me up and down he asks, "What experience do you have? Do you iron?"

Knowing who the shore agent is and where he is from, I reply in the polite, soft-spoken Sundanese dialect I have learned, "Yes, I am capable of what is required." In actuality, I have no experience at all in laundry room work. However, in that split second as the two of us intently look at one another, all uncertainties about my future somehow vanish. For in this moment during 1948, destiny's passage for me to see the world broadens as far and as wide as any ocean could possibly reach. I am twenty-one years old.

# 2

# EARLY SUMATRA SHADOWS

God has given you this day, live it well from dawn till end.
For when it's said and passed, you will want some treasure that will last:
a memory of love, God's love and your own.
Alva Pingel

I had become aware of prayer at a very early age. During the month of Ramadhan, our month of fasting within the Muslim religion, it was my father's habit to rise each morning before dawn while staying at the *kutubkhannah*, his library located in nearby Muara Pauh, a short distance from Sungai Batang. On these early mornings, *Ayah*, my father, would go to the water's edge of Lake Maninjau, which was close to the library. There he would step into one of the small fishing canoes tied up at the lakeshore and then slowly row out, his lips moving in constant silent recitation of verses from the Quran, our religion's holy book.

During special religious times, Ayah would remain at his library for prayer, writing and teaching. He would later leave his kutubkhannah and return home to be with us at the main house, only a mile or so from his library. Even then, it was still his habit to awaken early and be completely absorbed on reflections of Allah, God Almighty.

Echoing in the dawn, the slow deep reverberating beats and then faster rhythms of the *beduk* (drum) followed by *muezzin* -- a single voice atop the minaret from the *mesjid*, a mosque -- not far from our home, announced the call for *Subuh*, early morning prayers to our community. The voice resonated through the morning air, ushering in the dawn of each new day.

6

*ALLAHU AKBAR, ALLAHU AKBAR!*
God is great, God is great!

*HAIYA'ALASSALAH, HAIYA'ALASSALAH!*
Let us pray, let us pray!

As usual, in Minangkabau manner, I would be sleeping on the floor of our great room outside my parent's bedroom. Welcoming the day, Ayah would come out to where I lay sleeping. He would stop and softly snap his fingers several times, quietly calling out my name. I would hear him whisper, "Dud, Wadud, *jago-lah sembahyang*, Dud, Wadud, come; it's time to pray."

I remember the sound of Ayah's feet stepping through the house. I would get up and follow him as he went to prepare with *wudhu*, the Islamic cleansing ritual of washing face, hands, and feet with water before recitation of prayers. As if not a moment has passed since those early days of my childhood, the image of my father, who he was, and his love for me remain in the corridor of my memories.

I was born in the village of Kubu, Sungai Batang, Maninjau, West Sumatra, Indonesia, on June 7, 1927 (*6 Zulhijjah 1345 H*). I did not know the actual date of my birth until 1952, after my brother Abdul Malik recovered this information from one of our father's journals. My parents gave me the name Abdul Wadud Karim Amrullah, and I am the youngest child among the seven children of Dr. Haji Abdul Karim Amrullah. My father was an *ulema*, a Muslim scholar, and one of the leaders of the *Gerakan Kaum Muda*, a popular youth movement held in high regard for the reformation and modernization of Islam in Minangkabau.

My mother, whose name was Siti Hindun, was my father's second wife. Ayah never divorced my mother as he did other wives through the years. *Amak* belonged to the *suku Malayu*, people clan, while my father's suku was *Jambak*. Within the Minangkabau culture, our society is matrilineal; thus, I followed my mother's lineage of her suku Malayu.

Even though I am the youngest of my father's seven children, my mother had also previously given birth to two other daughters, both of whom died while they were very small. My other brothers and sisters were children from three other wives. The oldest was Fathimah, a daughter with

Ayah's first wife Raihanah, who passed away in Mecca while *Ayah* studied there. Then there were Abdul Malik (Hamka), Abdul Kuddus, Asma, and Abdul Mu'thi -- all four children from *Ayah*'s third wife, Safiyah. A son Abdul Bari was born ten years prior to my own birth, and was the child from my father's fourth wife Rafi'ah. Even though my six other siblings were from different mothers, within the Minangkabau culture we are not considered half brothers and sisters because we are all from the same father by birth.

Throughout the Minangkabau region, my father was well known and highly respected. Many called him, "Inyiek De ER" or "Haji Rasul." (The word "Rasul" means "a messenger from God," one who receives revelation of scripture.) Through the years, my father married twelve times. Ayah married my mother after his first wife, Raihanah, died in Mecca.

Two wives he never divorced. One was my mother Siti Hindun who remained married to him for thirty-eight years until her death. Our Muslim religion permitted him four wives simultaneously. However, my father always made certain to divorce, so as not to have too many wives at one time. When I was still small, during the Muslim fasting month of *Ramadhan*, I remember my father would not rotate his turns of staying with each wife, as was the custom of Minangkabau men who had two or more wives. However, during my childhood, both his wives were Amak, my mother, and my stepmother Dariyah, who I called Etek. Ayah did not have any children with Etek who lived in Kampung Tangah, a village several miles from the kutubkhannah, library, in Muara Pauh, where it was easiest for my father to stay.

Because Ayah remained at his library throughout the *puasa* fasting period every year, he always woke up during these times at about three o'clock in the morning before *Subuh* prayer to go out and fish quietly by myself. I later learned that even before I was born, my father used his library for praying and teaching during each year's fasting month of Ramadhan. Since he did not have to rotate visits with other wives who lived further away, it was simpler for him to stay in Muara Pauh. When I was still small, both Amak and my stepmother Etek would sometimes come there together during the fasting month. Both would bring their specially prepared delicacies for *buka-puasa*, the breaking of fast. I would come along with my mother, and if we remained for the night, all of us would sleep in one large bed. I do not think it was for any particular reason, but I remember that my stepmother would rest on my father's right side, while my mother would be on Ayah's left. I would be soundly sleeping on my mother's left side nearest the wall.

As I was growing up, I often heard that my mother was always the person helping influence my father in choosing his new wives. Two of her strongest criteria regarding the women were that they had to be beautiful and be virgins, since her husband was a person of prominence known as *orang jemputan,* a worthy person sought after in Minang tradition. My father often received marriage proposals. The parents of potential brides were always very willing and proud to have an *ulema,* Muslim scholar, join their family.

When allowed by my mother, I very much liked staying with Ayah at his library. As I grew older, I would lie on the floor on my stomach. My head resting on propped hands, knees bent and soles of my feet upward; I enjoyed this position while looking through publications with pictures. I usually had the companionship of one of Ayah's cats beside me. My father would be nearby preparing his teaching materials. This image of contentment remains forever in my mind.

CHILDHOOD HOPES… In the days before starting school, my father often took me with him to Padang Panjang where he lectured at several schools. At that time both of my cousins, Salimah and Halimah (daughters of my aunt Jamilah), were studying at Diniyah School where Ayah was also one of the lecturers. As we traveled to Padang Panjang, the hired car typically provided for my father stopped in the town of Matur. Here we would lunch at our favorite restaurant specializing in Minang food. Each time, I very much enjoyed the treats of my favorite spicy dishes.

Sometimes Amak came along with us. It was during one of these occasions she went to the *pasar,* an open-air market place to do her shopping and had me come with her. We usually walked by a store which sold a selection of bicycles. I always wanted to have a tricycle, and each time passing the store brought to mind again, how much I wanted one. I would have my mother stop long enough so that I could take one more look then attempt to convince her to buy me a tricycle, even if it meant becoming whinier rather than convincing in my efforts.

Because I had repeatedly asked for a tricycle, Amak quietly let my father know about our brief stops at the store. Finally, during one of our trips, my parents surprised me with a shiny red tricycle, which I then brought back to our village with great boyhood joy. That was a happy day, and I immediately shared riding the new tricycle with my friends. This was all much more fun, because prior to being the proud owner of that tricycle, I had used my imagination in pretending to ride a smooth rock, shaped like a bicycle seat in front of our house. "This now is great fun!" I thought. To have a real tricycle with real wheels that moved me from place to place was fantastic!

At age five, I began practicing one of Islam's most important religious duties of following the *ibadah puasa*, which is the habit of fasting for thirty days during the month of Ramadhan*,* regularly observed during the ninth month of the Islamic lunar calendar. During the fasting month, I went to visit my grandmother Tarwasa (who was Ayah's mother and whom I called *Andung*). She always tried persuading me to fast for only half a day because I was too small. My grandmother worried I might become ill because of feeling hungry. Andung did not want her grandson *diambek jalan lapa* -- a Minang expression meaning that if walking on the road of fasting followed too early, hunger would discourage me. Therefore, Andung always prepared goodies for me in her kitchen, delicious treats usually left over from *sahur*, the last meal eaten prior to sun-up and start of the day's fast.

Even though I knew I was supposed to obey my grandmother, I would feel disappointed if I did not at least try to fast just a little longer on that day. Thus, I held my hunger, because even at such a young age I wanted to show people that I was willing to obey Allah's commands even though I was a little boy. I never knew Amak's mother however. My grandmother, *nenek Sarat*, died when I was born. However, I still knew *kakek Thoyib*, my mother's father, because he lived with us in Sungai Batang. When I would later leave the village, my grandfather Thoyib was still alive.

With child-like zeal, I was also serious in following the *ibadah solat*, the Islamic act of praying five times a day. If my parents did not wake me up for the *Subuh* morning prayers, I would become very upset and begin crying.

Starting at this young age also, I was fearful each time I saw a blazing red sky appear above the lake at sunset. I ran home quickly because it seemed as if the heavens would fall onto the earth and cover the lake. I was very afraid that God would put me in *neraka,* (Hades). In my thinking, it meant that if tossed into the fiery flames of *neraka,* I could no longer be with my mother. Perhaps because I was her only child and she had already passed the age of forty when giving birth to me, my mother really spoiled me very much. Whenever Ayah was away from home, I always slept with Amak until I was about seven years old. When I started going to school, I felt reluctant to sleep with my mother because I was afraid my friends would find out and then tease me.

Being a wise, kindhearted, and soft-spoken woman, Amak also taught me never to take anything that did not belong to us. Even fruit like *jambu,* rose apple, from someone else's trees or a kernel of *sipulut,* sweet-rice, from a neighbor's supply was wrong. She always taught me to ask permission first from the owner. My mother also reminded me to love orphans, and told me that even the kind act of stroking their heads would eventually reap me rewards from God.

The impression of Amak's words remained with me. Opportunity to follow what she had said, would sometime later come by way of my two cousins: Jamaluddin (nicknamed Anyah) who was orphaned, and Arifsuddin (we called him Utin), who still had both his parents. Utin would complain that I was mean only to him and not to Anyah, because I showed favor to Anyah. This was probably because I was rather temperamental while we played our games, and according to him, I never reacted harshly enough whenever it came to Anyah. What could I say? I wanted to make him understand what my mother had told me.

During those days, both Utin and Anyah were my constant playing mates, but Utin wanted to make certain he would undoubtedly remain number one on my list of favorites. What he did not realize was that even though we had relation as cousins, he was already number one with me as a friend.

FROM WADUD TO AH-WAY… As I got a little older, I wanted all my friends to call me *Awe* (pronounced "Ah-Way"). When they called me by my given name Wadud, I pretended not to hear them. Therefore, my nickname *Uo Awe,* older brother, first began with those who were smaller than I was.

At that time the Muslim Muhammadiyah organization (which my father had established in the Minangkabau area) had their own boy scout troops called **H**izbul **W**athan or initialed HW (Indonesian pronunciation: "Ha-Way"). Thus, even when I was five years old, I already wanted to be a Boy Scout when I became big. I enjoyed watching the older school boys march around through the narrow streets of our village. The marching was neatly in step, always following the beat of several drums and many bamboo flutes. Fascinated by all this, it did not take long for me to want to lead a marching band of my own since it reminded me of leading soldiers or warriors into battle. I did this by gathering all my little friends together and using at least one large discarded empty kerosene container on which I loudly banged and clanged.

One time, it was already dark, and I failed to go home on time. After swimming, I went to watch *pencak silat* in front of the *surau*, which was our village's communal meeting-prayer house located in front of the mosque. The *surau* was the place young men and boys learned the Minangkabau art of self-defense, *pencak silat* (like martial arts).

Since night had fallen, my mother came looking for me. Carrying an *obor*, torch, to light her way, I could hear my mother repeatedly calling me from a distance, *"Wadud, pulang-lah,"* "Wadud, come on home." Even though I heard her voice coming closer, I still pretended not to hear. I did not answer, delaying a reply as long as possible. Once she reached me, I knew just by seeing the expression on Amak's face that I had done wrong and better obey, but her voice merely told me to come home and eat.

Not long after this she asked me, "Why is it you don't answer me when I call you?" Even though I was only six years old, I explained to Amak the reason why using initials from the **H**izbul **W**athan Boy Scout troops pleased me. From that time on, my mother also humored me and called me *Ha-we* which to her became simply *A-we*. Thinking back on my village life in Sungai Batang, located alongside the water's edge of Danau (Lake) Maninjau, I always remember family and community. Intertwined through those days were my parent's love for me and room for boyhood dreams and childhood fantasies.

When my aunt Jamilah opened a small *warung* (stand) in front of her house, she sold candies, cigarettes and other goodies to neighbors. Around four o'clock in the afternoon, the *Asar* prayer call sounded, and my aunt would have to leave her little shop to go inside and pray. I was usually the one asked to watch over things; but if my friends came by during that time, I gave away candies and other delectable sweets without charging them. In my thinking, since we were family, Aunt Jamilah's *warung* also belonged to me.

It did not take long for some of my friends, who were rather mischievous, to begin smoking and talking me into giving them several cigarettes at a time. I soon wanted to give smoking a try myself.

One afternoon I thought I could achieve what my friends had been doing with the cigarettes. Next to the *warung* was our house, which had outside stairs leading to the front door. I crept under the house by the stairway, believing I could hide myself there, and that my mother would not know what I was doing.

After several daring attempts at puffing a cigarette that I had lit like the bigger boys, I inhaled the smoke just as I had seen my other playmates do. I was so intent on practicing what I had seen, that I did not realize the smell of the burning cigarette was traveling up the stairs. Soon my stomach started feeling uncomfortably queasy followed by rolling waves of nausea. I am sure that if I looked in a mirror, I would have seen that my face had taken on a serious tinge of gray. It did not take much longer for the nausea to rise to its peak. There underneath the stairs near the open front door and Amak's ears I released all the contents of my earlier meal. My punishment had rudely arrived!

I sat there, breathing deeply and exhaling slowly as small beads of sweat broke out on my forehead and neck. Neither the quiet of the afternoon, nor the slight breeze brushing past my face brought any comfort. From that time on, neither Aunt Jamilah nor my mother ever needed to teach me any lessons about smoking cigarettes.

# 3

# VEILED MYSTICISM

*"The older generation may have a hard time keeping up with the younger,
but let's remember that as long as we are still breathing,
we are leading the way."*
Billy Graham

When I think of the past and my childhood at beautiful Lake Maninjau, I will never forget the exquisite beauty of the place of my birth and the lake, formed as a centerpiece within a basin ringed by rising lush green hills. This area was often described as *"A little piece of Heaven fallen to the earth."* At certain periods of the day, the sunlight would shine on the water, giving the lake a gem-like appearance. It was like a diamond radiantly gleaming -- cool, clear and clean. When thirsty, we scooped handfuls of fresh water and drank from its abundance.

Even though Danau Maninjau was beautiful, the lake was also notorious as *Danau Busuk.* That described my beloved lake as being a spoiled or rancid site. In early childhood days, it was hard for me to understand the mystical meaning of Danau Busuk. As a boy, I was yet to discover why the place of my birth was also the area in Indonesia notorious for being the strongest spiritual realm of practice with *guna-guna*, black magic and witchcraft. I later learned that my father, at a younger age, had played an important role in the battle of demolishing this spiritual darkness.

In order to rid the region of the black magic, my father also studied in-depth about these practices, traveling to Mecca a second time in 1904. While in Mecca, Ayah learned from several renowned mentors of Islam and returned to West Sumatra two years later in 1906. After arriving home, my father was determined to reform and cleanse Maninjau of the occult practices. Through the years, *guna-guna* had intertwined with the Minangkabau *adat*, traditional laws and Islamic religion within the territory. My grandfather had also been more than just a follower of these beliefs.

Around the middle of the nineteenth century, my paternal grandfather Sheikh Muhammad Amrullah, known as a great Minangkabau *ulema* (scholar), also went by the name Tuanku Kisai. My grandfather was one of the leaders of Tarekat Naqshabandiah, a mystical order of *Sufism*, which encouraged its followers to lead highly spiritual introspective lives. Tarekat Naqshabandiah also taught adherence to a strong belief of secretive occult practices within Islam. This trend of Sufism penetrated the Minangkabau region through the span of many years. As Sufism belief increased within Islam during that era, so did my grandfather's popularity, both as *ulema* and leader within the Tarekat Naqshabandiah organization.

So popular was he that people believed he had powers to heal and give physical strengths beyond comprehension to those who sought him. During those days, it was a regular practice to chew beetle nut leaves, known as *makan sirih*. When he finished chewing his *sirih* and spewing the remains into a spittoon, a follower would then quickly retrieve the remains and re-chew it. All this was in hopes of receiving my grandfather's supposed mystical powers.

Besides remembering stories told by my father about my grandfather's importance, I also heard from my brother Malik that throughout our grandfather's lifetime, he married eight times and had forty-six children. Known to be a very generous man, he often purchased properties surrounding Nagari for his daughters and for his nieces, since he held the position within the family as *mamak rumah*, guardian uncle. According to Minangkabau *adat* law, this made him additionally responsible for the children of his sisters. In later years, this included my mother who was a relative and would become the wife of my father.

After returning from Mecca, *Ayah* began speaking in opposition to teachings of the *Tarekat Naqshabandiah*, and *Kaum Tua*, meaning the old sect of Islam. My grandfather was a leader within the *Kaum Tua* movement. Although there were great differences of views between father and son, Ayah nevertheless held the highest respect for his father and always remained sensitive to protect their relationship. When my grandfather died in 1909, my father intensified his aim at reformation and steadily influenced the renewing and modernization of Islam. He was able to accomplish this through his leadership of the Kaum Muda, the "young order" movement.

*Note:* **Muhammad Amrullah Tuanku Muhammad Abdullah Saleh** *(Author's grandfather) West Sumatra, 1840 - West Sumatra, 1909 also known as Tuanku Kisai, was a great scholar of Minangkabau, and an ancestor of two major figures in the Malay world. One man is his own son,* Abdul Karim Amrullah. *Muhammad Amrullah was one the followers of Tarekat Naqshbandi. Amrullah is listed as one of Kaum Tua movement ("the elderly") leaders, and at the time, he created the [terminologies] Kaum Tua and Kaum Muda ("young people") when these movements had not yet become widespread. His own child, Abdul Karim Amrullah, was a pioneer and major figure in the struggle, including Kaum Muda. Abdul Karim Amrullah rejected the Tarekat Naqshbandi deeds, while rejecting the bond 'taqlid.' (From: Wikipedia, the free encyclopedia)*

*Note:* **Dr. Abdul Karim Amrullah** – *(1879–1945), known as Haji Rasul, (Author's father) was a Muslim reformer who led reformation of Islam in Sumatra. Haji Rasul was born in Sungai Batang, Maninjau, West Sumatra on February 10, 1879. His father was Muslim ulema, Syekh Muhammad Amrullah Tuanku Kisai and his mother Andung Tarwasa. In 1894, he went to Mecca, studying Islamic law under Shaikh Ahmad Khatib. After he graduated, he taught Islam in Mecca until 1906.*[1] *Upon his return to the Dutch East Indies (now Indonesia), he founded an Islamic organization known as Muhammadiyah in West Sumatra. In 1915, Haji Rasul founded Sumatera Thawalib in Padang Panjang. Thawalib was an Islamic school that produced many progressive students. (From: Wikipedia, the free encyclopedia)*

Since my grandfather passed away before I was born, I never had the opportunity to know him personally. I am grateful that my father was able to share many of these stories with my brother and myself. Through Ayah's accounts, we learned that after my grandfather's death, his grave in Nagari became like sacred ground. From time to time, my mother would allow me to go to Nagari (close to our house in Kubu) and visit relatives there. I would make my way across the rice fields in the direction where Ayah's family resided, either accompanied by some friends or by myself. This also gave me opportunity to go to my grandfather's mosque, which was located in Nagari, built years before in homage to him. During his popularity, this mosque was the place where my grandfather had taught and influenced many lives.

Later, while passing through the memory corridors of my adventures, I know that it was in the scenic highlands of West Sumatra by exquisite Lake Maninjau where I awakened to life. It was there that powerful parental love and a strong religious belief system shaped me. This environment introduced me to the fervent ways of Minangkabau traditional life, our religion of Islam, the affection from my close family, and awareness of my deeply rooted heritage.

NEVER-ENDING WATERS… Even while knowing the facts of its past, my love for Lake Maninjau and its waters there never waned. However, as much as I loved Lake Maninjau, I remember the terrifying experience of learning how to swim all by myself. For some time, I had watched older boys who already knew how to dive, and thought I had looked carefully enough. Their movement in the water seemed simple, easy, and fun. I thought I was ready to do the same.

One morning I went to a designated spot near the mosque located by the water's edge. I looked about and saw other people diving into the clear water from cement steps built there years ago. From where I was, I thought that looked rather effortless. So I too dove in headfirst as I had seen the older boys do.

Perhaps because of the speed with which I hit the water, I continued going farther down to what appeared to be a never-ending descent into the deep waters. When I was unable to push myself back up to the surface, overwhelming fear attacked me. Soon my lungs were desperate for air. In panic, I kept trying to kick upward to the surface, which was just too difficult. I struggled, losing power with each passing second. In those days, there was no one to guard the safety of swimmers. The other boys I had watched earlier were also a distance away. Thus, while I was under water there was no one to help me. Going down deeper as I struggled, darkness and a sense of alarm entirely consumed me.

Suddenly something made me completely surrender to what was happening and then there was calm like a blanket surrounding me. I floated in the space encircling me. Then, just as quickly as the fear had grasped me, I found myself rising to the top of the water. No longer sensing the need to struggle, I let my legs tread freely, pushing my body towards the surface. Amazingly, I did not drown!

Despite that initial terrifying lesson, my love for swimming remained. Whenever possible I was by my favorite spot (usually twice a day). In the early morning, I walked the short distance from our house and cross the road over to the water's edge. I would then briefly swim before going to school. I would try to swim again in the evening before *Maghrib* prayer. If I stayed in the water too long, I would do the *wudhu* washing at the same time before returning to the house to recite early evening prayers with my parents.

GAMES WE PLAYED… Besides swimming, playing soccer was also one of my favorite ways to spend time. In those days, any object we came across that my friends and I could kick around would quickly become our pretend ball. On the way home from school, if we came across a discarded kerosene can on the side of the road, this too would quickly turn into the object of our game. My friends and I would kick with all our might, noisily passing the can to the person on the other side of the road whose turn it was to receive. The bigger the can, the more noise we made. However, our favorite and most often-used object was the large grapefruit-like *jeruk Bali*, pomelo fruit, which grew abundantly.

Whenever we did have some money, we would collect a half cent from each person that had it, and buy a ball costing about three and a half cents. Although it was not a real soccer ball, we were satisfied. Once purchased, we would wrap the ball with layers of *getah karet*, rubber tree sap we had dried in the sun. By doing a little extra work, my friends and I would have a ball with more bounce and longevity. The only ones allowed to kick the ball, however, were the friends who had contributed their half cent to purchasing the ball. We all knew this was the rule, unless we had agreed to play a competition game with boys from the nearby villages of Kukuban or Muara Pauh. Only then would we pick others to participate and be part of our team. Of course, if they were good players we chose them even if they had not contributed any money.

Since a real soccer field was still too big for us, my friends and I would go to one of the nearby rice fields. Rice fields were excellent soccer spots before they were prepared for planting. However, this was not the place we held our big contests, because there were too many holes. Since I liked running around the field without shoes, I would often get hurt and sprain an ankle when accidently stepping into one of these holes.

Sometimes it was much more convenient and fun to have a soccer game on the side of the *balairung*, the village's community pavilion regularly used for meetings. Our frantic running after the ball and concentrating on kicking as hard as we possibly could made us oblivious to the high rising dust around us. There was no regard to the sweat and grime sticking to our bodies. As long as we could show off our playing skills, we were inside an imaginary stadium with make-believe spectators cheering us on. Neither heat of the day, holes in the ground, or dust in the air were ever problems for us.

SOLDIERS AND SCARECROWS… Even with school and all the other activities, if we had our way, my friends and I would swim all day long. When I went home and stepped into the house, my mother always took one look at me, sniffed my hair and said, *"Wadud, waang lah bak baun gaciek bajamue"* - "Wadud, you smell like a puppy dog naked to the sun." Then the inevitable came as my mother insisted I take a real bath, using soap. Afterwards she would again take a whiff of my hair making sure I really used the soap. It was also my mother's usual practice whenever I came home from playing outside to ask me if I had said my prayers yet. If I had not done so, it was the first thing she asked me to do.

After I started school, it was my father's habit when he was home to wait for me so we could eat together. He would always say that I looked like I really enjoyed eating what was on my plate, and that I never seemed to lack an appetite. Just watching me enjoy my meal would further stir his appetite. Ayah always enjoyed and appreciated the delicious food my mother prepared for us.

When I was still small, unlike other little kids, I did not like anyone to *suapin* me, (hand-feed). However, when I had to eat meat, my mother always kept a watchful eye, making sure that my bites were not too big. Amak wanted me to eat little by little, so as not to look like I was *changok*, greedy for food. She sometimes shredded the meat into little pieces and then lined it all along the edge of my plate; just like little soldiers standing at attention. I really liked that because she made me feel like a happy soldier too. My mother would pretend not to look as I quickly scooped up all the little pieces with my hand, and still put everything in my mouth all at once. Then, Amak would look at the plate again, mimic surprise, and ask, *"Kama saradadu nan babarih tadi?"* "What happened to the soldiers standing there earlier?" I replied, "They are all dead." *"Alaaa, ibo bana awak, anak den!"* she would exclaim, "Oh my goodness, what a pity, my child!" Amak always acted out her role well, that of being very surprised her little soldier was so quick. Later I realized my mother had shredded the meat so that I would not choke on the bigger pieces.

I also enjoyed very much going with my mother on the days that she worked in the rice field or other land we owned. The rice field was at Air Bamanyiek located near the lake. While Amak carefully worked the field, she allowed me to swim.

When harvesting time approached, we were busy chasing away *unggas*, birds that flew overhead in great numbers. As these birds attempted to pick at the ripened rice plants, my mother made *juek-juek,* scarecrows, decorated with pieces of torn clothing and paper streamers attached to rope. Amak would position the juek-juek to scare away the birds. In order to keep me busy, I was trusted with the task of yelling as loud as I could while also continuously and rapidly shaking the rope to distract and startle the annoying birds.

In the corridors of my memories, lodge the feelings from happy moments that we spent together during those days. For lunchtime, Amak usually brought *rendang*, the Minang dish of stewed beef, red-hot spices, and coconut milk. This she had prepared days before. Amak would sometimes also bring fried *belado bada masiek,* a particular kind of anchovy found only in Lake Maninjau, which was smoked and then stir-fried in hot red peppers. Both were favorite dishes of mine, *"Rasanya istimewa sekali, mmmmmm!"* "The taste was really good, mmmmmm!" We enjoyed eating together in the small *dangau*, a covered cottage-like shelter in the middle of the rice field. How I enjoyed the *rendang*, or *balado bada masiek*, with cold rice and drinking the cool tea. I took pleasure in every bite!

After we ate, Amak needed to continue her work. She always encouraged me to take a nap, and I willingly obeyed. Cool breezes from the lake took me into peaceful sleep. While I lay inside the simple *dangau*, the woven palm leaf roof shielded me from the midday sun while adventures played in my afternoon dreams.

After I passed a prerequisite school qualification test – able to reach my left ear by passing my right hand across the top of my head – it was the sign I was ready for school. So great was my desire to learn, I always asked my mother if we could please stop and ask one of the teachers to measure me each time we passed the school. It was an exciting day when I received the long awaited news. I had finally passed the test and could start elementary school the following school year. Thus, I began school at the age of seven in 1934.

In the mornings, before I was off to school and just having had a *mandi,* bath, my mother usually combed my hair very neatly. As was the way for children then, she would put a little talcum powder on my face as the final touch. When I left the house, I would make a quick stop along the way to rinse my face again with the not-so-clean water from the rice fields, while also running hands through my hair. I did this, so as not to have my hair or face look too neat or clean. A part of me feared that my friends would see and make fun of me. On the other hand, I also felt somewhat guilty, not wanting to hurt my mother's feelings in case she found out. Amak was proud of my longing to learn, it was only natural that she wanted me to look my best.

Our village elementary school taught basic subjects in the Minang language for first and second grades. This was followed by third grade and up in Indonesian. I attended school Monday through Saturday from seven o'clock in the morning to one o'clock in the afternoon. On Fridays, we had half days because of *sembahyang Jumat*, our Friday prayers. Each day I would rush home for lunch, and then in the afternoon I went to Islamic Ibtidaiyah School from two to four o'clock in the afternoon. Here, I learned the Arabic language and history of Islam. These included stories of prophets mentioned in the Quran.

After *Maghrib* prayer at sunset and before the *'Isa* prayer, I learned to *ngaji*, (reciting the Quran) at the mosque. I would then go home, have dinner, and do my homework. In between all these activities, I often still managed to have quick dips in the lake.

Each day, my schedule was a lively course of routine. Nevertheless, I was happy to have reached school age. Although busy, it was not difficult to stay disciplined in the daily activities. I enjoyed learning and even at that young age wanted very much to know more about new things and faraway places.

My yearning to experience *merantau* arose while I was in school. Like other Minang men before me, to *merantau* meant following the Minangkabau custom of leaving home and seeking a way for the future. Someday I wanted to discover what my fate was for making my fortune elsewhere. While I was in elementary school and safe in my village, my life held a sense of eagerness and innocence. These qualities would later guide me into my youth, birthing high hopes of dreams for my future.

# 4

# ADVENTURES OF BOYS AND MEN

The future belongs to those who believe
in the beauty of their dreams.
Eleanor Roosevelt

I had older friends, who after finishing village school, usually slept at the *surau*, a prayer house located next to the mosque. Religious studies also convened there. Another reason why older boys remained at the *surau* after reaching the age of thirteen or having advanced from the fifth grade Government School, was because they were embarrassed or ashamed to sleep at home in their mother's house. According to Minang tradition, the family house belonged to sisters within the family.

Thus, it was at the *surau* that some of my friends would stay at night and hope eventually to go *merantau*, especially those of us in Maninjau. Land surrounding the lake was limited to the use of planting rice or farming for those living in the vicinity. Therefore, Minang men customarily traveled the countryside and highlands of West Sumatra, making their way to different cities. Sometimes others were encouraged to continue studies abroad.

Within Minangkabau custom, when a couple married the husband went to *merantau*. This meant leaving his young wife behind in the village at her family home. If feasible, the husband would occasionally return to the village. Eventually, when the husband found a place to settle, the wife would join him. However, the women would sometimes wait for years for their husband to settle in another part of the country. During these times, the women back home typically received income by mail or packages sent by their husbands.

23

Maninjau was known as *daerah wanita*, the area of women, and it was indeed; since many of the men were often away. With whatever they received from *rantau*, the women were able to save, plan and build nice homes. Even though the women would build homes (usually on family-owned property), husbands returned for their wives. When the women joined their husbands, these houses remained empty. Sometimes people hired others to live in the homes while owners were away.

Thinking back on life in Sungai Batang, is always reminiscent of family and community. There were many religious ceremonies and festivals for us to celebrate, each with its own colorful expression and purpose. At the end of Ramadhan, we also celebrated *Rakik Rakik*, which was usually the night prior to *Idul Fitri*, the ending of the fasting period. On days of this particular celebration in our village, there would always be a contest of beautifully decorated colorful canoes. For this, adults designed a large *ondan*, a bamboo platform-like raft, which when placed on top of canoes, held replicas of our Minangkabau *rumah gadang*, the traditional Minang house or mosques. With *tambur* drums loudly struck atop the canoes paraded on the lake, neighbors and families of all ages cheered from the water's edge with joyfulness.

During time off from school, my friends and I would as always stay near the lake. We then planned and built our own *ondan*, raft. Instead of heavy bamboo, we built it from harvested *batang pisang*, banana tree trunks. These trees grew in abundance behind our house and elsewhere in the village, and were an excellent source for building a raft.

It would take about three or four of us to drag each banana trunk to the lake, one large trunk at a time, pulling it to the spot where we were building the *ondan*. We created with the active imaginations of nine and ten year olds.

Several trips back and forth, bringing more of what we needed would do the job. Five or six thick banana trunk stems still somewhat moist, arranged tightly together and horizontally skewered with strong *bamboo runcing* (sharpened bamboo spears), usually was enough. After building and decorating the *ondan*, it was time to plan our own "festival for celebration."

With our *tambur* drums (empty decorated kerosene cans) also placed on our newly built raft, we would then put the *ondan* out into the water for a test. I, of course, would be the one to pilot, standing on it with one other friend. Parading our *ondan* proudly in honor of our own fantasy celebration, we noisily beat our drums, clanging in different pitch tones according to the size of the cans while jubilantly cheering and yelling as loudly as possible.

Usually the boys carrying our dry clothes followed us from the shore. In particular, there were Salman and Khalid, sons of our next-door neighbor, *Uncu* (Aunt) Dalipah, and sometimes my cousin Rasyid, the son of my father's younger brother Yusuf. We would tease Rasyid by calling him *Si Gaek*, the old person, because he was *selalu ompong*, always toothless. The boys following us on the shore were usually the ones who took their responsibility seriously in guiding us from the water's edge. Actually, we did not allow them on the *ondan* because it was not large enough to hold us all, and because they did not know how to swim yet. Adults watching from shore would shake their heads while laughing, watching us having fun floating on the lake.

It was during these days when I was about nine or ten years old, that I sometimes invited about six or eight friends to hike and climb the hills through *Kelok 44*, the winding road of forty-four hairpin curving turns. The road led upward from our village market place Pasar Maninjau, to the top of *Puncak Lawang*, translated Top of Scepter Viewpoint (because of the curves). In my child's imagination, I thought that when we reached the top and looked down onto the lake, we had reached the city of Medan, which in reality was far away on the northeast part of Sumatra.

Reaching the top of the viewpoint, with the morning sun on us as we climbed, took about three hours. We were naturally hungry by then. Before we had left for our hike, we had asked our mothers if we could take lunch to go play. Amak and the other mothers usually prepared *nasi bungkus* lunches. Wrapped in banana leaves these always included rice with the vegetables or fish our mothers were preparing for the family that day.

We did not tell them where we were heading though. Our parents would never believe we had plans to play that far away from home. When one of us did not bring food or refreshment, the group shared with them.

While eating, we would sit and enjoy the beautiful scenery of the lake, admiring the surrounding panorama brimming with lush green foliage. Usually the view was clear during the morning until noon or a little after. The lake looked like a precious jewel shining brightly. In the afternoon, fog usually set in covering the lake and the encircling hillside area. We knew this indicated that it was time for us to head home. It would sometimes start raining while trekking down the hill, and we would be soaking wet by the time we reached home.

People asked us along the way, *"Dari ma kalian?"* "Where have you been?" *"Lah payah ranggaek kalian mancari kalian."* "They have been looking for you, everywhere." Chuckling, we would answer, *"Dari Medan,"* "From Medan." Looking back at that time later, I wondered if this was one of the boyhood signs of a desire to lead. Ah, those wonderful childhood days were such fun, although it surely must have worried our parents when we were mischievous. This was however, still a time of early friendships and innocence.


BOYHOOD TO MATURITY… The one particular special event of my life, which I cannot forget, was when I reached the age of ten. It was time for my ceremonial circumcision during *Sunat Rasul*, the festival specifically for this very important ritual. Together with my two cousins Salman and Muhammad Zein, the three of us on that day took this step of maturity.

Personally, I had anticipated this for quite some time, because I was looking forward to the big *selamatan*, village feast, which took place after the rite was over. In Minang language, it referred to as a *baralek*, celebration. This was when we felt like "king for a day." Lots of delicious food was prepared and served especially in honor of us who had gone through the ceremonial rite that day.

Early morning of the big day, my mother had already advised me to go and soak myself in the lake. Believe was, that at circumcision, the physical pain experienced was less. Thus, I closely followed Amak's advice.

At sunrise, I went to the lake alone after *sembahyang Subuh*, morning prayers. Stepping into the water, which was still chill from the night air, I swam and remained there for about one hour. I then came out of the water and returned home for breakfast. Mak Faqih, the *tukang sunat* designated to perform the circumcision, was already waiting at our house when I arrived.

Soon after we finished our meal, my two cousins arrived. Neighbors and family members (minus women) came along to witness the ceremony.

I insisted on being first in line and was not at all hesitant. This was a long awaited moment.

All males present entered into one of the side rooms of our house. As I sat on the edge of a designated bench, prayer recitation by the adults began. Remaining seated, the circumcision was done with a small knife, utilized also for killing goats. I was able to keep my eyes on Mak Faqih making the incision. Even then, it was very important to me to show my cousins that I was not afraid.

When it was over, I looked at Salman and Zein, whom I knew had not soaked in the water earlier that day. Both looked gripped with fear, their eyes wide and unblinking. I do not know their exact thoughts at that instant, but each of their expressions said enough. After Mak Faqih was done with me, both my cousins knew they were next in line. Because of my time spent soaking, I was the only one who did not cry when the circumcision happened.

Since the knives used were very traditional and there were no antiseptics or anti-biotic for my wounds, the sores quickly became infected. The only medicine available to remedy the situation was powder scraped from a coconut shell, directly rubbed onto the infected area. For several days, I could not wear pants, only a *sarung* (loosely draped cloth). This I held away from the wound when walking. I of course waddled like a duck.

TUMAYO BRIDGE CROSSING... After I finished fifth grade of the village elementary government school, my mother wanted me to continue at the Ibtidaiyah Tsanawiyah School, a junior high-level school focused on religious teaching. However, this was a girl's school. Many boys, after finishing village school, went *merantau* looking for work. At that point, I did not like the idea of being the only boy attending.

After my placement into the fourth grade of Ibtidaiyah Tsanawiyah School, which was located in Nagari not far from home, lasted only a short period for me. Since I handled all the lessons without difficulty, I quickly advanced to the fifth grade. Nevertheless, being the only boy, I soon became bored.

As the teachers tried to make me feel comfortable, they soon allowed me to bring a companion to sit with me in class. I asked my cousin Arifsuddin (Utin), to join me. I began thinking that the only reason I was accepted in the girl's school was that its administrators respected my family and wanted to please my parents.

Even though I received extra privileges, Sa'adiyah, my teacher, often came to our house looking for me since I repeatedly skipped school. Worried about me, she did not want me in trouble with Amak. I knew however, the reason my mother wanted me in the school was to keep me busy rather than spend all my time playing outside.

A story had spread regarding the escape of convicts from a prison. Rumor had it that they were wandering the area looking for little children, and collecting their heads for strengthening the foundation of a bridge being constructed, connecting the villages of Kubu and Kukuban.

Thus, all the children in our village had to be home before evening prayer at sunset. However, on days when I did not go to school, I would sit by the bridge watching laborers at work. As I sat on my spot, I would intently peer at the foundation of the bridge looking for clues.

To me, the Tumayo Bridge became the longest bridge I had ever seen. It was not until much later that I learned the story about the escaped convicts really was just a convenient tale from elders, especially since there were no large prisons anywhere near our village.

Meanwhile, the terrifying thought of our heads used as the foundational base for the Tumayo Bridge successfully put enough fear in me. I do not know about any of my other little friends, but for me it was sufficient. It effectively kept my friends and me from misbehaving any further, including skipping school.

I realized much later in life that the attention we give to our surroundings and things we hear or see as young children are very different when we became adults. This tale telling is what we referred to in the Minang language as *katak dibawah tempurung*, i.e. words under covering of a hidden meaning, or literally "a frog under a coconut shell." In this case, I was that frog who wanted to quickly grow up, hop across the Tumayo Bridge, and expand my horizons.

MATTERS OF EDUCATION… After my father discovered that I did not want to attend school with the girls, he asked me what I wanted to be when I grew up. Ayah allowed me to choose between becoming an *ulema* like him, or being what he called "an intellectual." Thus, my education became a matter of family discussion, which included my older brother Malik.

If I wanted to become an intellectual, Malik suggested to our father that I should enter INS, a vocational national school, at Kayu Tanam. It was at INS that writers and artists were developed. This school for creative students was under the leadership of Engku Muhammad Syafe'i, (who became Minister of Education and Culture after Indonesia's independence).

However, if I wanted to be an *ulema*, it was better for me to attend Thawalib School in Padang Panjang. This school was under the administration of Engku Abdul Hamid, one of my father's former students to whom Ayah had given the nickname *Engku Mudo*, Young Scholar.

My father founded Thawalib School in 1915, which specialized in Islamic education, and training, producing many advanced students of Islam and leaders. To please my father, I let him know I chose to become an *ulema*. Thus, I stayed in my village until I was twelve years old and then left for Padang Panjang to further my education.

After acceptance at Thawalib School, I went back into the third grade. Regardless of whom my father was the rules and regulations had to be adhered to even at this school.

Engku Mudo paid all my expenses while I was at school. According to him, my father's position as one of the founders made his contribution immense. Engku Mudo had great respect for Ayah, and wished to express his gratitude by making certain I was well cared for while away from home. This even included giving me an allowance of fifty-cents a week, which was more than sufficient for my twelve years. His wife, every week also prepared for me a *rantang* of stacked containers with food like preserved *rendang* or *goreng ikan teri*, fried dried fish and more.

After receiving my fifty-cent allowance, I usually still went straight to the Pasar Baru marketplace to feast on *sate padang Mak Said*. This included five skewered sticks of barbeque with *ketupat*, rice-cakes. This only cost *sebenggol* (two and half-cent). If I was not full yet, then I added *bakmi goreng*, fried noodles or *nasi rames*, which is rice served with an assortment of side dishes in a banana leaf. Again, this was only an additional two and half-cent of my fifty-cent allowance.

My mother also often sent my favorites from the village, like *goreng bada masiak*, the smoked anchovies that Amak fried until very crisp. She would add *sambalado*, made from ground chilies. Amak would always include her rendang for me to enjoy.

While attending school, I stayed in housing with other Thawalib male students. Some were graduates beginning their writing careers. Because I usually shared food provided for me, it would sometimes run out. On these days, I went to *Uo Imah*, my oldest sister Fathimah who lived at Jl. Guguk Malintang, only a short distance from where I was staying.

One of Engku Mudo's children named Irfan also lived at the same boarding house. Seeing all the attention his father lavished on me, Irfan became envious. Irfan approached me one evening around ten o'clock and dared me to fight him outside the boarding house at the nearby *Jembatan Besi*, Iron Bridge.

I usually did not confront first. However, if provoked I will not back away either. I agreed to meet the challenge for that night and word quickly spread. Other students always ready for excitement came out to watch.

Whenever there was some sort of challenge, the intent was that someone would put a rock between the two who were going to fight. One of us would have to start. Once the rock was in place on the ground, it represented the head of one of our fathers. That night we could not find a rock. Someone suggested the soccer ball we had used for playing earlier in the day. Once the ball placed between us, the dare was on.

Not wanting to be the one to step first on Engku Mudo's "imaginary" head, I hesitated. I remembered however, what my father had taught me about fighting. I should be the one to start with the first punch, not allowing my opponent an opportunity to hit back. That night, I did exactly what I remembered were Ayah's instructions and I threw that first punch. Irfan, not expecting that from me, was startled. I however did not stop punching, since my opponent's size was larger than I was. Finally, one of the bigger boys who also lived at the boarding house separated us. At that moment, I felt I was the winner because Irfan never had a chance to hit me back.

The next day, Engku Mudo found out what happened the previous night. Both Irfan and I received summons into the office. Irfan, with lumps visibly evident of our fight, received a firm scolding. Engku Mudo wanted him to realize my father was not indebted to Engku Mudo or Thawalib School, but instead everyone was highly indebted to my father because of

Ayah's progressive teaching and leadership. That, Engku Mudo told his son, was something they could never adequately repay.

Sitting in the office, I listened to Irfan receive the reprimand from his father which was given without Engku Mudo ever raising his voice. I then began to understand that my previous night's victory was not so triumphant after all.

When Engku Mudo was finished with Irfan, he looked away from his son. Sitting behind his desk, he turned to me and just looked at me with disappointment in his eyes. Being a very wise and kindhearted man, he did not say one word, which was far more difficult for me to take for hitting his son. What I had expected did not come. This however, was worse. Ashamed to meet Engku Mudo's eyes, I lowered my head. Irfan did likewise. The two of us still in our seats, Engku Mudo then quietly suggested we shake hands and be friends.

At first, we were both reluctant. Who would be first to give the hand to the other? I glanced at Irfan's face; he in turn quickly glanced at me. While Engku Mudo looked on, we slowly reached out toward each other. Once clasping the others hand, we briefly shook and were both relieved it was over and that our misunderstanding was resolved.

My days remained filled with much schoolwork and extra activities. I passed necessary exams for third and fourth grades with ease. For a second time I was moved into fifth grade again.

Although I had started school while still in the village at a somewhat later age, the curriculum was not difficult for me. It was frustrating however, that I had to repeat classes when my grades were good, causing me to become easily bored. It was only with the Arabic writing lessons that I needed to be a little creative, since at first that did not come as easily. Nevertheless, I always tried my best. I knew when attending Thawalib School that even if I had to repeat a grade I already passed, I must keep on doing my best no matter what.

No one was aware that during afternoons while in Padang Panjang, I would often sit at the railroad station by myself. Because I missed my mother very much, just sitting at the station platform, taking in the smell of burnt coal and seeing the hissing smoke escaping the trains, gave me the sense of being able to go home soon to see Amak. These momentary escapes at the railroad station helped me through those lonely days, even though in actuality there were no trains going to Maninjau. But just watching people entering and exiting the trains gave me comfort and hope of sooner being able to return home.

The more I learned at school, the more my longing of going on a long journey increased. If possible, I wished to voyage around the world. I was thinking I would at least first go to Medan, which was located toward the northern tip of our big island. From there, I would then find passage to Japan, which seemed half a world away from West Sumatra.

This desire to sail intensified while moving toward adolescence. Because Thawalib School had many books available, I read fervently. This sparked my dreams about travelling to other countries even more. As I reached the age of thirteen, added enthusiasm from what I read fueled these dreams. I was inspired with hope to visit those places someday soon. I also wanted to learn further about progress around the world. The year was 1940.

# 5

# COLONIALISM AND LIFE

*"Do not go where the path may lead,
go instead where there is no path and leave a trail."*
Ralph Waldo Emerson

Whereas Dutch colonial rule existed in Indonesia for a very long time, the West Sumatra Minangkabau region stayed governed somewhat different from other areas in our country. Administration of colonial rule had not been successful in West Sumatra due to *Pengulu* leadership strongly maintaining their stand regarding Minangkabau traditions. The Pengulu staunchly rejected Dutch mandates. Attempts to enforce absolute colonialist control in our region persistently failed. While the rest of our population suffered oppression, life in our region remained somewhat more bearable.

Although repeatedly warned by the Dutch, my father had never been afraid of the colonial government. It was undeniably his intent to continue speaking out and encouraging the people to remain strong in their belief of Islam and upholding our Minangkabau customs.

While Ayah spoke fearlessly, the people and Minang leaders listened. Thus, the Dutch needed him removed from the public platform. Since they were unable to prevent his influence, they considered him dangerous and a nuisance as well.

It became common for hecklers to disrupt when my father lectured and sometimes while he preached in mosques. When they believed Ayah was over-criticizing the Dutch government, it was their job to prevent my father from speaking his message. Appointed by the Dutch, these men received financial compensation.

Some were Minang, and our family was personally acquainted with several of them. At that, age it was difficult for me to accept the betrayals from those who regularly reported my father's activities.

As a thirteen year old during 1940, I saw my father as a bold warrior and courageous pioneer for people. Wherever Ayah travelled and whatever he voiced publicly was not only for the Minangkabau populace but also for our entire country. This resulted in the spread of nationalism throughout the region.

AYAH IMPRISONED… Eventually the Dutch government arrested my father, holding him in custody at Bukittinggi Prison. This happened while I was away at school in Padang Panjang. Ayah, although considered a serious threat, continued challenging the three hundred and fifty year Dutch colonial rule.

The day I learned my father was in custody, Engku Mudo summoned me to his office early in the morning. I could see from his expression that something was terribly wrong. Looking at him, my heart began beating fiercely in my chest. I sensed trouble.

Even though my mentor had not yet spoken one word, questions were already racing in my mind. Looking at him across from where I was sitting, I felt a lump growing inside my throat when Engku Mudo began speaking. I knew how much he loved and respected my father. Looking at me compassionately, he spoke quietly, his voice sounding grieved. I found it difficult to hear him, not because he did not speak loud enough, but because my own heart was beating so intensely within me.

He said, "Wadud, I have to tell you that your father was arrested by the Dutch, and has been placed in confinement at the prison in Bukittinggi." I could only stare at him, paralyzed and unable to move or take another breath. The blending of fear and anger rising up within me was tremendous. Although I had lived with the knowledge that Ayah's arrest was imminent, it was now here. How I wished I could take my father's place.

Engku Mudo proceeded to tell me that the authorities had come to Muara Pauh, and taken my father into custody at his library, and then transported him first to Maninjau where the office of the Dutch *Controleur* (district head) was located. After the transfer to Bukittinggi, they decided that Ayah indefinitely be held there.

Taking in what this news really meant, I became more fearful of what the Dutch would do to my father. I knew that these kinds of arrests only came by order of the highest Dutch authorities.

I told Engku Mudo I wanted to go to my sister's house. Perhaps not knowing what else to say to me, he permitted my request. I got up from the chair and he nodded while watching me leave his office.

It was not until I was making my way to where Fathimah lived that the tears, which I had been holding onto, burst forth causing my body to shake with its power. Worry about what my father was going through and the sense of helplessness overwhelmed me as I cried.

I asked myself how much harm could come to him while in prison. His health and advanced age worried me. Although always active, he was sixty-two years old and battling asthma. I was thirteen so how could I possibly help. I also thought of Amak, and it seemed that home and my mother were so far away.

Once I arrived at my older sister's home, she confirmed what happened. Fathimah gently reminded me what our father believed in and stood for, and that he had already expected this would eventually happen.

Every Saturday thereafter, I boarded the train from Padang Panjang to Bukittinggi. Going by myself, I hoped I might be able to visit my father. There was a part of me however, that knew each week I would not be allowed anywhere near Ayah. Once there, I was only able to stand and then slowly walk back and forth in front of the prison. Even though I could only see the outside of the building, I repeatedly did this, hoping to have even a small glimpse of my father.

Week after week, month after month, I still came but was not once allowed a visit with my father. Although refused, I would just stand outside the prison as long as possible. I did this on purpose, never losing hope that my father would perhaps see me from within his prison cell.

While I was in Bukittinggi, I always stayed at the home of Sheikh Muhammad Jamil Jambek, also a well-known ulema in West Sumatra in those days. He was one of my father's closest friends and an astronomer, a fact that interested me.

Before, when I used to go to Bukittinggi with my father, we always stayed at Inyiek Jamil Jambek's house. During this period, this was the safe place for me to spend those weekends of waiting. On Sundays, I returned to Padang Panjang, and managed to do so with a pocket full of money given me by *Ummi*, Inyiek Jamil Jambeks' wife, who loved me very much.

Incarceration lasted eight long months for my father. When released and we were together again, my father told me he was able to see me all those Saturdays, by peeking from behind the barred window of his cell. He told me that he knew I would do something like that. I was so happy knowing that my steadfast vigilance in front of Bukittinggi prison had not been in vain after all.

EXILE IN PLANNING... After Ayah's release, the Dutch Government, wanting to get rid of my father in *Ranah Minang*, decided to send him into exile in Sukabumi, West Java. They allowed my father one wife and one child under the age of eighteen to join him. Because Ayah had two wives at that time, he had to choose which one would go first.

Earlier during the 1920's, when he was teaching and lived in Padang Panjang, my mother was the one constantly at his side. Because she had so often been away with Ayah, it became apparent he was thinking about choosing my stepmother Dariyah to be the one to travel with us first. Ayah had discussed these plans with both of his wives and they agreed that my stepmother would be the one joining us.

With the decision made, Amak had given me the freedom to choose whether I wanted to go with my father or remain with her in the village. I was my father's youngest child and the only one of all my siblings under the age of eighteen. Thus, my age permitted me to be the only one of his children to stay with him.

I chose to go to Sukabumi with my father because I also thought about school. Being with him would make the hopes I had more attainable. If I stayed in Sungai Batang with my mother, options for my education would be too limited.

My mother, though it must have saddened her, blessed my decision. In all of her wisdom and love for me, she realized that she could not do much in raising me by herself. I was then only fourteen years old, but felt the weight of my parent's decisions since the imposed stipulations. The distance between the islands of Sumatra and Java already seemed too far apart. This became one of the saddest points in my life. I soon realized that I should not be so troubled with the heaviness I carried. It was part of

Ayah's plan, since he was not permitted to return to West Sumatra, that I would travel back home once a year. First, would be the responsibility of accompanying my stepmother Dariyah back to her village of Kampung Tangah and then return to Java with my mother.

Thinking it would only be for a year at a time, being apart from my mother would not be that difficult. After all, I had been at Thawalib School for two years and stayed at the boarding house, so I had become somewhat familiar with the idea of being away from home.

As we prepared for departure into Ayah's exile, I did not know that looming political circumstances within our country and the world would eventually hinder our way. Although I did not realize it then, life, as I had known it prior to my father's imprisonment would have huge leaps of change. These changes would affect every detail of my existence.

GOING INTO EXILE… When I had to leave Amak behind in West Sumatra, I tried to remain brave so as not to sadden my mother more, while also consoling myself with the thought that we would see each other soon. Having come with us to Padang, the final embrace from her loving, comforting arms that day at the harbor would always stay with me. Her voice and quiet reminder, *"Wadud…Jago Ayah yo,"* instructing me to take care of my father, and the kind expression on her face would be the last image of my mother to be stored deep within my heart.

Thus, on August 8, 1941, my father, stepmother Dariyah, and I left Padang on a KPM ship to Sukabumi West Java, the location of my father's political banishment. Departing from Teluk Bayur Harbor outside of Padang, my father was still thinking that his arrangements for his wives would take place the following year. However, the chance of my traveling home to our village and returning to Sukabumi together with my mother was not to be. On that day, however, I was not aware of it.

*Note: The Koninklijke Paketvaart Maatschappij (KPM) was a major Dutch shipping company that maintained the sea connections between islands of Indonesia (formerly Netherlands East Indies or NEI). (From: The Ships List www.theships list.com/ships/lines/kpm.shtml)*

Three days later, we arrived in Sukabumi. I thought the city was much like Padang Panjang. The somewhat cooler weather was refreshing. What also impressed me was that the streets were not as busy as I had heard about Batavia (later named Jakarta), the capitol of Indonesia.

I was relieved that the exile of my father was in Sukabumi. I later learned from my brother Malik that the Dutch Government initially planned to send Ayah to Boven Digul, West New Guinea. This was the place to which those considered to be communists and dangerous were exiled.

However, Mr. Mohammad Yamin, an Indonesian member of *Volksraad* Dutch Colonial Parliament, had spoken up for Ayah. In his defense, Mr. Yamin told the Dutch that if Dr. Karim Amrullah's exile was to be in Boven Digul, they might as well execute him immediately since he was already in declining health and advanced age. Concluding that the wretched conditions in Boven Digul were too brutal, my father's exile was to this West Java town instead.

While in Sukabumi, we stayed at Tjikirai Straat No. 8. The Dutch authorities arranged for us to live there, after first keeping us at a small hotel near the Sukabumi railroad station.

News had circulated quickly that the exile of Dr. Karim Amrullah was in Sukabumi. The Minang people there helped prepare for our stay among them. This also included housing for us. Engku Iskandar, a man from Pariaman, helped us and became our neighbor. Behind the house provided, a mosque was located and in the front was a Catholic School.

In addition to my father's exile in Sukabumi, the Dutch Government held many other well-known Indonesian leaders in confinement there. Among them were Dr. Mohammad Hatta, Sutan Syahrir, and Dr. Tjipto Mangunkusumo. There was no communication permitted between any of us.

In returning to school, I was glad when accepted at *Taman Siswa*, one of the few existing national schools in Indonesia. Pak Abdullah Salim, a leader in the Muhammadiyah organization, registered me. Since my father had established the Muhammadiyah in West Sumatra during the 1920's, he and other members helped us.

Because I lagged behind in the Dutch language at that point, I was required to take separate lessons. At Taman Siswa, I was in the same class with Djazuli, also a Minang who befriended me. In later years, he became a colonel of the Indonesian army in the Department of Topography.

While we were in exile, the Dutch Government did not keep their promise of providing us with daily needs. Never neglected however, we had assistance come regularly from other Minang people owning businesses in Sukabumi.

Even during these difficult times my father continued teaching. The people helped us, and others consistently came to the house where we stayed. While Ayah taught, it was my responsibility to write on a black board in Arabic the verses that he was speaking about from the Quran or *Hadis* (Hadiths: sayings or doings recognized as from the Prophet Mohammad). According to my father, my Arabic handwriting was very good.

No matter what the surroundings or circumstances were, my father remained active with his teaching. Even while in exile, the Dutch could not stop him. For my father, land boundaries or banishment from his beloved West Sumatra never prevented him from speaking to all who were eager to learn from him.

We were also often visited by Aoh Kartahadimaja, a well-known writer and poet who I considered to be like my own brother. Working for the tea estate Parakan Salak at that time, he often surprised us with breads, butter, jams, and cheese for our enjoyment at breakfast. Although I found these quite delicious, I still preferred the cold rice with leftover *kerak rendang*, the last bottom of the pan's crunchy leftovers of my favorite Minang dish.

*Note: In later years after Indonesia's independence, Aoh Kartahadimaja became poet for Radio Hilversum in Holland and then with BBC England. (From: Author)*

Since the Dutch Government forbade my father to go outside of town boundaries, it became our habit to take walks every Sunday morning. We would take different routes and pass by large houses with beautiful gardens on quiet, tree-lined streets. We usually started our walks early during the cool morning hours.

These walks often took two to three hours. It was during these times that I had even more opportunities to hear many stories from Ayah. He told me about his experiences when he was young and the extensive education he was able to receive while studying in Mecca.

With his cane in his right hand, Ayah held my hand in his left or sometimes placed his arm around my shoulder. We leisurely walked side by side, simply enjoying each other's company. These moments I savored greatly because I was free to ask him many questions, especially his opinions about the teachings of Islam. He always answered me with patience, wisdom, and clarity.

What I most appreciated about my father was the firm belief he held that we should not be *taklid buta*, meaning we should not just blindly follow what is set before us. My father's intent in sharing this with me and other people was because he strongly believed that, created by God; humankind should freely use the intellect that was God-given. He taught me through this not to merely accept what I heard, but always investigate the truth.

Ayah had so many funny stories, and because he was even funnier in giving excellent illustrations, we would sometimes roar together with laughter while walking. Especially funny were my father's stories about his hilarious experiences while studying in Mecca during his younger days. People, seeing an elderly dignified man strolling along tree-lined streets with the rather lanky, taller, young boy, would never have imagined the rich humor we shared. I also learned that my father's travels took him far, not only in destination, but also in academic standing.

One particularly interesting event took place while he was studying in Mecca, and his visit to Egypt to attend the World Congress of Islam. It was here that he met with Islamic leaders from all over the world and received his "Doctor Honoris Causa" Degree during 1926.

It was stories of adventure and laughter that filled our walks. For me, it was moments of learning, never taking for granted the man so highly respected. At the same time, he was my father to whom I would never stop being the young boy, his son.

If we had strolled too far out of our way, we took one of the *delman*, horse-pulled carriages back to the house.

I had also always been amazed with Ayah's gift of memorization. In the same way, I remained in awe of how he was able to explain the meanings and interpretations of verses from the Quran. To me, my father was so intelligent, brave, and wise.

Since coming to Sukabumi and experiencing exile together, our relationship grew even closer. Being his youngest child with him during my father's banishment, became for me one of the most valuable seasons of my lifetime. It was through his stories and examples; who he was as a brave leader and as my father, which instilled in me an even stronger desire to explore. Ayah planted the passion within me for eventually seeing the world created by a great God.

JAPANESE INVASION… As World War II spread throughout South East Asia, Japanese forces began occupation control toward our country. News reached us that the Japanese attacked Pearl Harbor in Hawaii on December 7, 1941. We knew it was their intent to likewise overpower and rule other Southeast Asian countries. After the Japanese forces succeeded in Singapore, they also invaded Indonesia, still known as the Dutch East Indies. In March of 1942, the Dutch and their army yielded to the Japanese in what history would later call the Battle of Java (February 28 – March 12).

Increased turmoil and conflict constantly brewed and made its way throughout the Indonesian islands. We cautiously watched the Dutch and Japanese combat one another for our territories as they stepped into deeper battle.

I still vividly remember the morning when sirens, disturbing the quietness of the day, suddenly sounded their shrill warning signals. I ran outside with great haste from the house. Not only did the sirens sound the alarm, but I also heard another strange noise coming from the distance. It began as a faraway droning in the sky and gradually grew to a roar. I was supposed to run for shelter. Instead, my curiosity caused me to ignore my safety instructions from school.

Standing in front of the house looking upward, I cupped my hands above my eyebrows, slowly moving my gaze from left to right and turning in an almost semi-circle. Trying to see into the distance, my eyes searched the blue sky above.

At first, I saw only some white clouds traveling over rooftops of houses, various buildings and tips of green palm trees. Trying to get a closer view, I kept staring intently into the distance. The sound grew louder and the roar even closer.

Suddenly, with the noise appeared six Japanese fighter planes seemingly coming out of nowhere, and what looked like directly toward me. Even with all the chaos created on land and the fighting not too far away from where we were staying; this was the first time for me to experience such a sight.

It was not only my fascination with the roaring airplanes that had stopped me in place, but also the trail of shots and noise of apparent machine-gun fire that accompanied it. The warplanes that I had only heard about flew a short distance away. This was an attack on the Dutch, who were already penetrating inland areas. The Japanese assaulted them from the air. The planes now and then released rapid-fire aimed at the ground. Te-det-teded-ded!...Te-det-teded-ded!...Te-det-teded-ded! The noise went on and on, echoing in my ears.

Continuing to look upward, I actually saw the unyielding spray of what appeared to be ammunition coming out of those planes in a steady, endless stream. It seemed an indescribable strength bore down on me, as I felt glued to the spot.

During those same moments of fascination and much to my own disbelief, a sudden confusion awakened within my senses. "Wait," the question rang within my head. "If the Japanese are attacking, why is there no retaliation sound being fired? Is nothing coming from any of the Dutch forces nearby?"

Just earlier in the day, I had seen the uniformed soldiers passing the house. "This is incredible," my thoughts raced on. "Where are they all; where have they gone?" This entire incident did not take more than ten minutes!

It was not until the planes almost entirely disappeared from view that I realized I was still standing in front of the house. I should have been under cover; what was I doing here? Suddenly aware of what had just taken place, my body spun itself around with surging speed, my heart beating loudly within me. I ran and flung myself back into the house with whirlwind haste. The door slammed shut behind me with a noisy bang. Nothing was holding me back now to get myself to a safe spot.

Once in my room, I slid under my bed with such a plunge, it caused me to land and then slide with a thud against the wall. I thought I would be safe in this spot. Remaining silent, I consciously tried first to slow down my breathing. My heart seemed to be pounding in my eardrums. I waited there until the sirens sounded again, letting us know that all was clear. This was the first time I ever saw and experienced enemy forces flying in this fashion and so up-close.

After waiting a little longer, I slowly crawled out from under the bed. The house seemed quiet. My room still shuttered in darkness, I opened the door and peaked outside it. Ayah was still in his study and had waited until the turmoil outside had passed. Even with the danger touching us, my father remained calm; always firmly believing his life was under Allah's hand.

After the all-clear siren had sounded, the day eventually continued as before. Some friends came by a short time later, and with much animation described to me what they had just seen and urged me to come quickly to look.

Throughout the last months in Sukabumi, I had seen numerous Indonesians having joined the *KNIL*, Dutch armed forces. I hurriedly followed my friends. Once we arrived at the nearby site, I saw with great astonishment the many uniforms that lay strewn about in heaps and in the open gutters, thrown there by soldiers who must have become terrified by the turn of recent events.

It was not long after this that the Japanese forces fully entered, establishing themselves in Sukabumi. Since the Japanese army occupied our country, they demanded immediate respect. I saw none among them of tall stature; nevertheless, they tried to make their appearance intimidating to the Dutch.

I remember an incident, which was rather comical for my fourteen-year old eyes. The Dutch, who were physically tall, had no choice but to look down onto the shorter Japanese soldiers. These same Dutch men, moreover, refused to bow themselves down to their guards in the *keirei* bow.

This was blatant disrespect to the opposition, and one of the Japanese soldiers became particularly angry with one obstinate Dutch man that day. More angered by the minute, the Japanese soldier turned and saw a wooden chair nearby. He grabbed it and placed the chair in front of the guarded Dutchman. The soldier then stepped up onto it and with all his might struck the Dutch man fully on his face, an action meant to be more humiliating than any other manner of insult.

Having watched from across the street, it still astonished me. The Dutch had had colonial power over the Indonesian people for 350-years. Then in that one moment, I witnessed one of them taken down by a single under-sized Japanese soldier standing on a chair.

The brutality and oppression of war ensued in its severity. To show us who was in control, the Japanese made an example of another incident and many more like it. One day, I heard from people in my neighborhood that there was a *kepala orang Belanda*, a Dutch man's head, lying out in the street in front of the Police Academy building. Understanding that it must be a shocking sight but always curious, I walked to the area by myself. I saw people clustered together not far from where the decapitated head had been left. The sight initially horrified me. Of course, the unnerving gruesomeness sent cold chills through my entire body.

As I looked at this middle-aged person's face, there was not much blood spilled on the street itself. Obviously, the execution of this man must have been somewhere else and then left in the street on display as a hideous reminder. My heart felt compassion and I wondered about this person's life.

People in the street looked on the ghastly sight amid eerie quietness; fearfully cautious of what lay before them. All of us understood too well the message given with this incident. This repulsive act and countless more like it were committed as an example and show of force. The Japanese intended to restrain and terrify us with this.

With the Japanese invasion in Indonesia, transportation between the islands of Java and Sumatra was no longer available. This meant I was unable to return to my village to bring back my mother to be with us. The disheartening reality had now arisen before me. With no transportation with which to go home, how could I possibly see my mother?

# 6

# CROSS ROADS TO SURRENDER

I will go before you and will level the mountains;
I will break down gates of bronze
And cut through bars of iron.
Isaiah 45:2 (NIV)

Since the Dutch Government surrendered to the Japanese armed forces in March of 1942, everything immediately changed for us. For our country, the 350-year Dutch colonial rule ended with the Japanese occupation of Indonesia that would last for three and a half years. Despite Japan's invasion, the path of my own life began expanding. For my father the restrictions of exile stopped. Without much warning, we faced a new and unexpected gateway through which we could pass.

A month later in April, we had already been in Sukabumi for nine months. My father, stepmother Dariyah and I were suddenly free to leave Sukabumi. Since the Dutch were no longer in control, there was not even a formal release of my father. Therefore, we made immediate plans to leave for Jakarta. With the period of Ayah's exile behind us, we would continue to walk on toward a more peaceful existence… so I thought.

Once we moved to Jakarta, we stayed at Gang Alhambra in the Sawah Besar area. This time we were able to remain a while at the house of my stepmother's uncle, Engku Sutan Pamuncak and his wife Ibu Upik. It was he, who initially arranged for our move and then came to Sukabumi to accompany us to Jakarta.

After staying a few months at Sawah Besar, a house was available for us in the Tanah Abang area at Kebon Kacang IV, no 22, located in central Jakarta. Again, with the help of Minang people greatly respecting my father, we were able to obtain household needs, including regular daily provisions. The rather large house was more comfortable and became the place for my father to continue his work.

Soon, every afternoon people began coming to the house for learning to *mengaji*, how to read the Quran. My stepmother was very knowledgeable in teaching the reading of our Holy Book and people enjoyed learning from her. Since she knew I had developed a rather strong ability to read in Arabic, she asked me to help. She trusted me with some of the teaching because I regularly helped my father to write out verses in the Arabic writing.

Since first having started school in Sungai Batang, one of my main subjects was mastering reading of the Quran. Even while attending Thawalib School in Padang Panjang I received the grade of 10 (i.e. Excellent). Thus for me, helping others to read the Quran was not difficult. I viewed this and especially writing in Arabic as an artistic expression, since every single swirl had meaning. Being fifteen years old in 1942, this sometimes came to me easier than other subjects in school. When my stepmother asked me to help students with reading the Quran, and practice the Arabic writing, it was an easy task to fulfill.

Certain scriptures in the Quran became constant reminders for me. One favorite verse was from *Sura Al'Ahsr' 103 Ayat (verse) 1-3*. Namely, its instruction was that unless faithfulness to God, performing good deeds, patience, endurance, and devoted worship are evident; with passing of time humanity is lost. I regularly recited this verse in my prayers. In Arabic:

*"Wal 'Asri. Innal insana la fi khusrin. Illalladzina amanu wa 'amilussalihati wa tawasau bilhaqqi wa tawasau bissabri"*

"With time man is lost, except having Faith, and doing righteous deeds, joining together in Truth, Patience and Constancy."
(Translation from Quran)

Well suited as a guide in the "time corridor" of my own life; the principles of this verse later directed the compass for my future through many years to come.

TAMAN SISWA SCHOOL... During our stay in Jakarta, life was active. Because streets were crowded and busy, my father did not allow me to have a bicycle. I went to school by public tram. The trip was from Tanah Abang to Gunung Sahari where I attended *Sekolah Taman Siswa* (translated: Students' Garden School) located on Jalan Kadiman under the leadership of Pak Sa'id.

At Taman Siswa, immersion into learning the principles for freedom of our land caused my spirit of nationalism, *jiwa nasional,* to soar. The general leader Ki Hajar Dewontoro established the first Taman Siswa School's in 1922.

Despite political conflicts and educational restrictions, still keeping our country bound; emphasizes on independence for the people and academic significance, remained the primary focus of the school. On this foundation, Taman Siswa had built its reputation. The ideals of freedom taught to us and application of these disciplines, birthed an increasing fiery spirit of national pride in those attending these schools throughout Indonesia, which included me.

Being a student at Taman Siswa developed a loyalty for my country that lived passionately within me. I understood that we deserved the right to be independent people under Allah, God who gave us life. I was in my teens and began giving serious thought to the restlessness within my own soul as I saw the conditions of our land and people.

At school, I met Murad Aidit, who was about the same age as myself and quickly became my best friend. Another classmate was Tisnaya, also a good friend of mine. I graduated from Taman Siswa School in 1943 together with these two very close friends. Although considered mischievous, the three of us, received the *Ijazah Istimewa,* a special Certificate of Recognition from the school. Told we had earned this commendation because of our outstanding academic achievement and leadership qualities, we welcomed the acknowledgment at that time.

After graduation from Taman Siswa, Murad and I hoped to continue our education, but were only able to enroll at *Sekolah Menengah Pertama – SMP Parapatan,* considered junior high school level. I had reached the age of sixteen years and both of us were already past that grade level. But with the struggles of war we had to be satisfied continuing school in whatever way or place we could, even if that meant repeating classes. We just wanted to go to school.

Having my education constantly interrupted, made issues of life more challenging. But I was intent on receiving as much education as possible.

As I grew older, my relationship with Ayah became even closer. I had never received a harsh scolding or physical disciplining from my father. This was one reason also why I respected him so much. I always wanted to do my best, making sure not to give him reason for anger or being disappointed with me in any way.

Many of my father's students became successful, especially in the realm of Islamic leadership. Although I always had opportunity to study under my father's teaching, he never insisted I do so. However, to satisfy my own longing to learn from him, I attended the lectures when he would speak.

National leaders such as Haji Agus Salim, Muhammad Natsir, Muhammad Yamin and Dr. Ali Akbar, (Ayah's personal physician) regularly visited our home. When my father had meetings with these important people, he always encouraged me to sit near him and listen to what they were discussing.

My father's intent was to teach me to be familiar with the company of these notable people and be able to speak with them without having feelings of inferiority. However, I knew that Ayah expected me to be humble, and that if I made a commitment to anything, to do so wholeheartedly.

As Indonesia remained under the occupation of the Japanese during the year of 1943, their government attempted using my father for their propaganda purposes. Because of his influence among the ulemas, my father received many titles by the Japanese in order to attract other Islamic leaders throughout Indonesia. Upon Japanese invitation, Ayah, then considered *Penasihat Tinggi* (High Advisor), attended a meeting with other well-known ulemas from Java.

Many things impressed me about my father. What especially influenced me were his faithfulness, endurance, and bold steadfastness in defending Islam, which he believed to be unshakeable truth, *teguh kebenaran*.

In a book, *"The Story of Indonesia"* author Louis Fischer wrote the following regarding my father.

*"On one occasion Dr. Haji Abdul Karim Amrullah, a famous Moslem divine from Sumatra, was the only Indonesian invited to sit on the platform with Japanese officers at a 1943 meeting in Bandung. When the officers rose to bend worshipfully to the Emperor, Dr. Amrullah remained seated. This was an offense to their Shinto feelings, as offensive as refusing to stand when the national anthem is sung or a national banner is carried past – and in wartime. Yet nobody touched the brave doctor. In fact, the injunction to perform the Emperor Bow was withdrawn shortly thereafter." (From: "The Story of Indonesia" by Louis Fischer Harper & Brothers. Publisher New York 1959, Page 69)*

The Japanese government realized that it was not easy to attract and use my father for propaganda purposes. Instead, they respected him because of his faithful courage in upholding defense of his religion. This incident was also primarily an example and encouragement to the other ulemas who attended that meeting. Word spread quickly about my father's daring action on that day.

Later, according to Bung Hatta (Indonesia's first Vice-President and foremost political leader), my father was referred to as the first ulema among Muslim clergy during the Japanese occupation, to declare by his actions *a spiritual revolution.*

# 7

# SEPARATION AND SORROW

*A mother is someone who dreams great dreams for you,*
*but then she lets you chase the dreams you have for yourself*
*and loves you just the same.*
Anonymous

In early 1944, news reached Ayah that my mother had passed away. On that day when I returned from school just after noontime, I first went to my room, put away my schoolbooks, changed clothes and prayed *Zuhur (or Lohor)* midday prayer. When finished, I went to the other side of the house to Ayah's room to greet him there.

My stepmother as usual prepared our meals each day. She then placed the dishes on the area designated for eating. My father still liked waiting for me to return home, so that we could sit and eat together.

Being hungry, I soon focused my attention on the meal and busied myself with the food on my plate. It was not long before I noticed that my father was strangely quiet. I glimpsed at Ayah and saw he was not enjoying the food with his usual appetite. I thought he perhaps might not be feeling well or have other matters on his mind.

After finishing our meal, Ayah asked me to sit closer next to him. Already sensing that something must be wrong, I moved over and waited for my father to speak as he turned toward me. Looking at him, I noticed drawn lines on his face. At the same time, I could feel my own body grow tense with anticipation.

My father then proceeded telling me, "Wadud, I received sad news today." Ayah looked me in my eyes, pausing a moment and then went on to say, "Your mother passed away at home in the village."

50

It felt like the air squeezed out of my lungs as I stared at him in disbelief. While continuing to look at me, he went on to speak softly, "Your mother had been ill for a long time, and I want you to realize that she has returned to God who created us and has the right to take us back to Him."

I was stunned. Even with the heat of day surrounding us, my entire body shivered. It seemed like the area where we were sitting had suddenly grown oddly cold and hot all at once. Looking even more intently at me, Ayah waited a moment, and then reached out to embrace me in his arms. My father just held me close to him kissing the left side of my head.

In disbelief I remained where I was a little longer. In those moments, I felt safe in my father's embrace, at the same time remembering my mother's affection and love, which would never wrap around me again. Holding myself close to Ayah and sensing he too felt comfort as we held on to each other, I was unable to speak. The pain of the news was a crushing load, making it almost impossible for me to move. Time stood still. After he held me a while longer, I heard my own voice come out in a strange hoarse whisper. My father slowly released me, pain marking his face. I knew he too was grieving for his wife, of thirty-eight years.

I did not cry in front of my father. Once in my room, having closed the door, I just sat on the edge of the bed. I felt overcome with sadness as I glanced around the room, finally focusing on design of the tiled floor. "Who would ever love me like that again?" My thoughts flashed back to the years with Amak in our village. My voice within me cried out, "God, why did this have to happen now?" I had had big hope of eventually going home to Sungai Batang and bringing my mother back to us.

I remembered the day we left Amak at the harbor in Teluk Bayur. As we departed, I knew instinctively that she was trying to remain brave for me. I remembered the tears in her eyes as she quietly let go of me, and Amak's kind, gentle gaze fixed on me, while our ship pushed away from the harbor's dockside edge.

Now my mother was gone and I had not even been able to say a final goodbye to her; nor had I been able to bring my mother to her final resting place. Suddenly the thought arose, "What day was it when she left this earth?" Sitting in my room, painful sorrow pressed into my soul until mournful sobs escaped. I only wanted to feel the warmth of my mother's affectionate embrace.

Through death's separation, a gaping chasm, too far and too wide, lay stretched out before me. Although I was sixteen years old, I knew that I could not possibly cross its vastness. I still needed Amak's presence. "O God," I silently cried, "Where can I find my mother?"

I do not even remember how long I stayed in my room that day. Somewhere in the long hours, I laid down on the bed exhausted, as my body curled itself around the sorrow I experienced. On that day, my mind refused to accept why Allah did not allow me to see my mother just one more time.

Soon after my mother's death, I realized that I did not possess even one single photograph of her. This only saddened me even more. She very seldom had taken pictures, but I still hoped that there might be one of her at home in West Sumatra. Perhaps our family kept some in the village in Sungai Batang.

Even without my mother's face captured on paper, her image remained printed within my heart. Most important was the legacy Amak left behind with me. My mother had lived her life rich in virtue. A woman filled with love and quiet affection, she was always humble, gentle, patient, and very generous.

Never refusing to help anyone, Amak did not expect anything in return, always giving to others with pleasure. She had indeed been patient, receiving trials and tribulations in her own lifetime.

What shall forever remain with me as her son, are my mother's words in Arabic, *"Innallaha ma'assabirin"* reminding me, "God will always be with those who remain patient."

Although I did not fully understand that then, my mother's image never once dimmed within me. No matter where life would eventually take me, our bond would never be broken. The virtuous examples she taught me to live by from early on would travel with me through the passage of life and long distances of merantau.

I heard later that on the day of my mother's funeral, all schools in Sungai Batang and surrounding areas of Maninjau remained closed.

WINDS OF CHANGE… Wavering political uncertainties consistently lurked around. Although these events relentlessly encircled our lives, my father remained busy with his teaching. Following my mother's death, Ayah seemed even more active with his lectures. Opportunity also arose for constructing a new mosque in the neighborhood of Senen, Jakarta.

My father was then able to speak more freely and lectured regularly in many mosques in the capital. No longer were there hecklers positioned throughout the crowd as like during the Dutch rule in Indonesia.

Time never stood still for the ongoing quest of becoming a free people in our own country. The two driving forces behind the nationalistic movement to gain independence for Indonesia were Dr. Mohammad Hatta and Soekarno. In 1924, before I was born, Dr. Hatta together with others had formed Perhimpunan Mahasiswa Indonesia, the Indonesian Student Association.

Soekarno and other leaders formed the Indonesian Nationalist Party (PNI) in 1927, which accomplished adopting *Bahasa Indonesia* as our country's official language. The PNI organization had also embraced a more aggressive policy of being non-cooperative with the Dutch government. This was due to the main conflict between Indonesian nationalism and Dutch colonialism during those years. Thus in 1944, freedom's torch burned on and the pursuit for independence steadily moved forward through Soekarno and Hatta.

While we were living in Jakarta with the constant unrest nearby, Ayah preferred that I accompany him to the mosque in Tanah Tinggi every week for Friday prayers. He would even ask me to come along when he taught there on Sundays. I knew this was my father's way of making sure I remained safe.

The Mesjid Tanah Tinggi was one of the many mosques built with Ayah's influence after our move to the city. On Fridays, my father would give the sermon during *Jum'at prayer*, our Muslim day of worship. On Sundays, he regularly taught on the verses of the Quran.

Afterward we often ate lunch at one particular Padang restaurant upon invitation from the owner who attended Ayah's lectures. The restaurant was located at the market place of Pasar Senen, to which the owner accompanied us.

I always looked forward to this since the restaurant specialized in *masakan Padang*, Minang cooking. I enjoyed it when, in typical Minang style, whatever was on the day's menu came served in small dishes. Once these were set on the table we could choose to our heart's content whatever we liked. It was here that Ayah often visited with other acquaintances to enjoy a meal together.

The Padang restaurant was located next to a small church that was not of the same caliber like other large church buildings I had seen in Sukabumi and Jakarta. The design of this little church was in the same style as the restaurant where we ate.

I was aware from previous Sunday's that the church had a name consisting of the word *Pentekosta*. I was wondering about the meaning of *Gereja Pentekosta* (Pentecostal Church). My curiosity increased with each week's visit to the restaurant.

I knew that *gereja* meant church, but in the Minangkabau language, a portion of the word *Pentekosta* had an unfavorable implication. It seemed strange and most inappropriate to me that for a place of worship they even considered such a word. Since I was always curious, I could not help but want to take a quick look.

One Sunday after we had finished eating, I wanted to find out what was really happening inside the little building. I also wanted to know what the *orang-orang Kristen,* these Christians in particular, did when they went to their place of worship. I wanted to know why it was so small. The few other churches in the city seemed to stand out due to their larger sizes.

That Sunday, while my father was still conversing with the restaurant owner, I let him know I was going to take a walk to next door. Although I was outside, I could hear the sound of singing coming from within.

I remained standing at the church's doorway listening to the songs. As I glanced from side to side, I could see that the group inside was about forty people. I could also hear music from a piano playing melodies that sounded nice. It was difficult to hear the exact words of the songs from where I stood, but felt a strange sense of well-being.

After the songs ended, an elderly man about sixty years of age stood up. He walked toward the front of the church. Turning to the people, he stood for a moment, and then began telling a story. First, he thanked God, being glad that he finally obtained a light bulb. I thought, "A light bulb! Who talks about finding a light bulb in a church?"

It was indeed difficult to acquire light bulbs during the Japanese occupation. "This is interesting," I thought to myself. Listening closely as the man told of his experience; I saw his shy manner disappear, and he became livelier. His expression of thankfulness to God impressed me.

I was puzzled however, that someone needed to share about something like that. Why would this man speak about a light bulb in a place of worship? Why were these people telling such stories? If they were worshipping, why were they not just reciting prayers to God? I understood the difficulty of finding something like a light bulb in those days, but wondered why it was something to express in a church?

My mind filled with many questions, especially why they so freely told such a story among those gathered in that small space. When I made my way back to the restaurant, I was thinking how happy those Christians were while they were thanking God and singing songs.

Still puzzled when I arrived back at the restaurant, I told my father what I had just seen at the little church next door. I began telling him about the man who thanked God for helping him find a light bulb.

Ayah sat calmly looking at me while I animatedly explained what had happened with the light bulb. He just looked at me, smiling quietly. My father waited patiently until I was finished and then told me that we should always thank God just like that older man had done. *"Alhamdulillah,"* Praise Be to Allah, for everything that He has given. Ayah said, *"Karena itulah dinamakan berkat,"* "Because that is, what is called a blessing." My father never became angry with me about this. Instead, he helped me to understand.

TIES THAT BIND… My brother Malik whom I called *Uo Aji,* i.e. Brother Haji, used to tell me that I was the most fortunate among all of our father's children, because I had opportunity to be with Ayah longer than my other siblings had had when they were growing up.

Uo Aji had already gained status as an author and as Chief Editor of the Islamic magazine Pedoman Masyarakat. My brother became popular with his writing under the pen-name HAMKA, which was a combination of the first letters of his name given at birth; **A**bdul **M**alik **K**arim **A**mrullah. After having made the *Haj,* which was his religious pilgrimage to Mecca, he became a Haji, thus the letter **H** preceded the others in the use of his pen name.

Since I was the youngest child, there was a large difference in age between the others and me. Uo Aji (HAMKA) was nineteen years and three months older than I was. I viewed what he said about my being the most fortunate in our family as partly true. Uo Aji felt that I was the only one close to our father, and that I was the recipient of a deeper love and affection from Ayah; especially as our father was growing older. However, other events demonstrated that Ayah loved us all.

On one occasion, Uo Aji visited us in Jakarta from Medan (Northern Sumatra) where he lived and worked for many years. At that time, his visit with us was also with the purpose of bringing a message from other Muslim scholars in Sumatra to my father; with hopes of persuading him to return to the area.

When my brother was to travel to the city of Jogja in central Java, to meet there with his colleagues of the Muhammadiyah organization leadership, he became ill with malaria.

My father, upon hearing that Uo Aji was very sick, had me go to Bandung to look for him, and make sure he had proper care. I did as my father asked, and left to go find my brother hoping he could return with me.

After arrival in Bandung, I checked at the Preanger Hotel. Informed that my brother had already left for Jakarta, I hastened back to the train station that same day. The trip back also took a little over two hours. Reaching home, I found my brother there, together with Ayah. Although he was still ill, it appeared the worst of the malaria attack was already over. Uo Aji was comfortably resting.

Because at first he had been so concerned about what happened to my brother, and not knowing about Uo Aji's exact condition, Ayah was happier and at peace since his son was at our house.

My brother stayed another three weeks under the care of Dr. Ali Akbar and recovered, enabling him to return to Medan. It was at this time I realized how much my father loved all of his children, even though the others were already grown adults.

During my earlier years at home in the village, I did not have much opportunity to see my other brothers and sisters. Not only were they all older than I was, but my father's sons and daughters lived in various parts of Sumatra. Having their own families and careers, they were away from us for long periods.

In our family, Uo Aji was one of my four brothers. My second brother Abdul Kudus, who was a little younger than Uo Aji was, lived in Palembang and constantly moved around. The city of Palembang was located on the southern portion of the island of Sumatra; far away from us in West Sumatra.

From when I was smaller, Kudus well known for his acting talents, traveled as a performer in *sandiwara* stage productions. One of Kudus's achievements in particular was the play "Si Malin Kundang," which was popular with audiences. I did not see him regularly. My sister Asma lived in Deli, located in the eastern portion of Sumatra. She had moved away to that area, to merantau with her husband who had settled there and raised her family. Like my other older siblings, she very seldom returned to the village. Therefore, while I was still small we seldom had contact.

My third brother Abdul Bari was thirteen years older than I was and an author. During those early days, Bari was the only one who remained nearby in Maninjau, not only to concentrate on his writing, but also to take care of his mother. Since Bari was living near our house in Sungai Batang, I was able to see him and his mother Rafi'ah often to share a meal together.

Bari's mother, whom my father divorced in 1929, would come to visit Amak, asking her if she could possibly help persuade Ayah to return to her. Seeing one another regularly also on market day, they would catch up with family happenings. While still in our village, I always felt like Bari's home was my second home.

The Dutch imprisoned my brother for writing a manuscript entitled "Suluh Yang Gilang Gemilang," "The Torch of Brilliant Brightness." They arrested him for writing and speaking out against Dutch colonialism.

In 1923, "civil freedom restraint" placed on our people, limited the freedom of assembly, speech and expression in writing. Having opposed these restrictions through his writing, my brother remained jailed for many years. Bari died in 1939 while incarcerated.

In our family there was also my brother Abdul Muthi, who was Ayah's fourth son. From what I understood, Muthi's lifestyle was always rather rebellious and met with staunch displeasure from Ayah. Being young, I did not understand much about their conflicting relationship. I knew only that Muthi very seldom came home, and until the age of fourteen when I left Maninjau, I had seen him only two or three times.

While I enjoyed the rare occasion when my brothers were all home together, I did not like it when they tried persuading me to *pijit,* give them massages. Perhaps because I was the youngest, they thought I could be easily coaxed. I so disliked their asking me for a massage that I would purposely walk out of the way to avoid them as they sat relaxing and swapping stories with one another regarding their most recent accomplishments. Somehow sensing their requests ahead of time, I intentionally pretended not to hear them when they tried to cajole me. My brother Bari, who perhaps knew me best, was the only one who would not try persuading me. However, it was seldom that they were all home together, and I enjoyed the time spent with my older siblings.

Ever since I was small, my oldest sister Fatimah and I were very close. Although married to A.R. Sutan Mansur, who was Ayah's protégé, I saw Fatimah often while at school in Padang Panjang. Some of her children were my age, and when she brought them home to visit, we all played together as I had a special friendship with them.

From what I heard through my siblings and other family members, relationships between my father and his other children were indeed different from what I was experiencing. If it was because life was just different during Ayah's younger years when he had focused on travel and lecturing, I do not know. But perhaps with age, my father became more mellow and affectionate. I most certainly knew that no matter what, Ayah would always be our father and loved each of his children in his own different way.

PASSING AND LETTING GO… During 1944 and 1945, I watched my father's declining health take over more of his days. He most often battled with asthma. The disease would flare up and affect him especially during the rainy season in Indonesia.

Witnessing his physical struggle, I felt helpless seeing this once strong man fight for each breath through attacks of asthma. When we were in Sukabumi during Ayah's exile, he would also become ill. I would gently rub his back to try to ease some of his discomfort. The medicine made available to him was usually not enough to remove his discomfort. Often unable to speak from exhaustion, I knew, as he looked at me that he appreciated what I was doing.

While we were in Jakarta, during May of 1945 my father became even more ill. The doctor informed him that he needed hospitalization, but Ayah refused. Instead, he insisted on treatment at home.

My stepmother Dariyah and I were constantly at his side. In addition, Dr. Ali Akbar, Ayah's physician and former student, stayed with us almost every night. He faithfully accompanied us in the care of my father.

My father continued in this serious condition for over two weeks. Throughout this time, I could barely rest or sleep. Taking care of his needs was of utmost importance to me. Watching how difficult it was for my father to breathe, I was always ready to hold him so that he could lean toward me as I gently rubbed his back.

Besides giving my father medications and remaining by his side, I was also there to assist him with his praying. Although his body was weakening, Ayah insisted that he maintain his five times of prayer without fail each day. This meant that with every prayer time I would help him.

Starting with the *wudhu* washing during early morning hours of the day, I would bring a basin filled with clean water specifically for this purpose. Then standing beside him, I would assist my father to sit upright toward the edge of the bed. I would then scoop a small handful of water out of the basin to begin the wudhu.

The pre-prayer washing began with my brushing the clean water over his face, head and ears. I then proceeded with brushing more small scoops of water over his arms and feet. Once Ayah was finished with the wudhu, I would then help him turn his body towards the *Qiblat*, Mecca, in order for him to begin his prayer recitation.

As the days went by, it became more difficult as Ayah made every effort to go through each of the physical motions required for prayer. I would remain by his side and hold on to him securely when he needed to bow his head and lean his body forward, prostrating himself in submission before God.

During the last hours with my father, after just having finished praying, he told me that he wanted to pray again. It was about three o'clock in the early morning. Since he had remained on the bed, there was no need for me to repeat the wudhu washing for him. His words to me in an almost inaudible whisper were, "Wadud, I want to pray, hold me." Then my father began reciting his prayer.

Not long after he had started the recitation, he began bowing forward and back, forward and back, repeatedly. Having positioned myself behind him on the bed, I tried to hold and support him. Ayah's sudden movement of repeatedly bowing in prostration startled me. In that moment however, I suddenly had a strong sense that my father was preparing to leave us.

While he softly continued resaying verses in Arabic, I gently pulled Ayah's weak body toward me and slowly turned him, resting his head near my right shoulder. His breathing was then very labored and his voice barely a hoarse whisper. With each passing moment, my father was fading. He looked very tired as he leaned on my shoulder. The struggle to regain another breath was futile. Holding his head and body against my chest, I kept my gaze on Ayah's face, as he became very pale.

While in my arms, my father's life was draining away. He could no longer say anything; his eyes just stared at me. My heart was breaking. In this precious moment while we were alone together in his room, I very softly began reciting to Ayah the *kalimah syahadat*, the Muslim profession of faith.

*"Asyhadu an la ila ha illallah*
*Waasyhadu anna Muhammadar rasulullah"*

"There is no God other than Allah,
and the Prophet Muhammad is His messenger"

(Translation from: Kamus Indonesia Inggris)

As I quietly repeated these last words, while still holding my father just a little longer, I was also letting Ayah go. Soon after this, my father gasped one more time, took his very last breath, and then peacefully died in my arms.

After holding his lifeless body, I then very carefully laid Ayah down on the bed, and with my hand gently closed his eyes. The exact time my father passed away was Saturday June 2, 1945 at three-thirty in the morning. He was sixty-six years old.

Staying alone with him just a while longer, my heart felt shattered once again. I wanted to keep my father there and hold on to this moment. This great man admired by so many was my beloved father, who had finished his purpose on earth.

As my father's body lay on the bed, I left the room closing the door softly behind me. I walked the still dark hallway to the back of the house to look for Dr. Ali Akbar who faithfully maintained his vigil there. My stepmother was also waiting on the open veranda, where in the cool quietness of that early morning, I told them that my father had passed away.

The doctor quickly rose from where he had been sitting and immediately went to the front of the house where Ayah's room was located. My stepmother and I followed him. When inside the room, Dr. Ali Akbar walked toward the bed and then bent over Ayah's body to examine and confirm that indeed my father had died.

Looking at Ayah, my heart was so sad but I was not in shock in those moments. I was just relieved that my father would no longer have to suffer. After waiting for the doctor to finish his examination, I then picked up a clean sheet on the bed next to Ayah's body and covered him carefully as my stepmother stood by me and looked on.

Having confirmed the death, Dr. Ali Akbar told me he was going home and would return soon. The light of dawn was just breaking into a new day. As the doctor left, I too went to the house of one of the Minang neighbors.

Early morning *Subuh* prayer sounded as I knocked on the door, which Uo Makmur opened. Telling him my father had died, I asked if he could help me to notify Pak Nur Sutan Iskandar, our very close family friend and leader of the *masyarakat Minang*. I knew he would then contact the Minang community who would be first to hear of my father's death.

Once word reached the public, arrangements for my father's burial began. It did not take long for others to come also, and the Islamic rites for burial commenced. As required by our religion, men arrived to bathe my father for the last time. Having placed the body nearby the well of our house, the final ceremonial cleansing followed.

After Ayah's body had been prepared and swathed in white cloth (according to Islamic rite), my father was carefully placed on a *tandu*, the stretcher-like funeral bier. The men carried him to the front area of the house where his body remained for viewing. Before others arrived, I was able to go in and be with him by myself.

Looking at my father's still remains, I bent over him and silently kissed his forehead, tears filling my eyes. I said my goodbye to Ayah soundlessly, telling him silently how much I loved him. No words could express the immense loss I felt pressing into my soul. The crushing weight of grief was once again upon me, so soon after having lost my mother the year before. I tried very hard not to cry, because I knew I was not supposed to do that, but tears slowly rolled down my face nonetheless. I quietly remained there by my father's body, remembering his words to me. He always said that we should not express long crying or sounds of wailing emotions upon the death of someone we love because Allah has every right to take away life since He is the one who gave it.

*"Inna lillahi wa inna Ilaihi raji'un"*

"To God we belong and to Him we return"

Many people surrounded Ayah's body throughout the next few hours. In my sadness, it was difficult to distinguish who came to our house to pay last respects. Having dedicated his life to teaching, defending his religion and country, people considered my father as one of Indonesia's renowned leaders and heroes of that time. Various well-known national leaders attended Ayah's funeral. These included Kyai Haji Mas Mansur, leader of the Islamic Muhammadiyah organization, who was also one of the four pioneers of *"Empat Serangkai,"* (the Center of People's Power) political organization during those crucial years of Indonesia's historical development.

*Note: The Japanese created "Empat Serangkai" (Four Stems) organization in March of 1943 and included other leaders like Soekarno, Hatta and Ki Hajar Dewontoro who established the national Taman Siswa Schools. (From: Author)*

About five hours after Ayah's passing, his body was again carefully lifted onto the shoulders of men selected to give this last honor and carry him to Mesjid Tanah Abang, the mosque nearest to our house, for final recitation of the *Janazah* funeral prayer.

By about eleven o'clock that morning, the funeral procession continued on to my father's final resting place, Kuburan Karet, the cemetery almost twenty minutes walking distance from the mosque.

There were other prominent figures present at the gravesite giving their last respects to my father. Among them were Haji Agus Salim, another national leader, and Prof. Purbotjaroko, our neighbor and renowned professor of Javanese culture.

From all of my father's seven children, I was the only one present at his funeral, since Muslim rites required that burial take place as soon as possible after a death occurred. I was very sad with the loss of my father, but felt thankful Allah took him back and he would no longer be fighting the battle of illness.

Before Ayah's death, he had often reminded me, not to place any grave marker with his name on it at his burial site. This request was very important to my father. He told me he did not want the location to become a shrine like his own father's grave, my grandfather Tuanku Kisai.

A few days after losing my father, I had in fact turned the age of eighteen, although then; I had not yet learned the exact date of my birth. (It would be seven years later that I received information as to when I was actually born.) However, during that year of 1945, I realized that the moment had arrived for me to take steps in caring for myself. I knew the point in time was before me to move forward as an adult. This included discovery of life, which eventually forced me to walk through passageways of uncertainty and pain for survival.

# 8

# INDONESIA'S FREEDOM GENERATION 1945

Freedom is not won on the battlefields.
The chance for freedom is won there.
The final battle is won or lost
in our hearts and minds.
Helen Gahagan Douglass

From my earlier years, I had noticed there was a huge lack of a fair and suitable educational system for those native to our country (then still known as the Dutch East Indies). This was not so obvious to me when first attending school in my village of Sungai Batang, since the majority of my friends also went to school there. However, life in those days was generous to my free spirit and I was certainly too young to notice otherwise.

I did realize then, that because of my father's position I had been able to receive somewhat better opportunity for schooling. Since he was highly respected, I knew there were doors opened to me that were not opened for others who also deserved the basic right of learning how to read and write. The matter of equality or lack of it was not as obvious in West Sumatra as in Java or other islands, but it was evident nonetheless. A rather large community of *Indos* (of mixed Dutch and Indonesian descent) resided in the city of Padang, West Sumatra's capital.

It was while I was attending school in Padang Panjang that I first noticed the difference between treatment of the (indigenous) Indonesians, versus the Dutch (*Belanda Totok*) and (*Eurasian*) Indo people. I remember seeing small Dutch and Indo children go to the *Vreubel School*, Kindergarten

School. At age twelve, while standing across the street from the school, I wondered why the majority of our children were not educated. Later I became aware of blatant differences among those who called Indonesia home and the matter of their receiving an education.

While my parents had sent me to school in Padang Panjang during 1939, this lack of education for the Indonesian people and broad contrast of inequality within it would eventually become cause for interruptions in my own education, resulting in repetitive grade levels for me. The matter of inequality was an obstacle in the path of my life's journey already set in place by the Dutch during the colonial era, long before I was born.

*Note:* "*At the start of the twentieth century, the number of secondary educated Indonesians was almost negligible and from this time on, the Ethical Period saw the colonial government expand secondary educational opportunities to indigenous Indonesians.*" (Wikipedia – Indonesian National Awakening, Reid 1974, pp. 2-3)

*Note: Years later, it was appalling to me, discovering that by the end of the colonial era only about 6 % of our people could read and write (from the 1930 Census). This meant an astounding 94 % of Indonesians never received any basic education! (From: Author)*

It seemed impossible for our people to receive even the most basic education. In the eyes of many, it was unreachable, but for me it became a personal hurdle, which I was later determined to overcome. Sadly, the majority of our people accepted the fact that they or their children would not be able to attend school on a regular basis.

Therefore, most Indonesians assumed life was to be lived in an inferior manner. Additionally, it was a reality that most could not earn enough income due to lack of education under rule of the Dutch. As I grew older, I wanted to see the gap closed which colonialism had lain out.

One advantage for the people was when H.I.S Schools (Hollandsch Inlandsche School), defined as Dutch School for Natives, were established throughout the country. National organizations like the Muhammadiyah, established the H.I.S schools, which followed elementary level Dutch-style curriculum, including the Dutch language. There was one such school also in Padang Panjang and later even one in my village of Sungai Batang.

Although my father was one of the founders of Muhammadiyah in West Sumatra, he had me attend Thawalib School in Padang Panjang instead. At Thawalib School, the curriculum focused on Islamic studies as well as basic education.

Even though I attended the Thawalib School, I had already heard much about the national Taman Siswa Schools. During the period of my father's exile, I had jumped at the opportunity when asked if I wanted to attend there. I was glad to be a student at Taman Siswa for it was there the blaze of nationalism truly ignited within me. I would learn and respect even more the vision of the handful of national intellectuals who led the courageous forward march and yet to come victory for us as a country.

When my father passed away during 1945, I had suddenly leaped into adulthood. Without my parents, the usual nearby shade of their love and guidance, no longer shadowed me. I intuitively knew that I must first keep a course of action before me to continue with school, gleaning from it whatever I could and achieving results in a short period. After my father's death, while still living temporarily with my stepmother Dariyah, I remained at Sekolah SMP Prapatan, Middle School, although I was of high school age.

After the Japanese invasion in 1942, Sekolah SMP Prapatan, like the few other existing national schools, had also fallen under strict Japanese dictate. While I still attended school there in 1945, each day's curriculum consisted of four main objectives.

First, it was required that all students master the Japanese language. This class was taught by an Indonesian named Pak Mahyuddin, a Minang who amazingly enough had learned the language fluently shortly before teaching it to us.

Second, there was *Kyoren*, daily military training focused on the art of fighting. This was included every day without exception.

Third, we were engaged in a rigorous physical exercise routine twice a day. Known to us as *Taysho*, this took place in the morning and prior to our dismissal for the day.

Fourth, the Japanese expected that students work in construction labor within Jakarta wherever needed. This included assignments in repairing roads and digging trenches along streets. The purpose of these trenches was to protect the Japanese in case wartime fighting broke out. This labor was mandatory.

The period of Japanese occupation was difficult for my peers and me. If we wanted to learn, it meant attending these schools and obeying the extreme discipline. All our people had to follow the methods controlled by them. It however brought opportunity for everyone to receive an education.

Suddenly we faced a "no age limit" for those wanting to read and write, causing both young and old alike to seek it. It quickly became very clear to us that if we desired to learn, we needed to register ourselves and be prepared to follow their orders.

One of the strict mandates immediately enforced was the complete shaving of our heads. My friends and I regularly took turns shaving each other. At one point, some of the older students wanted to grow out their hair again. Surprisingly, the Japanese permitted it and we all soon followed.

Every Thursday it was required we attended presentations of propaganda films. My friends and I looked forward to this, because the films provided entertainment and helped interrupt the boredom. After the viewings, we usually dismissed to go home.

A problem arose one Thursday when instead of allowing us to leave, we were suddenly ordered to run through the Jakarta streets and back to the IKADA Stadium, supposedly as part of our military training. At this time of day, heat was reaching its peak and students naturally began complaining. It upset me that there was no regard for our well-being. I then made the decision not to do the run and encouraged other students to go home in defiance, which we did.

The following morning we all expected there was going to be trouble when our school Principal Pak Soebroto and a Japanese officer entered our classroom and stood sternly in front of us. Pak Soebroto, a man of distinguished appearance, and the middle-aged officer silently glared at each of our faces from one end of the room to the other.

Then it came, the scolding expected by all in the classroom. First Pak Soebroto harshly reprimanded and reminded us what could possibly await us. As our principal looked sternly at our faces, he asked, "Who was the one responsible for this act of disobedience?" Of course, no one responded. I stood up from my seat and replied to the principal and officer that we had all been tired explaining to them the difficulty of having to run that far in the hot afternoon heat. When I finished, I was ready for anything. I expected punishment for myself by having to do even more strenuous exercise in the blazing heat of the day. I also wanted to show that I was not afraid to face consequences.

Seemingly surprised that I dared speaking up, and acknowledging my actions of the day before, the Japanese officer looked at me with his continuous, merciless glare. He then proceeded to order the entire class to shave our heads as punishment. Even though he spoke with a tone of reprimand in his voice, I did manage to catch a small flicker of compassion in his eyes. As he spoke, the announcement came also that we could no longer grow out our hair until further notice. Even with the discomfort of intense discipline under the Japanese, we had a sense that things were changing.

*Note: Many of our people however, continued living within the condition of hopelessness, especially in education. Even with opportunity placed before them, they were fearful to step forward and reach for what could become a better way of life. This mindset, brought on by hundreds of years existing under colonial repression would not quickly disappear. At that point, the Japanese had yet to gain, the trust of Indonesian people. (From: Author)*

An immediate mandate given by the Japanese after occupying our country in 1942, was that anyone native to the land, who did not attend school or lacked proof of legitimate employment would become a *romusha*. This meant doing forced labor for the Japanese. Our young men who chose not to learn or hold valid jobs were then sent to work for the Japanese, either within Indonesia or different countries like Burma, Thailand, Philippines, Malaysia or other Japanese occupied territories. This forced labor meant internment in camps and working to build bridges, airports, and roads in these areas.

During the Japanese occupation of our country, there was horrific inhumane treatment in the forced labor camps. These accounts would later fill pages of our history books describing the unbearable cruelties experienced by the Dutch, the Indo's and the Indonesian people alike.

*Note:* *Experience of the occupation varied considerably, depending upon where one lived and one's social position. Many thousands of people were taken away from Indonesia as forced laborers (romusha) for Japanese military projects, including the Burma-Siam Railway, and suffered or died as a result of ill-treatment and starvation.*

*Tens of thousands of Indonesians were to starve, work as slave laborers, or be forced from their homes. In the national Revolution that followed, tens, even hundreds, of thousands, would die in fighting against the Japanese, allied forces, and other Indonesians, before Independence was achieved. A later United Nations report stated that four million people died in Indonesia as a result of famine and forced labor during the Japanese occupation. Including 30,000 European civilian internee deaths. (From: Japanese Occupation of the Dutch East Indies WIKIPEDIA the free encyclopedia)*

After World War II ended and Imperial Japan surrendered to the Allied Forces, immediate turbulence flared up in Indonesia. When the Japanese occupation ended on August 15, 1945, the instantaneous threat of the Dutch, returning together with the British was too realistic a scenario for us to accept.

Civil unrest escalated rapidly. Within days, Indonesia propelled into volatile directions. The explosive climate of incidents immediately affected my own way of life.

I had just finished the second level at SMP Parapatan School and was preparing to enter the next grade. Personally, those few days became momentous regarding decisions I needed to make quickly and steps I had to take for my future.

On August 17, 1945, Indonesia proclaimed independence two days after the Japanese had surrendered. After many years of combined efforts of national leaders and their organizations, the time had arrived that the *seed of freedom* for our people was finally coming to fruition. Years later, I would eventually come to know the results and milestones of these events, including the crucial part they played in the shaping of my beloved Indonesia.

Chaotic days and weeks followed the proclamation. Word spread especially among our country's youth who like me had received nurturing in schools like Taman Siswa, which inspired the spirit of nationalism for daring beliefs of a free nation. We no longer accepted the idea of life once again bound by oppression of colonialism. We refused any more domination by the Dutch as we had suffered for 350 years. We were not afraid to fight for the freedom we could experience just like other nations of the world.

Courage is not simply one of the virtues,
but the form of every virtue at the testing point.
C. S. Lewis

INDONESIA'S YOUTH MOVEMENT – API (1945)… The first indication of additional change in my life arrived one afternoon toward the end of September 1945, a few weeks after the declaration of independence by Indonesia. My friend Murad Aidit and I were making our way home from school around two o'clock in the afternoon through the area of Kwitang. Murad suggested we stop by *Menteng 31*, the new headquarters for the *API – Angkatan Pemuda Indonesia* – Indonesian Youth Movement.

As we leisurely walked, Murad described to me how the youth movement was organized (under leadership of Wikana, Chairul Saleh, D.N. Aidit and others), and how they were progressing with the strategy of keeping Indonesia free from the threatening return of Dutch colonialism. The youth movement mobilized into action, in order to defend the independence proclaimed by Soekarno and Hatta. The API Movement had officially established in Jakarta earlier that month on September 1, 1945.

Murad, being the younger brother of D.N. Aidit who headed the API Jakarta Raya faction, was able to tell me first-hand what happened most recently. His brother D.N. Aidit was only twenty-two years old, but had already been actively involved with underground youth groups in Jakarta, even during the Japanese occupation.

Murad had recently signed up with the API Movement. He told me what he heard about the days and moments leading to the courageous steps taken in declaring independence for Indonesia.

According to my friend, the activist youth had been involved in the kidnapping of Soekarno and Hatta. Bringing the two political leaders to

Rengasdengklok, they insisted that the two men make public declaration of Indonesian independence as planned.

*Note:* To further the cause of Indonesia's independence, Soekarno and Hatta appeared to cooperate with the Japanese authorities. In reality, however, Indonesian nationalist leaders went underground and masterminded insurrections in Blitar (East Java), Tasikmalaya and Indramayu (West Java), and in Sumatra and Kalimantan. (From: *Asian Info – Indonesia's History and Background*)

*Note:* While the formal preparation of the declaration, and the official independence itself for that matter, had been carefully planned a few months earlier, the actual declaration date was brought forward almost inadvertently as a consequence of the Japanese unconditional surrender to the Allies on August 15 following the Nagasaki atomic bombing. This historic event was triggered by a plot, led by a few more radical youth activists such as Adam Malik and Chairul Saleh that put pressure on Soekarno and Hatta to proclaim independence immediately. (From: *Proclamation of Indonesian Independence* – Wikepedia, the free encyclopedia)

*Note:* The Allies had no consistent policy concerning Indonesia's future apart from the vague hope that the republicans and Dutch negotiate peacefully. Their immediate goal in bringing troops to the islands was to disarm and repatriate the Japanese and liberate Europeans held in internment camps. Most Indonesians, however, believed that the Allied goal was the restoration of Dutch rule. Thus, in the weeks between the August 17 declaration of independence and the first Allied landings, republican leaders hastily consolidated their political power.

The situation in local areas was extremely complex. Activist young people, the pemuda, played a central role in these activities. As law and order broke down, it was often difficult to distinguish revolutionary from outlaw activities. Reactions to Dutch attempts to reassert their authority were largely negative, and few wanted a return of the old colonial order. (From: *The National Revolution 1945 – 1950* countrystudies.us/Indonesia/16.htm)

Murad, who was naturally easy-going of character, spoke to me about all these events on that afternoon. His explanations added fuel to the passionate blaze already ignited within me. Those passing by us on that day would not have believed what it was we (as young boys) were discussing. My ears were attentive to Murad's every word. With each comment spoken, my interest increased greatly. So much so, that I wanted to join my friend in fighting for Indonesia. I had been waiting for this opportunity.

Once having reached across town, we stopped at the Menteng 31 building. Murad checked in as part of the daily routine. Even though I came with my friend, I registered my own name as well and therefore committed to being an active member of the *Angkatan Pemuda Indonesia – API* youth organization. Age did not really matter, but three months prior to my enlistment in 1945; I had turned eighteen years old.

Having received constant military training during much of the three and half years of Japanese occupation, my classmates and I were prepared to instantly blend in with the ongoing activities of the API movement.

One of the first experiences soon after signing up was when Murad and I received instructions to go to a bicycle factory in the area of Kramat located in the center of the city. Our orders were to remove the Japanese flag and replacing it with an Indonesian red and white flag.

Our arrival that morning coincided with the still maintained daily Japanese flag raising ceremony. Determined to follow orders, we approached the Japanese officer in charge who looked at the two of us confounded. Everything came to a halt as I determinedly walked to the front of a group of over two hundred workers already gathered. Facing them with Murad at my side, I announced that they were to fly the Indonesian flag only. We then proceeded in lowering the Japanese one, and raising the Indonesian red and white flag. Not a single person stirred as the Japanese officer and his men looked on in astonishment. Murad and I were prepared for what could possibly happen to us.

In looking back, I clearly had not given much thought to the broad meaning of what happened that day. I only know that I never felt fear or hesitancy in those moments because of the fire already burning within me for my country. Knowing what we had to accomplish, there was no time to think about anything else but our orders.

Events continued shifting very quickly. There was a vast surge of nationalistic energy intensifying among the youth, much like a firestorm beyond stopping. A hard-to-contain passion was building up among all of us dedicated to seeing a free Indonesia. The Japanese departure was near on the horizon, but the possible threat of once again coming under Dutch control (since the Dutch were part of the Allied Forces), was the greatest incentive driving us at such young age, to willingly offer our lives. During those days we were not afraid to die, and would rather sacrifice ourselves so that others would know freedom in the land we greatly loved.

The leader of the API organization was Wikana as General Chairman. But Dipo Nusantara Aidit, Murad's older brother (known to us also as "Bang Amat"), was the local API Chairman within the city of Jakarta. As weeks passed, I would often see national officials like Adam Malik and Chairul Saleh at Menteng 31. These were just two of the intellectuals who for years had diligently paved the way establishing youth movements all over Indonesia.

Following my enlistment, I still attended school in the mornings. Afternoons I spent at Menteng 31, the API Headquarters. There we daily received more training and instructions from Wikana (and others) in forming the *Kamlin Keamanan Lingkunan*, neighborhood watch groups.

Attending Japanese school with the daily discipline of strict military drill regimen had actually prepared us to fight for our own emancipation. We had been instructed during those years how to mobilize our neighborhoods in the event of enemy attack. Thus, for circumstances of that time, we were able to use military tactics, taught to us by the Japanese.

The API youth army's purpose, was to prevent the Dutch from returning and re-claiming particular *kampung-kampung*, neighborhoods within the city. It was our responsibility to protect the people by being "the wall," which the Dutch would have to break through to re-establish their colonization.

Forming the Kamlin Keamanan Lingkunan neighborhood groups was to mobilize them into action to fight the return of Dutch arriving with the Allied Forces. Never knowing when the attacks would begin, our people needed to be prepared to protect themselves against an invasion by Dutch military forces.

Since my father had passed away and was no longer waiting for me each day, I did not come home until late evenings. My stepmother was very much aware of my participation in the youth movement and constantly reminded me to make sure of my safety.

My deeper involvement in API developed rapidly. Since I was already living in the area of Tanah Abang, I became API group leader in that section of Jakarta one month after my enlistment. This also included organizing the guarding of other areas in Kampung Bali, where the API headquarters was located. I replaced the leader in charge in Kampung Dukuh, since he left the city and returned to Central Java where outbreaks of fighting were advancing.

My good friend Adri Munir, was appointed as my secretary within the API organization. One of his responsibilities was to pass on to me instructions received from our command center. It was then my duty to mobilize these orders into immediate action.

Being selected group leader was an enormous honor for me during this time of our struggle. This important responsibility was a duty not taken lightly, especially because I thought there were other older, more experienced people than me. I soon learned that this kind of trust from my superiors was also rare.

Events continued changing daily. The Allied Forces (British and Dutch -NICA) had already landed and begun occupying large cities like Jakarta and Surabaya. It was our task to protect certain areas, so the Allies would not be able to infiltrate into the smaller residential neighborhoods.

While they did not know our strength, we intended keeping these forces out of specific areas. If the Allied Forces were able to penetrate into the smaller neighborhoods, it meant to us that we already lost that portion of the territory. The opposition, not aware of what the Japanese had trained us for, underestimated our degree of strength at that crucial time. Heavy fighting continuously broke out on main streets of the city.

We recognized the unexpected fortune for our cause. Applying military training previously imposed by the Japanese ultimately enabled us to defend ourselves during the revolution. What the Japanese intended for their own strategic purpose became an unforeseen benefit and advantage for the Indonesians.

We held back the opposition with whatever firearms available. Employing any accessible weapons to defend ourselves, this included the use of Molotov cocktails. These became standard arsenal for our fighting. We devised these comparably small bombs by using empty bottles filled with gasoline and mixed with shredded pieces of rubber. By putting rubber in the bottles, after hitting an object, the ignited rubber would then create more damage with the spreading of flaming fragments. We topped off the prepared bottles with cloth, which then became its fuse. Once ignited, we hurled them quickly and simultaneously, creating blasts causing soldiers in the tanks to come out.

By using *homemade weapons*, as long as we carefully planned the timing, it was a suitable form of launching attacks for us *pemuda-pemuda*, API fighters. Twelve to eighteen of us would wait united with fixed concentration. The thought of danger to ourselves by having lit explosives in our bare hands did not even cross our minds.

We had heard the Russians used this particular method and weaponry, in fighting against the Nazi Germans. For us it became one-way of utilizing whatever means were available during the extremely dire conditions we faced defending our country.

We were also the youth fighting with simple pointed bamboo spears. By making these handmade weapons; sharpened bamboo spikes known as *bambu runcing*, we succeeded with tough resistance. Perhaps it was the fiery courage of our young age causing us to be so fearless through the critical period of Indonesia's history. I only know that we insisted on standing up and claiming our country, which was ours by birthright.

We sometimes received orders to abduct certain Indonesian officials used previously by the then occupying Japanese forces. Taking advantage of their expertise was important for our goals. As odd as it may have seemed, we then had them become members of the newly formed cabinet of the new Republic of Indonesia.

In looking back, it was the API pemuda-pemuda, youth, who were most actively involved in the Indonesian revolution. We achieved this with our carefully organized mobilization in confronting the opposition. Indonesia's older generation often remained hesitant and fearful, unable to see the potentials of our simple explosives and weaponry like bamboo runcing spears.

Those with pessimistic views also mocked our efforts. They believed the youth could not possibly win against allied forces with their combined strength and modern artillery. Although often underestimated, we remained undeterred. It was with our fiery spirit that we persevered. Eventually, we also seized weapons from the Japanese forces remaining in Indonesia. This we accomplished with loss of many lives.

Additional Allied Forces continued arriving. Among them, the British *Ghurka* soldiers of Indian descent. The API youth however, relentlessly fought back the Dutch in attempts of their reclaiming Indonesia.

Every day we listened to radio broadcasts from Bung Tomo, a highly respected revolutionary leader. His passionate speeches about fighting in Surabaya and other areas against Allied Forces including the Dutch NICA encouraged our spirits not to give up. Bung Tomo used these radio broadcasts to rally the country together for battle.

*Note:* "*During the early stages of the Indonesian National Revolution he (Bung Tomo) played a central role when Surabaya came under British attack. Sutomo spurred thousands of Indonesians to action with his distinctive, emotional speaking-style of his radio broadcasts. His "clear, burning eyes, that penetrating, slightly nasal voice, or that hair-raising oratorical style that was second only to Sukarno's in its emotional power." (From: "In Memoriam: Sutomo" Indonesia Frederick, William H. April 1982 – Cornell University Southeast Asia Program)*

*Note: In later years, when Bung Tomo visited the United States, and I was local staff of the Indonesian Consulate, the Consul General in San Francisco assigned me to accompany him as he traveled throughout America. (From: Author)*

History later referred to the last three months of 1945 as the beginning of the *bersiap tijd* (Combined Indonesian/Dutch words meaning, "preparing time"). Violence, chaos and lawlessness, spreading everywhere characterized this particularly volatile period.

When the Japanese occupied the Dutch East Indies (Indonesia) during 1942, they established and controlled internment camps. Their focus had been the Dutch-European Indos who at that time had become a displaced people group. Born in Indonesia yet were considered European, they also had become targets of the Japanese.

*Note: The Japanese sought to eradicate anything reminiscent of European government. Many of the Indies Dutch had spent World War II in Japanese concentration camps. All Europeans were put in Japanese concentration camps. First the POW's, then all male adults and finally all females with their children and adolescents were interned. The Japanese failed in their attempts to win over the Indo community and Indos were made subject to the same forceful measures. (From: Indo People Wikipedia, the free encyclopedia)*

Consequently, Indo people suffered during the Japanese occupation. They later continued suffering through the intense *bersiap*, preparing, period of our revolution. Re-internment befell tens of thousands of Dutch people under the new R.I. (Republic of Indonesia). This infuriated Indos having to enter the camps again; and refusing to believe the intention of Indonesians, wanting them protected rather than be in harm's way on streets constantly in battle. Additionally, they resented the API Pemuda youth army, of which I was an active fighter.

*Note: Liberation of the internment camps holding western prisoners was not swift. After four months of post-war internment, Western internees were released on the condition they left Indonesia. (From: Japanese Occupation of the Dutch East Indies – End of the Occupation Wikipedia, the free encyclopedia)*

The British could not prevent API pemuda fighters from viewing them as being pro-Dutch. Thus, the British became targets of the youth fighters as well. Even the Japanese became victims of the violence, since disorder was rampant and any situation could trigger a chaotic "free-for-all."

When I was in Tambun, West Java, training villagers in making and using Molotov cocktails correctly, an incident happened that stayed with me throughout my life. My group and I were in the area one late afternoon when I discovered numerous Dutch-Indo women in one of the houses we had to search. It was then common all over Indonesia that sometimes five to six families would have to reside in one house if they managed to remain outside of the internment camps.

Discovering the women hiding, they off course were terrified of us, but my heart went out to their plight. Seeing the expressions of fear in their eyes touched me, and with it came a sense of deep compassion. Even though we wanted a free Indonesia, the suffering of innocent victims affected me most. I did not know any of these women personally, but in those moments, I tried my best to communicate to them that we were not there to harm them. Since I spoke some Dutch, we were able to ask questions. They then told is about their situations.

My friends and I began helping the women find ways of returning to their relatives, some who were located as near as Jakarta. We wanted to reassure them our intent was to protect them. They reminded me of the Indo friends I also had in school who were from Dutch mothers and Indonesian fathers. This encouraged me to want to help these women and their children get to the safest possible place.

It was during this time; I also heard about the killing of nineteen allied soldiers in nearby Bekasi. Among British captured were Indian Muslim soldiers. These Indian soldiers later joined us in our fight.

Amid the turmoil, allied forces continued arriving at Surabaya and other main harbors throughout Indonesia. It was clear that devastation caused by events of wartime and this conflict, horribly affected the lives of the Indonesian people, the Dutch, and Indo population alike.

FREEDOM'S QUEST (1946)… Our food supply was extremely limited. Daily provision consisted of occasional *ikan asin*, dried salted fish and some *sayur-sayuran,* vegetables. With no plates or utensils available, we used banana leaves to eat our rice and vegetables.

Occasionally we received confiscated wooden boxes from the Pacific Compo containing products and food actually intended for allied forces. Each Pacific Compo box actually intended for two persons, we shared with more than two members in our group. Among the contents were British cigarettes, canned goods like *sardines and corned beef,* plus health and hygiene provisions. We removed these boxes from the allied forces convoy; bringing supplies to Bandung for their soldiers. When their train stopped at the Cikampek station, it gave us opportunity to seize the goods.

The API Youth movement and other organized Indonesian freedom fighting groups received orders from the new government to move out from Jakarta and go inland during November of 1945. While still in the Jakarta area, I instead, decided to join with the *TKR – Tentara Keamanan Rakyat* – the People's Security Army. With constant changes taking place, the TKR soon changed its name to *TNI (Tentara Nasional Indonesia)* Indonesian National Army.

I relocated with the VI Regiment, Siliwangi Division – Cicampek, commanded by Col. Mufreini. Our group initially consisted of six members. Two were my friends Agus and Adri, both having arrived with me. Three others joined us. They were Sutan Harahap, Nuril Rachman and Khaeruddin.

I soon left Jakarta with my friends Agus S. Indrakusuma, Adri Munir, and Ishak Dasaad. Before leaving, we received some extra money from Ishak's parents to help us buy food when needed. Their other son Benny Dasaad had left Jakarta before us, but was killed in the battle against the Dutch army at Bekasi.

When we arrived at Cikampek, our assignment was in the Military Police Investigation Section *(Polisi Tentara Bagian Penyelidik)* under command of Capt. Sofyan. All who joined this newly organized group were my friends. Adri Munir (my Secretary in API) and Agus S. Indrakusuma both originated from Lampung. Khaeruddin Nitikusumah (later became Brigadier General of Police), Nuril Rachman (eventually became a Member of the Indonesian Parliament BAKIN), Sutan Harahap (became a successful business executive), and Yudono (whom we called "Delman") were all with me in this TKR unit. We always teased Yudono who was the only one in our group who came from Java. His speech was always too *halus*, refined, for us. He had some trouble adapting himself with the *preman*, tough guy style dialect we used.

In addition to these close friends, there were many more *teman seperjuangan*, fellow freedom fighters with me in Cikampek. All of them were serving in this Siliwangi Investigative Division, although previously from different freedom-fighting detachments. We stayed in barracks with other recruits while awaiting new orders.

Despite the seriousness of our duties, our camaraderie developed into some of the most memorable wartime moments. One funny experience I can never forget happened during this time and involved our temporary housing.

For a few days, only our unit stayed in these quarters. This had previously been a coal storehouse for trains. We had reached the barracks late in the evening very exhausted. We each laid our weary bodies down wherever we could find a spot. Most fell asleep immediately. When we woke the following morning, each person enjoyed great hilarity at the black noses and nostrils of their companions before realizing they were themselves also black with coal dust.

With no mirrors on hand, no one at first acknowledged the black nostrils to the other, since we were unable to see our own reflections. Of course, it was not long before we burst into laughter seeing each other's faces. That was when the mischievous jokes began. More laughter followed when first one person sneezed, then another. Of course, each time one of us sneezed, more black soot settled above their lips. Even during those dire times, seeing this band of young tough fighters (forced by war to become men much too soon), rolling over in laughter like little boys, was hilariously funny. Through moments like this, we were able in a small way to relieve some of the unbelievable tension we lived with each day.

Since we were the newly formed army of Indonesia, there were not enough uniforms available for all of us. Since I had arrived in the area with no personal belongings, one of the men from the former *PETA* organization (an Indonesian volunteer army created by the Japanese during the occupation in 1943), gave me a pair of pants which he had also found somewhere along the way.

Thus, I wore European style riding pants known as a *rij broek*. These pants designed to fit loosely from the waist to above the knees, fit tighter around the calves. Below the knees of these riding pants, leather boot tops covered my legs, while the worn out soles of my shoes had twine string wrapped around each foot. Another friend of mine had provided me a shirt, which had also been part of a uniform belonging to a slain British Gurkha soldier. Because I was new to the Division, I was one of the few wearing a straw hat, to cover my head. These *topi rumput*, straw-hats, became the recognized representation of the Indonesian Revolution written about in history books of Indonesia years later.

We had made a pact to refrain from cutting our hair until the struggle for independence was completed. Thus, we kept our hair *gondrong*, shoulder length or longer, especially within my group.

As part of our reconnaissance operations, we regularly went out behind enemy lines. Our mission was to investigate their activities and know where our targets were moving. This was a period of extreme pressure in my life. I was in serious danger each time my friends and I went out to survey the positions of our opponents.

After a year of active duty, we were given a short period of furlough during late 1946. I used my leave to travel to the city of Yogyakarta in Central Java. It was here that I ran into a business owner from Jakarta who had mocked our purpose and me while I was active with the API youth movement.

I had regularly come to his store on errands for my stepmother. He had been among those who strongly believed, that we as young people with our *bambu runcing* spears, did not have a chance to win battle against allied forces. He had expressed his opinions in front of others, with rude unpleasant words.

The day of our encounter was in Yogyakarta (capital of the new Republic of Indonesia). He was traveling to Malang east Java to a meeting of the KNIP, Indonesia's first Parliament. This same person, who previously voiced we could never successfully fight against the Dutch and British Allies, had become one of the representative delegates from Jakarta.

I had gone to the luxurious Merdeka Hotel, which had become a recreational site for my friends and other fighters like me. As I walked around (in what was still) the plush hotel lobby, I noticed him. With my changed appearance and long hair, he may not have recognized me at first. But I purposely walked toward him, my mind replaying his crude words.

Upon my approach, he could not hide either that he knew me. After small talk, he invited me to chat, *ngobrol* in his hotel room. Walking with him, he talked nervously.

In the room, he asked more questions. I told him, I was in the TNI Indonesian army. Sensing he was avoiding mention of our last encounters, I waited for the right moment. While looking intently at him, taking my time, I spoke in a quiet voice, "You see, today this is the result of our struggle as young fighters, that you too, are appointed as one of the parliament leaders of the free Republic of Indonesia." It was clear he was embarrassed and uneasy. After finding his voice, he apologized to me for having been tactless and judgmental. I left soon after this.

I went directly to visit my aunt Halimah Ibrahim, a relative from my mother's side through her Malayu clan. She and her family were now living in this area. It was quite a distance from the Merdeka Hotel, but when I arrived, I felt welcome there among family. After one week of some good times in Yogyakarta, I returned to my army outfit located in Cikampek, West Java.

Having already been in the new TNI army for a year, I felt bored with life as a soldier. I believe this restlessness stirred because our group of six had dispersed, each of us received new orders. I was no longer involved in the deeper field fighting. My new assignment involved entering occupied areas in search of weapons, as far inland as Mojokerto in East Java.

FREEDOM'S STRUGGLES (1947-1948)… In the years following our 1945 Proclamation of Independence, fierce fighting continued throughout Indonesia. Considered *Extrimis*, political extremists by the Dutch, we remained adamant in our cause as Revolutionary Freedom Fighters. Wanting total freedom from the Dutch, we were unafraid. We did not care about the sacrifice, especially during the period of *Polisionil Aksi Pertama*, the First Police Action. This was when Dutch forces (having re-entered Indonesia with the allied forces) began attacking further inland areas to re-establish colonial rule in Indonesia.

Our recently formed national army TNI also led underground operations throughout former Dutch-controlled areas. This First Police Action took place in a two-week period from July 21 to August 5 1947.

*Note: AKSI POLISIONIL or Police Action, also known as the Dutch Military Aggression, is a military operation launched by the military Dutch in Java and Sumatra against the Indonesian Republic conducted from July 21 to August 5, 1947 (aksi pertama - first action), Dutch Military Aggression I, also known as Product Operations. This operation succeeded in occupying most of Java and Sumatra, because the TNI – Indonesian Army did not carry out resistance due to lack of weapons. However (it) resulted in the actions (activities) from the guerrilla's by the TNI – Indonesian Army, and Pelopor, the Pioneers (Forerunners) in other areas. From 19 December 1948 until 5 January 1949 (aksi kedua – second action), Dutch Military Aggression II (occurred). This police action in Yogjakarta directly attacked the Indonesian government, including (that) President Sukarno was arrested. The Dutch action, actually an attempt to destroy the (new) Republic failed, due to intervention of the United Nations. Finally, the Dutch recognized Indonesian independence because of pressure from the United States. (Indonesian Translation – From: Wikipedia, the free encyclopedia)*

*Note: "These Dutch actions ignited and fueled the anti-Dutch feelings and hatred towards anything related to the Dutch, including the Indo's, citizens of mixed Dutch-Indonesian parentage, who then became victims of the wrath of the freedom fighters. What did the Dutch government do to help them in their time of need??? Nothing!!! Their continued military offensives only further fueled the Indonesian spirit to defend their freedom from Dutch colonialism at all costs.*

*If the Dutch had ended their aggressive military quest for continued colonial government, loss of lives and deplorable atrocities on both sides could have been prevented. But, unwilling to recognize the changed political climate, they stubbornly refused to do so.*

*The revolutionaries fought to defend their freedom. Their previous Dutch masters gave them good examples of how to treat the enemy. Not only revolutionary opponents but also innocent villagers became victims of the Dutch colonial quest. As a result, Dutch citizens and Indo's had to suffer the revolutionary wrath and retaliation of the Indonesian independence fighters. Atrocities occurred on both sides." (From: "Indonesia: The Sukarno Years" edited by Hal Kosut Subjects: Indonesia-History -Revolution 1945-1949 Published New York: Facts on File, c 1967)*

During the First Political Action, I was already in Jakarta and had joined in with underground activities of a group known as *Kota CBI Klawar* under the command of Mustafa Dulah a.k.a Mahmud Jabar. A close family friend, Zainal Abidin Saleh, whom I considered to be like one of my older brothers, introduced me to this faction.

I was very happy meeting Zainal Abidin Saleh again. I always referred to him as *Uda,* the Minang word for big brother. I knew Uda Zainal since he attended the Qulyatul Muballighin School in Padang Panjang. He also often visited the home of my sister Fathimah there. We had last seen each other during 1939. He had come to our house to ask my father for a letter of recommendation for him to attend the SMT (Senior High School). After my father wrote a letter to Pak Adam Bakhtiar (who was then the principal of the school), Uda Zainal was accepted.

I did not meet Uda Zainal again until 1943. With all the wartime actions rapidly developing through the following years, we met during early 1947 and then continued together for the remaining period of freedom's struggle.

Between 1947 and 1948, it was via information I regularly received from Uda Zainal that my instructions came from the underground Kota CBI Klawar faction. By then, we both belonged to the group and I carefully carried out their orders, which most often involved the destruction of buildings re-occupied by the Dutch.

One particular mission almost cost me my life. This happened in 1947 during the First Police Action. Having received new orders, I left one morning at daybreak for the home of my friend Syafei. Our group usually undertook these strikes late at night.

My friend was already waiting when I arrived. It was our group's assignment to destroy specific buildings located nearest to the palace in the city. Because we were so young, we were daringly determined.

Syafei knew where to provide his support in helping me. We had to be extra careful, since we were following this particular order during daylight hours. With every movement cautiously planned and timed, we knew the procedure. Many others would join us at the targeted sight. All involved knew their part and responsibility.

My appearance at this time, with my hair cut short again, belied the fact that I really was a freedom fighter. Cautiously we made our way to the area known as *Jakarta Pusat*, the center of Jakarta. Under my loosely fitting shirt, attached to my waist were six hand grenades. We hardly spoke while walking until we reached the street where the *Harmonie* building was located. This building was the center of European society during colonial years, known as *De Soosietijd*. Reoccupied once again by the Dutch, that morning the aim of our group was to demolish the building with fire.

As Syafei and I guardedly preceded on foot, suddenly out of nowhere, a jeep driven by Dutch MP's, headed toward us; approaching quickly, but drove by. Passing us, their eyes never left us. All young men our age were highly suspect.

We immediately sensed the threatening danger, not only because of what we were about to do, but also because we knew what the MP's next moves most likely would be. If they caught me with the grenades on my body and Syafei on his, the arrest and punishments would be severe. They however were not on foot, we were.

Not wasting a moment, before the jeep had opportunity to turn around and chase after us, Syafei and I started running. We quickly dashed over a bridge across the Ciliwung River. We ran fast, heading straight into narrow alleyways of the Pecenongan neighborhood. Here, the houses were closely crowded together on countless small back streets. With grenades still fastened around my waist and Syafei holding onto his, we kept running and running, not daring to stop or look back for even a single moment. Sweat drenched, our lungs just about totally depleted of air, Syafei and I finally reached one of the houses we knew belonged to a Minang family, friends of Uda Zainal.

Met by the stunned family, we hid inside their house, catching our breath first and waiting until we knew it was safe the Dutch police MP's could not find us. Some three hours later, believing it being secure enough to leave, we asked if we could temporarily store the ammunition with the family, reassuring them we would return very soon. Knowing the risk involved, they still agreed to help us.

Therefore, it was because of such dangerous situations, that those in my faction and I would repeatedly almost lose our lives. There were six of us in the group, Anwar Rasyid (my nephew, the son of my sister Fathimah), Syuhaimi Luthan, Zarkasih, Uda Zainal and myself. Syafei, although not considered a regular member of the Kota CBI Klawar often partnered with me (depending on the assignment).

During this period, I stayed at a house rented by Syuhaimi at Kebon Kacang V in Jakarta. In order to accomplish our missions, meant nightly going out on foot. During daytime hours however, I still also tried completing school as best I could.

On nights of our undertakings, we remained cautious with curfews imposed by the Dutch. We avoided main streets, swiftly navigating mazes of the narrowest back streets in *kampung*, neighborhoods. Although we were young, nightly assignments on foot and coping with tension, physically and mentally drained us. Often working through the night, our weary bodies became fatigued.

After completing a mission, we returned to the house, quietly slipping in unnoticed (we hoped). Each of us would then find a spot to lay our weary heads, quickly welcoming sleep.

Resting usually meant doing so directly on the floor, most often without a *tikar*, woven straw mat. I would undress and slip my *sarong* (material sewn in tubular fashion at each end) over my head and cover the lower part of my body.

On one such night, our group managed to return safely to the house unseen – or so we thought. The house we stayed at had several bedrooms. Some rooms we shared, but that particular night I slept alone in one.

While we were all asleep, Uda Zainal, who slept in the front portion of the house, was the first to hear pounding on the front door. Startled by the sudden noise, he jumped up from where he lay. Boom! Boom! Boom! Boom! Boom! The pounding continued. Uda Zainal cautiously went to open the door. He nearly fainted at the sight facing him. Standing there, were at least twenty-five Dutch red-beret NICA soldiers.

While facing them in the open doorway, one of the soldiers pushed Uda Zainal forcefully in the chest, shoving him sideways; causing him to nearly fall backwards on the floor. Then the same soldier again grabbed Uda Zainal, in a loud voice shouting at him, *"Ektremis, ya? Ektremis, ya?"* "Extremist, right?" Trembling and weak in the knees, Uda Zainal could only silently stare back at the soldier.

Suddenly from within the group, several soldiers rammed their way into the house, entering each bedroom to search for the rest of us. Soldiers remained outside waiting and guarding the house, while in the first room some were holding Uda Zainal. Room after room they kicked doors open. My other friends, also awakened by all the commotion, were ordered to get up and go outside of their rooms.

One of the NICA soldiers, stun gun in hand burst into the room where I lay on the floor still sleeping. The room was pitch-black. Apparently, he saw something and letting out a hair-raising scream, bolted from my room, running from the house shouting loudly. The entire platoon, shocked by his terror, unthinkingly fled directly behind him into the night.

Uda Zainal, still shaken after the forced entry and then sudden strange departure of the NICA soldiers, quickly closed and locked the door. As fast as his weak legs could take him, he rushed into the room the NICA soldier had bolted from; where I was still sleeping. He later told me that seeing me there, he also almost fainted. It was no wonder the soldier had become so frightened and burst forth from the room. For there I was, lying on my back on the cement floor, arms resting across my chest, eyes closed with my body swaddled in the *sarong*. In blackness of the room, the manner in which the cloth wrapped around me must have made the soldier think I was a dead *mayat*, corpse or a *hantu*, ghost. Whatever else may have appeared to that soldier, none of us would ever know.

As much as the initial sight of me startled Uda Zainal, he erupted with loud uncontrollable laughter. It was not until I woke up from the boisterous racket, that I became aware of what had happened. As he shared how the chain of events took such an unexpected turn, Uda Zainal repeatedly said, *"Alhamdulilah Alhamdulilah,"* thanking Allah, God for the protection over us from the NICA soldiers; even if in such a hilarious manner.

Thinking back, the manifestation of my supposed *penampilan-hantu*, ghost-like appearance, which chased away powerful Dutch soldiers, still humored me for years to come. The fact that I had never awakened during that entire occurrence remained a mystery to all of us, most of all me.

If Uda Zainal, had not seen my *sarong* clad body on the floor that night with his own eyes; none of us would have understood what so terrified an entire platoon of NICA soldiers. These were moments when fate was moving. In looking back, it was also the beginning of a realization in my young adult life how the shadow of Almighty God already hovered over me.

# 9

# DESTINY'S DOORWAY

Surely the power of endurance
that God can give to the human soul
are beyond our understanding.
Amy Carmichael

My yearning to continue school emerged, when acceptance at *SMA Salemba* (High School) arrived for me. Located in front of Tjipto Mangunkusumo General Hospital, the school later moved to another location on Kramat Raya Street.

During the beginning of 1948, I reunited with my friend Murad Aidit in Jakarta. We had been close friends, especially during our API –Youth Movement days three years earlier. Meeting each other again, Murad asked if I had a place to stay. Telling him I did not, he suggested I stay with him and his older brother Basri at Gondangdia Kecil. I attended high school during the day and evenings had begun working with my uncle selling textiles.

Since my father's death in 1945, I was very much on my own. It seemed only *Pak* Adam Bakhtiar, one of my teachers (whom my family had known many years), took special interest in my personal well-being.

I was twenty-one years old during 1948 and after all the interruptions; I was still trying to finish my high school education. Knowing I had an unquenchable appetite for learning, Pak Adam Bachtiar continued being particularly concerned about me. No matter how difficult the matter of my regularly attending classes was, my faithful teacher fought to keep avenues open for me to resume learning. Sometimes when I missed classes for too long, he sent his son to look for me. Since I was staying at Gondangdia Kecil Street, it was not far from my teacher's house.

Because I was always busy, it was difficult for me to be at any given place during specific hours. However, those who looked for me always found a way to meet up with me. On one occasion I told Pak Adam, that since I had to earn money, I helped my uncle *Mak* Harun Sutan Siri (my mother's half-brother), with his textile business at *Pasar* Tanah Abang, open air market. I expressed to Pak Adam about my desire to learn; and how I felt concerning my education lagging behind due to the weight of responsibilities I carried. Even as difficult as life was for me at that time, I was able to share with him about the hope I had for my future. I sensed his compassion as he listened and I realized that fate was on my side through this man who believed I could accomplish anything I wanted.

After our talk, Pak Adam did all he could as well as several of my other teachers, Pak Takdir Alisjahbana, my Indonesian language teacher, and Pak Wagendorff, who taught me English. They also helped, by tutoring me outside of the classroom, willing to meet with me as often as I could make time. I appreciated their belief in me, and tried my best to follow all their instructions without disappointing them.

One evening while doing homework, my concentration focused on the Algebra book in front of me, I suddenly heard the sound of rushing and running outside the house. I did not realize that what I heard were the Dutch military police. Being so absorbed in the homework, I had not been aware of their entry until it was too late.

When I looked up, five rifles pointed at my head. Near the table where I was sitting, were many stacked cases of ammunitions on the floor. These reached across the room and other spaces inside the house where a larger quantity of the weaponry was stored. We had received instructions to transport the firearms further inland the following day.

Ordering me to get up from where I was sitting, the Dutch MP's immediately grabbed me. Murad, reading nearby on the floor was also apprehended. They forcefully shoved us outside and into one the waiting jeeps. We discovered later that one of our own had betrayed us.

Murad and I were taken to the *Hoofd Bureau*, Dutch Police Headquarters. There they interrogated us for hours. Because we did not divulge information, they separated us and we received rounds of beatings by MP's. Murad was the first one taken away. While I was awaiting my turn, I silently began reciting a prayer in Arabic, which my stepmother Dariyah taught me. She had told me to memorize this prayer and use it whenever danger confronted me. It is as follows:

*"Bismillahi amantu billah, wa'tasamtu billah, watawakkaltu 'alallah. La haula wala quwwata illa billahil 'aliul'adzim."*

The words and this prayer meant surrendering everything to God in fullness of faith, believing the outcome would be according to Allah's all-powerful will.

When my turn came, they moved me to another interrogation area. There were more MP's in that room, some not much older than myself. A barrage of questions and threats immediately spewed out of the mouth from the officer in charge. The CP, Dutch Police examiner, was Inspector Smit. This irate man separately interrogated both Murad and I.

When questioning me, they believed I was lying. Inspector Smit continuously used a large wooden ruler with a sharp metal edge on one side to hit my head at particular angles. I tried not flinching at the pain inflicted each time the sharp ruler struck my skull. The strikes however, were not enough to make me give in to their demands. What hurt most, was not the physical pain, but the indescribable betrayal I felt from those beating me. They were Indonesians who had gone over to the Dutch side.

As interrogating continued, the inspector addressed me in the crudest manner. When his onslaught of questions ended, we all waited, no one moved. I however, had decided to keep an unfaltering silence. Then the real beating began.

When the interrogation started again, my stubborn silence infuriated the already incensed Dutchman that much more. When I did not reply, a sudden fierce blow to my forehead sent me reeling backwards. The Dutch inspector continued his attempt to intimidate, by way of his position standing over me. While remaining obstinately silent, but brazenly holding my stare on the sweating Dutchman, I knew that I was aggravating the situation even more.

That first night, hours dragged on in the interrogation building. They ordered Murad and I to strip naked; then shoved us into a temporary holding cell. Intentional humiliation in this manner was to break us down.

Several hours later we awakened, when MP guards poured buckets of cold water over us, one after the other. At the same time shouting, *"Hei, anak Sukarno, bangun lu!"* – "Hey, Sukarno son, get up, you!" (Using *"lu"* is a demeaning slur). They then ordered us to leave the cell.

Murad and I stood lined up with other detainees. Our wet naked bodies shivered in the early morning hours. After ordering us to get dressed, the individual interrogations continued as did the beatings. The frustrated Dutchmen, who hours earlier were unable to retrieve anything from us, were again incapable of breaking our silence. Since they thought I was lying when I did reply, repeated hitting the side of my head with another very large wooden ruler began. I know that because I did not scream with their blows, they inflicted harder strikes on my person. Murad on the other hand, thought the louder he groaned with each punch, the more chance of slight relief.

After this, those in charge shoved us into a small 10x16 foot cell, which already held fifteen other prisoners, most whom were criminals. Due to the overcrowding in that narrow space, it was impossible for any one of us to lie down, forcing us to remain sitting-up on the filthy floor. Trying to sleep meant doing so in that same sitting position. Since not permitted to bathe, the stench of unclean bodies was especially bad.

Food allotted was only rice and tasteless *sayur*, a watery vegetable mixture, without a dish, bowl or leaf from which to eat. Since we did not have an empty can or container, they poured a scoop of rice and vegetables directly into our cupped hands. The food was never enough to satisfy our hunger.

Punishment for my stubborn silence came, when the Dutch interrogators ordered me to clean the *WC,* toilets each morning. These were actual open gutters with human waste. This labor was stomach turning repulsive, but I remained voiceless.

After detaining us for almost two months, Dutch officials concluded no information was coming forth from Murad or me. Much to our surprise, sudden release arrived with the only requirement being, that we report daily to police headquarters and immediately return to school. Disobeying this condition meant re-arrest.

Resuming school was a gift for me. This was very different from my daily toilet cleaning duties while detained. Through this experience, I gained true satisfaction in knowing; I overcame cruelty and through silence remained standing for Indonesia's freedom cause.

Once released, Murad and I decided that it was safer to separate. We each also had our own plans. I told Murad that it was my intent to go abroad, although I did not yet know how, but would look for a way. Murad told me he was going to remain in Indonesia to continue in the struggle. My friend then went to look for his older brother D.N. Aidit and family to stay with them. After this, I no longer saw my best friend. Many years later, I heard Murad contracted Tuberculosis and endured hospitalization for a very long time.

I also learned that Ibu Mus, owner of the house where our arrest took place, was tortured with both her hands completely shattered by beatings with a rifle butt during interrogations. She lost complete use of both her hands.


FATE'S PASSAGEWAY… Turmoil continued spreading out of control. I experienced many dangerous and sad incidents during that period. These included the numerous times the enemy had opportunities to kill me but were unsuccessful. After the Dutch released me, my participation with underground activities increased for a short time. As part of the revolution for total independence, these particular struggles would eventually become part of Indonesia's history. All however, would remain vivid memories for me. I kept this deep within my soul, and in due course, these experiences travelled with me throughout my life's journey into the world.

Even amid the constant turmoil, I remained optimistic and continued working and selling textiles with my uncle Mak Harun. At the end of every month, we divided profits equally. This helped me in taking care of myself, plus putting some earnings aside for my plans. The shop at the Tanah Abang pasar, market place, began flourishing, judging from the large stacks of merchandise we restocked monthly. I saved whatever money I could in order to go abroad soon.

Not only was I helping my uncle at the one open-air market during daytime, but during evenings, I often also rode around Jakarta on a bicycle stacked with textiles. I carefully managed to balance the merchandise through even the narrowest of streets. Some of the open-air markets only did business during evening hours. Most often, I biked to Pasar Manggarai. On some evenings, I went to another location called Gang Kancil. As seen from the *badaman*, bundle on the back of my bicycle, sales were quite profitable. With time, this grew larger. All this took place during the early part of 1948.

One day, while thinking how to juggle the different things I was doing, I compared it to when my cousin Utin (Arifsuddin) and I, sold cigarettes at the market place we frequented during the Japanese occupation. At that time we sold cigarettes "by the piece" which provided the two of us only a very small profit. It was enough to buy us some snacks. If we did not sell the entire package of cigarettes, (making sure not to waste anything), we smoked the rest ourselves. Since my father was still alive during the Japanese occupation, and while I still lived at home with both he and my stepmother, *uang jajan*, snack money, was good enough for Utin and I. However, those days of 1943 already seemed very long ago.

My dreams of going abroad by ship never faded. Even with all the turmoil throughout my teens, I firmly remained focused on my ambition; knowing I must keep saving money for this goal. Although I was, still physically present in Indonesia; the years of Dutch colonialism, Japanese occupation, and Revolution for our independence, never stopped my mind from traveling to worldwide ports.

I soon enough realized that the money I tried saving during 1948, would not be enough to pay for passage abroad by ship. Knowing it would take too long, made me somewhat change my plans. I decided that whatever funds I saved, I could use to bribe one of the *mandor darat*, shore agents, whose job it was to look for Indonesian laborers seeking work on out-going ships.

Being very much on my own, I felt I had begun moving toward a new passageway of fate. I believed my destiny was beginning to take its direction. I sensed Allah held a course for me in my future.

Having become so focused on working and saving whatever money I could, my schooling suffered. Once again interrupted, my education fell to the wayside almost to the point of total neglect. This forced me to decide, and I sacrificed finishing school. I had to make this very difficult choice to earn enough for daily needs, and following my dreams of sailing abroad.

Nevertheless, I was determined to pursue my education by the best possible means. Conditions being as they were, and understanding my plight, my teachers were still willing to continue helping me. I learned much later that recognizing my potential convinced them to keep providing me the extra opportunities to learn from them.

Because I had set my hopes rather high, I knew that for my plans to become reality it must be set into motion soon. I was already preparing necessary paperwork I knew I would need, if I were to leave Indonesia. First was acquiring a *Lieu of Passport* document, obtainable through the office of Indonesian Foreign Affairs, which had already opened offices in Jakarta.

Uda Zainal and I went there together, because he initially was also planning to go abroad with me. We had often talked about our dreams of leaving together, after our responsibilities with the guerilla group and revolution finished.

At the time, there was somewhat of an obstacle. Uda Zainal was already engaged to *Uni* Nurma, (*Uni* – meaning sister in Minang) the daughter of Sutan Iskandar (a prominent writer also from my village, Sungai Batang). Thus, desiring to sail but because the engagement made it more difficult for him to decide, I told Uda Zainal that if he was going to be married, he should cancel his plan of leaving Indonesia. He finally agreed with my suggestion so that Uni Nurma's heart would not be broken if he left her behind.

I was able to receive my Lieu of Passport document with the help of Pak Soerjotjondro, (one of my former teachers), who then worked at the Foreign Affairs office in 1948. While helping me, he asked about my plans to reach my goal. My reply was that whatever way possible, even if the first option was becoming a worker on a small boat sailing to Singapore, would be fine with me. Pak Soerjotjondro's only advice to me was, "Be careful Wadud; remain safe."

Looking back to those turbulent and uncertain years, my being able to obtain the Lieu of Passport document became evidence that God wanted this for my life. While Indonesian people still suffered much pain and sorrow regarding freedom in their lives, and when so many things were unreachable, I somehow received an open passage for my future. However, at the age of twenty-one in 1948, I did not yet clearly understand the importance of that fact.

HIGH HOPES AND DREAMS… I had heard that the Dutch Shipping Company *SMN (Stoomvaart Maatschappij Nederlands)* was looking for Indonesian laborers to work as machine maintenance assistants. Another Dutch shipping and passenger liner company, the *Rotterdamsche Lloyd*, also offered employment as *anak-sekoci,* laundry-men; but usually preferred Sundanese workers from West Java for these positions, while the *jongos-jongos*, steward assistants, were from Javanese and Madurese background.

There was a shore agent named Arifin from Bugis (Sulawesi), who lived in Tanjung Priok and worked for the SMN Company. It was his task to look for machine maintenance workers on the ships. I knew this from my friend Muhammad Ahmad, a schoolmate of mine. We realized later, we were also related because Ahmad was the grandson of *Datuk* Nan Putieh, one of the leaders of our Minangkabau *suku*, clan.

With hopes of getting work, we each, had already paid f30. - (thirty rupiah red money/gulden) as bribe money to this shore agent Arifin; trusting he would put us on a list of workers to be quickly placed on one of the ships. To save that much money then was very difficult for us, since we did not hold permanent jobs.

While waiting, our money situation became very tight. We were staying at the house of Ammi Umar a man from Bima, who was very kind to us. He was a very devout Muslim, and we often prayed together. He then asked me to teach his sons to read the Quran, Islam's Holy Book.

Ahmad and I waited at Ammi Umar's house for about three months. At first, Arifin gave us many excuses. One excuse was about certain requirements of a medical examination in order to be hired. Sometimes the other reasons did not make any sense at all. After this, Ahmad and I did not receive any more news from Arifin the shore agent. When discovering that he spent all the cash we had paid him, we realized he cheated us. Since all our money gone, we left Tanjung Priok, returning to Jakarta, where I was also able to stay at the house of Ahmad's family.

While I had been living at Tanjung Priok, I made friends with many seamen, but also associated with *preman-preman,* hoodlums around the harbor. They too were looking for work on the ships as well, even if that meant being smuggled onboard as *penumpang gelap,* stowaways. It was during this period I met Abdul Rahman from Gresik who, I heard, used to live in America. As he began sharing his experiences with me, I sought as much information as possible about America. It marked the beginning of a friendship that would eventually last decades.

While staying with Ahmad and his family, the two of us did not give up. Expectantly we continued looking for different ways to find work on one of the large ships docked at the harbor. Through other friends, we received information; the Rotterdamsche Lloyd Company was hiring experienced *tukang-tukang binatu*, laundry-men. We immediately registered ourselves as instructed.

Not long after sign up, Ahmad was first to receive the awaited call for a physical examination. The passing of the check-up was a requirement for being hired. How sad and disappointed I felt when Ahmad received summon, but not me. It seemed my dreams, hopes and plans were all in vain.

But I came along that morning on what became the fateful day of October 1948, when I boarded the bus with Ahmad to Tanjung Priok Harbor. Earlier that morning, he urged me to come with him. Although very discouraged, I went anyway with the intention to watch how they processed physical check-ups to those on the call list. It was then while sitting at the waterfront, atop the large wooden spool of coiled rope, emotions swept over me.

So no one would notice my sadness and despair, I had turned my face toward the wide-open sea. Looking out across the waters, I kept wondering how I could possibly cross that big ocean since all my money was gone. I thought about my fate in life, reflecting about living without direction, purpose or meaning. In those moments, despair tried devastating me. As tightly as the thick rope coiled around the wooden spool where I sat, I felt the limits of circumstances strangling all my hopes for a future. With my schooling constantly interrupted and work not steady, I thought about what would become of me if I remained in Indonesia. I knew I would not survive living an existence of aimlessness.

Although I loved Indonesia and fought for my country, my desire to go abroad was huge. I wanted to go overseas and did not care what kind of work I would be doing, as long as I could *merantau* to seek my fortune with integrity and have opportunity to go to school again.

This was a different personal struggle for survival. I had decided some time ago that I would not return to the house where I lived with my father before his death, especially since my stepmother Dariyah had already remarried. I had also said good-bye to my uncle Mak Harun, so sure was I of soon sailing away from Indonesia. Since having received my Lieu of Passport document, I steadfastly believed I would somehow become a ship's worker, even if on a small boat. I had repeatedly pictured in my mind how I might possibly reach Singapore; and then from there look for a ship going further abroad to Europe or perhaps America.

FATE'S JOURNEY LAUNCHED… Sitting on the dock that day, in my own way, I silently asked God to open a way. As ocean winds touched me I cried out in my spirit, "Where are you taking me, Allah?" I sensed something reaching deeper into my soul in that moment. While I continued looking out over the vast waters before me, my disheartened spirit again called out, "You are Allah, God Almighty, what are you going to do with me now? Show me the way!" In that moment of deepest discouragement, I thought about the hope and longing to continue my schooling. "How could I ever possibly achieve that?" I asked God.

It was then, I suddenly heard the shore agent Pak Haji Jakaria calling out a name listed for that day's call. Apparently, only nine men had shown up, yet the company needed ten laundry men.

Because I was still there and hearing the shore agents anxious voice, I instantly realized they needed one more worker. I turned towards him and seeing how agitated the man was, I quickly jumped down from the wooden spool where I sat. I knew those of West Java's Sundanese background were preferred for this position. Having approached the shore agent, I asked in the Sundanese dialect (I had learned while living in Sukabumi during my father's exile); if he would consider taking me as a replacement for the absent candidate.

Thinking about the urgency of the situation, Pak Haji Jakaria gave me a thorough looking over and then accepted me. When asked about my experience as a laundry worker, I reassured him I was capable. Pak Haji Jakaria then also asked me if I wanted to use the name of the absent person on the list, or use my own name. I answered politely still using the Sundanese dialect that if he did not mind, I liked to use my own name. Remaining cautious, so Dutch military police would not discover I left Jakarta; I gave my name as WADU (without the letter D at the end). At that time it was still binding, that I daily reported to sign-in at military police headquarters to avoid re-arrest for defiance of their orders.

Pak Haji entered my name WADU on the roster for physical examination that day. After assessments of all ten candidates, we interviewed one by one with the company's Dutch officials before final acceptance. Having passed the physical exam, and provided sufficient paper work, we were officially hired. Each of us received f.25 (gulden) *voorschot*, advance salary. The Dutch official who interviewed me asked if I could write. Pretending to be more timid than was my nature, I answered with deliberate reserve, *"hanya sedikit Pak"* – "just a little Sir" – then signed the Company contract with a signature unlike my own.

As a token of appreciation for his kindness in helping me, I wanted to give Pak Haji Jakaria all the advance money I had received. He was surprised and refused the money, telling me, since I had not even started working yet, I really did not have to give him anything. He said that when I returned home after sailing I could bring him some *oleh-oleh*, souvenirs, from places where I had traveled.

Although officially hired, we still had to wait for a ship assignment and departure date. It turned out Pak Haji Jakaria also owned a laundry business. While waiting for our ship, we were told to work at the business and help at his house in exchange for meals. Even though I worked without pay, by helping out at the laundry I became more knowledgeable about professional washing and ironing of very large items.

Pak Haji Zakaria wanted some of us to continue working for him until receiving our ship assignments. Instead, in order not to upset him, I gave an excuse that I needed to go and help my *bibi,* aunt, who also owned a laundry business in Jakarta. Pak Haji Jakaria believed me and accepted what I told him. Perhaps, because of the advance money I had given him anyway, he knew better than to try keeping me longer at his place of business.

One month later, I finally received the long-awaited news from the Rotterdamsche Lloyd Company. I was going to Holland with Jauhari, my friend who had a lot of experience in being a laundry man and who used to live in the United States during WWII. Jauhari also helped other former freedom fighters wanting to go overseas. Finding jobs for them on ships where he had connections, those former fighter's also had been able to leave Indonesia. Jauhari knew that I was one of them.

Before the departure date, I went to see my stepmother Dariyah to say good-bye. She assumed that I was going back to my village in Maninjau. I told her that we might see each other again in twenty-five years.

I later heard from my uncle Mak Harun that people from our *kampuang,* village, owning businesses in Tanah Abang, did not believe that I really went overseas. They considered me just a dreamer. The badgering angered my uncle, who upheld me through years to come.

# SECTION TWO

## *1949 - 1964*

# 10

# ONBOARD PASSAGE
# TO FREEDOM

Life's journey is a process and discovery painted by our passions and struggles.
Our journey eventually brings us face to face with God and ourselves.
Anonymous

In the middle of February 1949, Jauhari and I finally boarded ship and prepared to depart for Holland. We were sailing to the Port of Rotterdam. The Rotterdamsche Lloyd Company also employed *kapal penumpang,* i.e. working ship passengers, on the ocean liner *MS Willem Ruys.* These passengers worked onboard ship instead of paying their way. As fate had it, my friend Jauhari, whose name actually means expert or specialist, was the one appointed with the task of training me onboard ship as we sailed toward Europe.

On the day of departure, I too stood on deck excitedly with the many passengers. Leaving my beloved Indonesia made me sad, but my heart also overflowed with anticipation for adventure. The beginning of what I had dreamt about for so long was here. I was waving enthusiastically, gesturing farewell to the hundreds of people remaining on shore, although there was no one from my side among them. Neither family nor friends came to see me off, since none of them knew when I was leaving.

The ship slowly began moving, pushing its way out from the dock at Tanjung Priok Harbor. One single pilot-boat guided us out to sea. I stayed there on the ship's deck, which during those moments seemed very large and wide. Amid the hundreds of other passengers, most of them Dutch-Indonesian Indos, we all tried catching a last view of Indonesia's scenic landscape. Even to Indo people, Indonesia had been their home, their land of birth.

As we were slowly moving forward to the wide-open ocean, my heart felt freed, released from shackles that held me until that day. An even more amazing feeling of excitement came over me, as the ship made its way farther from Indonesia's shore. The MS Willem Ruys was taking me toward the beginning of my untouched destiny where adventures awaited me. I stood on deck, looking to the horizon with ocean breezes brushing my face. The farther out we went, the smell of ocean waters brought me that sense of freedom, such as I had never experienced.

I was twenty-one years old, and finally my hope of true-to-life adventure was no longer just a distant dream. With Allah guiding my journey, I understood that my highest expectations for the future were within reach. I believed that anything was possible for me.

Having done my duty the past four years, offering my life for Indonesia's freedom, I felt ready for whatever quests lay ahead in fate's path for me. My heart fearlessly elated; my spirit and body were finally separating from the oppression and suffering of war. I also felt, that time and destiny had aligned for my life journey.

Even though I was leaving Indonesia, I remembered to take with me all the teachings from early childhood in West Sumatra. These teachings from my parents, I kept close inside my heart just as I did during the wartime battles, which often had endangered my life. However, on this day, with the sea air embracing me, I clearly heard the voices of my parents deep within me. Their wisdom would voyage with me wherever Allah took me. I would always remind myself, that all things in my life; were to be done with awareness of the love taught by my parents since I was a small boy.

My mother through her own life had shown me to first love and care for those in need. My father displayed to me the courage to stand up for what was right, and dare to fight with endurance for justice; to which all human beings had a right. These examples would go wherever I journeyed through life. I knew my parents' life lessons were always to be the way that I approached the future.

Still looking out at the horizon and remaining on the outer deck of the MS Willem Ruys, I did not mind at all having to work as we sailed to reach distant lands. Allah had watched over me and heard my anguished complaints at the Tanjung Priok Harbor's waterfront edge. I reminded myself that I would work at anything as long as I could do so with honesty and integrity. This included my first job on the MS Willem Ruys as a laundry room assistant for my first sail.

Since there was not enough cabin space for all the workers, those of us new on the voyage had to sleep on tabletops in the *bediende or jongos*, servant's mess hall located near the kitchen. Therefore, we had no choice but to get up very early each morning. If we did not, the *jongos-jongos*, kitchen help and waiters, would wake us up by dropping piles of tin-trays on the floor. After deliberately making these obnoxiously loud noises, they would laugh and be annoying, although we were of equal rank as below deck workers.

The ship followed the route known as the *East Indies Route* with a first stop in Singapore, then Colombo, and on through the Suez Canal. We stopped at Port Said, sailing also on the Mediterranean Sea, and through the Gulf of Biscay, known for its severe storms and dangerously giant waves especially during the winter months. In 1949, the MS Willem Ruys, considered a modern ship, could sail from Jakarta to Rotterdam, Holland in only twenty-six days. This same voyage, took lesser ships almost six weeks to cover. The vessel could hold about 900 passengers. It was a wonder to me that I was actually onboard the MS Willem Ruys.

During that first trip, I also ran into several students, acquaintances whom I knew from Jakarta. Being children of well-to-do Indonesian families, they were traveling to Holland to continue their studies there or in other areas of Europe. I did not acknowledge to them that I was working on the ship. By staying quiet, I let them assume I wanted to continue my studies in America. I did this on purpose, being familiar with their sometimes-patronizing attitudes. Had I admitted to being one of the sailors, they would have embarrassed me in jest. Therefore, I decided that simply not telling them anything was best. I was just very happy being on the ship and going abroad.

Every day I walked on deck, breathing in, and enjoying the fresh ocean air. I especially liked, that as laundry room workers we usually finished our tasks early in the day. It gave me lots of free time without worries where my next meal would come from. All I was experiencing seemed too good to be true. Walking several times a day on deck, I thanked Allah that the goal I set for my life was coming in reach.

REACHING HOLLAND'S SHORES... We arrived in Rotterdam early March of 1949. When I came onboard, the only clothes I had brought were what I was wearing. I was not able to bring extra belongings, fearing that if the Dutch MP's on shore saw me with luggage, they would have stopped me. To be safe I walked onboard ship under pretense of returning to shore. The only two documents I brought with me were from the Rotterdamsche Lloyd shipping company, verifying employment as WADU, and my Lieu of Passport identification.

*Abdul Wadud (1ˢᵗ Left) with "Hermie" (2ⁿᵈ Left) arrival in Rotterdam, Holland on the MS Willem Ruys, 1949*

I only wore a white shirt torn on the backside, which I had sewn as neatly as I possibly could. With that white shirt, I wore my only pair of khaki cream-colored trousers. Having heard about the weather in Europe from other sailors, I knew I would be extremely cold in Holland during March, if wearing only this type of clothing.

Jauhari lent me some of his clothes when I was on ship, including a coat to keep warm. Mr. Volkamp, the Rotterdamsche Lloyd company representative, heard about my problem. He quickly came to my aid and gave me company uniforms, which were black wool jackets and trousers. Had help not come in this way, I would not have been able to withstand the cold weather at sea.

Once we arrived at Rotterdam and the MS Willem Ruys docked, passengers made their way onshore while we finished our tasks below deck. Having been at sea, just like the passengers, we too were looking forward to being on land. Before leaving the vessel, I was able to return to Jauhari clean sets of clothing he had lend me. I thanked him, appreciating very much what he had done for me.

I was almost twenty-two years old, and had so long wanted to go abroad. Just like my other sailor friends, I too hoped to spend time onshore with Dutch girls. I heard about this from their stories while we sailed. Since I received the Rotterdamsche Lloyd uniforms during the voyage, I had warm clothing to wear.

With a group of friends, I went to a nearby recreation area already familiar to those who had been to Rotterdam before. There we met numerous Dutch girls. I knew they liked going out with Indonesian young men because we treated them with respect and invited them to restaurants. After some fun at an eatery, all of us walked around the city together.

During that March of 1949, much of Rotterdam and the Netherlands were still in ruins after WWII. Many buildings were destroyed and debris remaining everywhere. Walking around the city with our group, I even saw little school children helping adults with the cleanup of these structures. Times were hard. I also noticed Dutchmen without any shame picking up tossed cigarette butts from the ground, lighting these and taking puffs from whatever tobacco remained in the cigarette waste. I became aware that Dutchmen were friendly and kinder in their own country, unlike those I saw in Indonesia.

On other days, I also watched hundreds of local people all riding bicycles, going to work every morning and then returning home in the afternoon. I had never seen such a wave of bicycles with as many people riding them in the streets all at once, not even in Jakarta.

In the morning, I enjoyed watching people eating what I learned was raw *haring,* herring fish for breakfast. Tilting their heads back, opening their mouths wide, and then putting the fish in one by one, to me seemed appalling. Actually, I could not stand watching this unappetizing habit at that time, but I was too curious. I heard from friends that Dutch people ate raw herring covered with freshly chopped onions, beginning early in the day. Later I learned that eating raw fish was a delicacy, and not only just with the Dutch in Holland.

As I traveled more, I also discovered further about the eating habits of other nationalities. Growing older, raw Japanese *sushi* would eventually become one of my most favorite foods to enjoy.

Since there were not many cars on the streets, the city of Rotterdam seemed quiet during the daytime. On weekends (weather permitting), the locals enjoyed walking in the park or going out of the city to the countryside. Someone told me that riding a bicycle, one could cover all of Holland in one day. Unfortunately, I did not have the opportunity to enjoy that kind of adventure.

About a week after arriving in Rotterdam, while waiting for our next ship, we had opportunity to work in the city if we liked. There happened to be openings at a *wascherij,* laundry business, which provided laundry workers for other businesses or private homes. It meant extra cash for us, but for me it was a chance to learn, and get some more experience in professional laundering of clothing and larger pieces.

There were many women working at the wascherij. They did tasks like ironing and folding clothes. The men did the more demanding undertakings of washing heavy loads in very large machines. It was here I really began learning how to iron the professional way. By the time, the Rotterdamsche Lloyd gave us our new assignments; I already knew how to iron as if I had done so for a long time.

While in Rotterdam, I did not see any laundromats, as I heard about from friends, where one could use washing machines do personal laundry. These practical businesses I would come across only in America after arriving there months later.

To pass the time, each Saturday after receiving our pay from the wascherij, I would go into the city with several friends to eat *petat frite,* fried potatoes (French fries), freshly made and hot, with *mosterd,* spicy mustard. We also very much enjoyed eating crunchy *ikan goreng,* fried fish.

After all the difficulties of war, then finally sailing gave me long awaited delight. The reality of my dream to go around the world was here, to not only sail the high seas, but also go wherever new adventures would take me.

In looking back, my longing to sail became even stronger when I met Abdul Rahman at Tanjung Priok Harbor. We quickly became good friends. There were so many stories I heard from him that made sailing even more attractive and making me want to leave for foreign countries even sooner. My interest especially sparked when he told me that people in America could afford buying a car, while working as a *tukang cuci piring,* a dishwasher in restaurants, or even as laborers picking fruit on farms. He also explained that before while working on the ship and then staying in America, he changed his name to *Hermand Jonas ("Hermie")*. He told me that most Indonesian sailors staying in America changed their names so that they could blend in easier.

Hermand told me, that during WWII and the Indonesian Revolution, he was already living in San Francisco. Even though he lived there, he was active in the Indonesian Association of "*Perhimpunan Indonesia.*" Among other things, one of their main activities was interacting with American labor unions to boycott Dutch ships transporting weapons to Indonesia.

Hermand, after deportation by the US Immigration, returned to Indonesia since he could only stay in the United States for the period of WWII. He wanted to return to America because while staying there, he experienced a better life and more opportunities for his future. After being in Indonesia a few years, he again looked for ship employment. My friend Hermand left for Holland about one month before me, but we met each other again in Rotterdam.

After staying in Holland for one month, I transferred to the *MS Japara* that was sailing to New York and other places on the East Coast of the United States and Canada. Hermand (I began calling him by this name, which later became Hermie) was on the same ship with me.

On the MS Japara, I began spending time with Dutch sailors onboard who considered me a friend and not their enemy. I took that opportunity to improve my Dutch language. Because many of my Indonesian friends on the ship did not finish their education, I helped with teaching them English, which I had learned in school.

With Hermie, I was planning to remain in the US. Kasim, another friend of ours who originated from Kalimantan, shared the cabin with

Hermie and me. He was cabin boy for the ship's captain. Because he always listened to our conversations, Kasim too became very interested in following us with the plan.

With time, I became more experienced at my laundry room tasks. Although not considered an old ship, we used coal on the MS Japara to warm up washing machines. Clean wash, interlinked with tied ropes later hung on deck to dry. When knotted in a specific way it ensured a strong hold. Otherwise, powerful ocean winds would blow the wash away. I learned quickly the best techniques of rope knotting. As we sailed, it was my responsibility to oversee the washing. My friend Jauhari took care of the ironing.

It took fifteen days sailing from Rotterdam to New York. Fortunately, I only became seasick once. After that incident, one of my friends told me to drink some seawater and I would never get seasick again. I followed the instruction. Whether true or not, I am not sure, but after I drank a few small gulps of the seawater, I never again experienced seasickness.

Onboard, I saw the difference in treatment of Indonesian crewmembers. For example, dishes used by Indonesians were tin-plates, *piring-piring kaleng*. Preparation of our food also did not get much attention. We did not even have a mess hall for eating meals. Seeing this really aggravated me. I refused accepting that kind of repressive treatment, which was the same as during the colonial era.

To protest, I told other Indonesians to gather all tin-plates, and throw everything overboard into the ocean. Watching what happened; the Dutch quickly realized their mistake. Since that incident, they permitted us to use the same dishes like the non- Indonesian crew. No disciplinary actions came against us. Instead, via Captain's orders, Indonesian crewmembers could use the officer's mess hall with rotating mealtime schedules. This plan worked out very well.

AMERICA THE BEAUTIFUL – First Visit... The MS Japara arrived into New York's harbor on a beautiful morning of May 1949. We passed by the Statue of Liberty, which looked magnificent in the bright sun. Seeing Ellis Island, I knew that was a place of history for immigrants arriving from all over the world. To me in those moments, watching the Statue of Liberty was a sign of America welcoming people coming from many countries. All different nationalities arriving here, to achieve their hopes and dreams in this free country.

My heart was content. Having recently fought in the struggle of keeping Indonesia free, I knew it was the day for more fulfilment of my dream to remain eventually in this country.

The weather was bright, cool and fresh that day we reached America's coast. I was very happy, and overflowing with wonder. I was in awe seeing how beautiful the city of New York looked from the ships' ocean side. I dreamt about this for so long and I absolutely knew in those moments that this country was where I wanted to be.

After the ship docked, I immediately prepared to go ashore. First, I had to pass through document clearance with US Immigration to enter the United States. Before I even went ashore, my heart was already pounding excitedly, waiting in anticipation for my first steps on American soil.

I thought, how very happy I would be, if able to stay in this country. I had imagined this for a long time. My heart was ecstatic, and aware of the gift that Allah was giving me. During those very exciting moments, I did not forget to honor God.

Once ashore, I immediately bought a street-map of New York City. I was ready to go by myself, because most my friends were still working. As I walked across busy streets, I did not feel like a stranger at all. Having just bought the map at a newspaper stand, the first location I looked for was the Empire State Building, and the offices of the Indonesian Delegation to the United Nations at that address.

I received this information from one of my friends in Jakarta, who had returned from the US. I knew that with the map I could find the subway station and train for taking me to Manhattan where the Empire State Building was located. I had heard about this also from other friends, and found it exciting to go on a train underground. I thought about how great America was to provide this for the people.

When I reached the Empire State Building, I looked at the directory for offices and floors where I should go using the elevator. For me, this was the first time entering an elevator. I had also heard about this from friends. The office of the Indonesian Representatives was on the sixty-first floor. I found out where it was located and entered. It was my purpose to ask for information about the possibility of staying in the US. An official who received me informed me that everything was up to me. He only warned that if the US Immigration found out, deportation back to Indonesia would happen.

I then went to look for the location where I knew an organization of Indonesians met regularly. I received this address also from the same friend who provided information regarding the Indonesian Delegation to the UN office.

I found the Indonesian organization without much difficulty. Arriving there, I met Malaysians and Indonesians who had lived in New York a long time. I had opportunity to ask many questions about staying in the US. Some of them warned I should be very careful because they knew about stranded seamen when WWII ended. I did not quite understand what that meant, but I was not afraid.

One question they asked me was how I found their location. I told them that when I came ashore, I bought the street-map and followed directions to the address given me. Chuckling and shaking their heads, they looked at my being so daring with amazement. According to their accounts, when they left the ship, they were so blind, not knowing what to do next. They also expressed with amusement, "We were not as smart as the boys nowadays."

That night I returned to the ship very content. Immediately telling Hermand where I had been, I asked what he thought about me leaving the ship while we were in New York. Wisely, he replied that the decision was in my hand. Thinking things over, I finally decided not to leave the ship yet because we also did not have enough money saved. Besides, I still wanted to go around the world and see other countries. We continued working on the MS Japara, even though that meant sailing back to Indonesia. We would be going to Semarang, Surabaya and Makassar, then back to the US through Belawan, a port city on the North East coast of Sumatra.

While the ship docked in Belawan, I met with friends there from school days in our village. They owned businesses at the Pasar Belawan market place. Another person from my village owned a beds and mattresses shop there. He invited me for dinner, and afterwards gave me a very generous supply of hot beef Rendang to take onboard ship. No matter how far I would travel, and pass through years of life's experiences, my love for Rendang and rice would never be lost.

REACHING AMERICA'S SHORES – Second Time... The Transfer of Sovereignty from the Dutch Government to the new Republic of Indonesia took place as our ship was on voyage from Indonesia back to the United States of America.

My first visit to the US was in May of 1949. Six months later in mid-November of that same year, the MS Japara returned to New York having traced the same route through the Suez Canal. We again stopped at ports in Singapore, Colombo, Aden (a Yemen seaport), and Port Said, a city close by S.E. Egypt in the Mediterranean Sea.

Reaching the US that second time, the ship sailed first on to Halifax, Canada, and from there to New York through Boston. The cold season had already begun, and due to icy weather (fallen below twenty degrees), water pipes on the ship froze-up. For me it was the first experience with those kinds of icy temperatures. Even though earlier that year I had been in Holland, the cold weather there seemed different.

After sailing up and down the east coast for six weeks, we arrived back in New York again. With start of New Year 1950, we were still in New York. The ship would berth there for only a few days. Having saved enough money, Hermand and I were ready to jump ship.

Our original plan was to leave the MS Japara after returning from Canada, before the ship would set out to New Orleans. Then after staying in New York a few days, we planned to go to San Francisco by Greyhound Bus. Traveling across country would take three days and three nights. Having heard that Immigration was very strict in New York, we had no intention to settle there. Remaining cautious, the two of us chose going to San Francisco, California. Since Hermand used to live there, he had many friends willing to help us.

With time off, we went to Lenox, an area where African Americans lived to look for a hotel. This was part of the preparation for keeping out of sight before leaving for San Francisco. The cost of renting a room at the hotel was only five dollars for a week's stay. I was able to cover cost of the room. Having secured a place and paying in advance, we returned to the ship.

Kasim was enthusiastically waiting for us when we arrived. He was excited wanting to give us good news. Our captain was looking for workers willing to transfer to the *SS Limburg*, berthed in San Francisco. From there, the ship was sailing to South Africa and South America. This was very good news. I believed, *pucuk di cinta ulam pun tiba* – the peak of what I loved and wished had arrived. What was important to me was that our captain requested three Indonesian workers, one laundry man, and two cabin boys, plus one Dutchman cook. By then I was not even thinking about the five dollars I would lose for the advance payment at the hotel. All I thought about in those moments was that this way I had more opportunity to continue my dream of going around the world.

I told Kasim to inform the captain immediately that the three of us were the only ones willing to transfer. I told him also not to let anyone else know about this news. When the captain woke-up from an afternoon nap, Kasim told him that he already knew of some boys willing to transfer to the SS Limburg. Later when called in by an administrator on board, Hermand and I with Kasim accepted the transfer. The three of us still travelled with the ship to Louisiana, where after a few days the MS Japara would depart from Lake Charles. The four of us, including the Dutch cook, would then take a train from Lake Charles to San Francisco, California.

After the MS Japara docked at Lake Charles, Hermand, Kasim and I would leave the following day. Some of the Indonesian crewmembers planned a small farewell dinner for us at one of the nearby port restaurants. The three of us also wanted to say farewell and thank our co-workers for their close friendship.

After enjoying a nice meal together, some of the men wanted to share a few words. They expressed appreciation for how I looked after them. Since I made sure, there was peace among the Indonesian crew by averting fights; due to the often heavy drinking, they regarded me as their caring friend and valued our bond. (To prevent clashes onboard or on shore, I usually gathered their weapons for safekeeping and their own protection.) As words of sincerity continued, they expressed feeling loss of a friend who always helped them, even with writing letters to their families.

A crewmember from Madura stood up and began crying. With emotion in his voice he told everyone about an incident between us when I had just come onboard. He said that one day; he saw me eating rice with only *sambal kecap*, hot soy sauce, and a small piece of *empal*, dried meat. He had grabbed my plate from me, and thrown it across the room. Instead of retaliating, I remained seated, not saying a word. He said, I just kept looking at him, and then slowly got up from where I was sitting. Coming very close, asked what the reason was for his flinging the plate like that.

He expressed, that in those tense moments, he could only reply that it angered him, how bad the food was for the Indonesians and no attention came from superiors. Adding that he had also heard about the incident on the MS Willem Ruys of our throwing tin- plates overboard, he thought that by starting a fight with me would perhaps bring awareness of the problem on the SS Japara.

Our friend then told everyone that what he had done was wrong, and that he never expected my reaction such as it was. He expressed that after what happened that day, he realized I also empathized with severity of conditions. After he finished speaking while still standing, he asked my forgiveness before us all.

The next day, Hermand, Kasim, the Dutch cook and I left for San Francisco on the Pullman Train, which to me was beautiful and clean. Traveling on this train included a bed and meals served in a dining car. Waking up in the mornings, an attendant had shined our shoes. The trip from the south to the west coast took three days and three nights. I thought to myself, what wonderful experiences I would have on my new adventure in the United States.

After journeying on the train those days and nights, we arrived in Los Angeles, California. At the Los Angeles Union Station, we transferred to another train going north to San Francisco, which I soon discovered ran along the coast. What beautiful views I saw between Los Angeles and San Francisco! This kind of beauty was very different from other sights in portions of the South in the US.

The California coastline allowed us to pass coastal areas, where directly on the right side of the train I saw rising hills with green trees and on the left clean beaches with beautiful houses along the sand. It was incredible to me how clean and smooth the roads were in America. In San Francisco, a representative from the Rotterdamsche Lloyd met us, and drove us to where the SS Limburg berthed.

Coming onboard ship, I had another pleasant surprise. I met my friend Suma again who would be my working partner on this next sail. Incidentally, Suma was also in the same regiment together with me in Cikampek during our days of fighting in the army.

After Suma had returned to Jakarta, he started a laundry business there, but for only a short time. Later, he worked on the Dutch ships as a laundryman. My friend had much experience, both on ship and ashore. He was able to teach me with patience and a lot of humor as we often joked around. Especially when we began sharing stories about our army adventures, we realized that the period of our wartime actions were recent and not long ago at all. My sailing time with Suma became very valuable. While he taught me about being the best laundry man, I could be, he also reminded me about my upbringing, and that I needed to appreciate what life had already brought me through. Suma also reminded me, I was not to forget what happened in Indonesia, even though I was now on the other side of the world.

The SS Limburg docked in San Francisco for another week before departure from the beautiful city by the bay. Hermand's friends who lived there invited us to attend a meeting of the Perhimpunan Indonesia Association, which established in the US during the time of our revolution under the leadership of Lari Bogok.

I saw about fifteen people in attendance when we arrived. The Indonesian community in San Francisco at that time was not large, and after introductions, those attending expressed they were very happy to meet us. Among them was Arsyad Ismail, also a Minang from West Sumatra, who had lived in Malaysia. There were Ray Makmur, Ali Usman, Atekan and a number of others who had already been in America for a while.

During the gathering, we told them about our plans to leave the ship. Lari Bogok mentioned that he might go back to Indonesia, but hoped we would return and stay in San Francisco to continue the organization. We told everyone that our plans of leaving the ship would be after our return to the United States from Africa and South America.

In the middle of March 1950, the SS Limburg left San Francisco for South Africa. We first stopped in San Diego, and then sailed through the Panama Canal on to New Orleans.

From New Orleans, heading for Capetown the weather continued worsening. Giant waves and hurricane force winds constantly struck the ship without ceasing. Our cabins were located in the back portion of the ship on top of the propeller, which was already very noisy. The storms and enormous waves caused our ship to shake severely. So dangerous did these situations become, that we had to use safety belts even while sleeping.

Sailing through the enormous storms, mounted thick strong ropes along the deck protected us from falling overboard. The deck was very slippery during these treacherous times. Holding on to the safety ropes; we stood better chance within the extreme sea motions.

It was terrifying when the ship sailed against very large winds, and a single wave could be as high as (what seemed) a mountain. The ship navigated under each wave, while thunderous rolling waters surrounded us. In those moments, our ship seemed miniature compared to the colossal waves.

Almost all of my friends were seasick. Fortunately, I had never gotten nauseous since we left Rotterdam, because on advice I drank a little seawater. My friends were rather annoyed seeing I did not get seasick like them. Not only were they unable to eat, just smelling food being prepared near our cabins, triggered constant retching. Since I was still able to eat and had a good appetite, they booted me out from the cabin and told me to eat somewhere else. It amazed me that my friends were in such bad physical condition, yet most of them worked on ships for years and sailed much longer than me.

SOUTH AFRICA TO SOUTH AMERICA... By the end of March 1950, after two weeks of rough sailing on the SS Limburg, we reached Cape Town. It was there that I became acquainted with others of Indonesian descent, called *Cape Malay* (the Malays of Cape Town).

I discovered that during the Colonial era, the Dutch government exiled many Indonesians to Cape Town when considering them too dangerous. Because of eventual mixed blood between the ousted Indonesians and other nationalities, their skin color was not as dark as those native to the area was.

Our ship docked in Cape Town for one week. We (Hermand, Suma, myself and other friends), were taken everywhere to meet with their families and others of Indonesian origin. I had the opportunity to help them read and translate old journals and books written in the Indonesian language, with some using the Arab alphabet written by their relatives and ancestors.

Because *apartheid*, segregation, was still in effect, the situation in South Africa was volatile. The non-whites could not enter places designated for the white people. On busses, recreational places, shops, even in parks, there were always signs, "For European Only." For me, this was not strange because this kind of treatment happened in my own country.

The Dutch Government during the colonial era attempted discriminating between ethnic groups and regions in Indonesia. We knew this tactic used by colonials, as *memecah belah sambil menjajah,* breaking-up while colonizing. In other words, "divide and rule."

I learned valuable lessons about the Cape Malay people during that stopover, especially regarding their tenacity for survival in that portion of the world. From Cape Town, the SS Limburg left for Port Elizabeth and Durban, South Africa.

In Durban the ship remained in dry-dock for repairs for one month. We had plenty of rest during that time. The *pedicabs*, cabs drawn by tall black people with incredibly long legs immediately fascinated me. Because their legs had such length, it enabled these men to leap upwards with giant steps, while then hanging their bodies unto the cab portion of their passenger vessel. They repeatedly leaped and bounced as they covered the distances. By holding their bodies and tossing them onto the carriage at that height, looked like they were flying. As they called out to potential customers, the pedicab drivers shouted with loud voices as if to purposely startle the people; but always with big smiles. The population in Durban was very friendly. I used to dream about meeting different people and seeing new places. I was then finally experiencing what I could only imagine before.

Once the ship finished repairs in Durban, we departed for Lorenzo Marquez, in Mozambique, a former Portuguese colony. Because the stop here was just for two days, I only had a quick chance to walk about in the city, but did not see anything special. Our ship then left for South America.

The first port stop was Buenos Aires, Argentina. Since I did not like to waste valuable time, I was always one of the first on shore. My friends already knew that my way was "better sooner than later." I did not like waiting around the ship until others were finished with their work. Ready to go ashore, my attitude was that there were too many interesting things to discover and people to meet. Going off on my own was just as enjoyable as going with friends.

When I was having lunch at one of the restaurants in Buenos Aires, I met a well-known Argentinean artist of that time, Mr. Sandro Carreras. Introducing himself to me, the artist was interested in drawing a sketch of my face with his pen. We had a very interesting conversation for a long time. Mr. Carreras later invited me to his residence at which time he gave me the drawing he had made of me.

Buenos Aires was very attractive, with its traffic well-regulated and clean city. I noticed that uniforms of their army looked like the uniforms of German soldiers during World War II. During that period, Argentina's president was Juan Peron.

Later, my friends and I also had opportunity to go outside of the city by train because the soccer team from the SS Limburg had a friendly game with a team from another ship. I was almost tempted to leave the ship in Argentina, because I was attracted to what I saw there. However, one of the Chinese men who had been living there for years came to the ship and during our conversation advised me to live in the US. His reasoning had been that it was easier to find work in the United States.

Leaving Argentina, the ship then sailed north upward South America, making stops again in Montevideo (Uruguay), Paraguay, and Bahia (Brazil). From Brazil, we headed for Panama through Trinidad. Crossing the Panama Canal I was amazed to see how engineers had designed and built the canal, connecting the Atlantic Ocean to the Pacific Ocean.

Going through the Panama Canal, the distance to the other side of Panama was approximately 82 km (50 miles). This route saved approximately 13,000 kilometers (8,077 miles) compared to a voyage through the Strait of Magellan, located by the southern tip of South America.

Construction of the fascinating Panama Canal began in 1880, and finished in 1914, taking thirty-four years to complete. Originally started by the French, the United States later took over. In total, about 80,000 workers labored for this project. In the process, approximately 30,000 workers died because of serious health conditions. In crossing this canal, we passed the man made Gatun Lake. The SS Limburg arrived at Pedro Miguel only nine hours later on the Pacific Ocean side.

From Panama, we continued on to the California ports of San Diego, San Pedro and San Francisco. Looking toward land from the ocean side, what a beautiful sight San Francisco was, as I saw it again. The city built on seven hills, made me more enthusiastic than ever before. The scenic beauty also encouraged my heart to make the decision to leave the ship and live in San Francisco.

I especially felt that since I had already been to many countries in a short time, my vision had become reality. However, the beauty of San Francisco *menggiurkan hati saya*, seduced my heart, in a way that could not possibly compare to any other place. San Francisco was more attractive to me than any other metropolitan city. I felt I had achieved my dream of going around the world.

SAN FRANCISCO – CITY BY THE BAY… Our ship the SS Limburg docked at a San Francisco pier on a Saturday late afternoon, in the month of June 1950. As was usual procedure, workers received their pay after arrival at each harbor from the *hofmeester*, the chief steward in charge. However, because it was a Saturday, all offices remained closed, including the office of the Rotterdamsche Lloyd. The chief steward told us we would receive our money at arrival in Portland, Oregon on Monday after the weekend.

Hermand, Kasim (who changed his name to Max Cosem) and I, decided to leave the ship that evening. Our plan was not to return after being on shore. I however, did not want to miss salary that I had worked for up to then. I decided to ask Capt. Everdingen, our ship's captain, if I could borrow some cash from him.

I waited and approached when I saw him coming down the steps with other officers. With the explanation that I wanted to eat outside, I politely asked him if he could possibly lend me some money until we arrived in Portland. Looking at me as if he was a little bothered, Captain Everdingen asked me how much I needed. I answered him that all I needed was ten dollars. Taking out his wallet, he happened to have only twenty-dollar bills. He handed me one, with the reminder to re-pay him when we received our salary.

At that time, as a laundryman, our salary was not much but we also received a bonus depending on the amount of washing we had done during each leg of the trip. This meant that we earned more than cabin boys did.

After receiving the money from Captain Everdingen, all three of us, Hermand, Kasim and I, brought only some of our clothes with us. At the dock, Atekan one of Hermand's friends, waited for us with his car.

While crossing the San Francisco Bay Bridge, we looked to where our ship docked. Waving good-bye to the vessel that had brought us to the United States of America brought me a sense of elation, never experienced before. In those moments, we did not even consider the weight and consequence of the wrong we actually were committing. As young and daring as we were, we were ready to face whatever it took. However wrong, the actions of these steps were for us the only way. That night we slept at Atekan's apartment. Early the next morning, he drove us to Penryn near Sacramento the capital of California.

Immediately after arriving at Penryn, we first worked at a pear farm. I quickly realized, numerous ship jumpers from Indonesia clustered here because the supervisor was an Indonesian. He too had changed his name to Alex Dixon, but had already been living in the US for a long time. We called him *Bang Ali*, Brother Ali, who accepted us with open arms. At that particular farm, I met many new friends. Among them, I still remember were Peter Ananda, Tony Ardy, Anton Hutagalung, Aris Munandar, Derek Ayal, and others.

To avoid recognition by the US Immigration Department, I also promptly changed my name to *Willy Amrull*. (In later years, whenever asked why I changed my name, I always jokingly replied that this was my stage name just like Hollywood actors.) I never felt awkward or guilty about deciding to use the name Willy Amrull instead of my birth name. Even my father, having returned to Indonesia from Mecca, had eventually altered his own name from Rasul to Abdul Karim.

On the farm near Penryn, we worked daily picking fruit and earning seventy-five cents per hour as our first wage. Since the work was not too heavy, we were satisfied. The food was always very good because our friends from Indonesia were the cooks. They raised goats for the purpose of slaughter, and prepared *Sate kambing*, skewered barbeque or *gule kambing*, Indonesian-style curried goat for us.

Sunday was our only day off. We usually spent that time going to the nearest towns like Penryn and Auburn. My friends and I would hitch rides with other friends who already owned cars. Sometimes we went all the way to Sacramento to see a movie at the theater, or on other weekends go to another farm to watch boxing matches.

This was when Dewi Dja, a renowned Indonesian dancer who had been living in the US for a long time, also came to visit. Since the early part of the 1940's, together with her husband Alli Assan, they lived in the Los Angeles area. Before meeting her, I had heard a lot about her from Hermand while we were still on the ship. When she came to visit us at the farm, it was a time of real camaraderie for everyone. We shared good food, sang *Keroncong*, Indonesian folk style songs, and of course reminisced about our beloved Indonesia. Within the Indonesian community through later years, Dewi Dja became the reflection for memories of the Indonesia we had left behind.

On farms everything flowed by seasons of the year. After the pear season was over, we immediately looked for work picking peaches. When this finished, we relocated further to the Stockton area to harvest asparagus. In this case, only a few Indonesians were willing to do this particular work. We always needed to be on the move from farm to farm and do so quickly, wherever the next season would take us.

In order to pick the tender light green stems of asparagus, we had to work harder than any other period of the year. When harvesting asparagus, earnings came by contract, and not hourly wage. I quickly learned this job was quite different than picking any other type of fruit or vegetables. Farmers usually preferred skilled Filipino workers for harvesting asparagus. They were more experienced, faster and generally hard workers. Laborers picking asparagus did so while bending over, quickly moving non-stop and slicing the vegetable at the same time.

To avoid intense sun heat during the day, work started at two o'clock in the morning, long before dawn. This would continue until ten o'clock in the morning. During the remainder of the day, resting was important for workers. The asparagus needed cutting exactly on time. If the harvesting was late even by just one day, the blooms would be open and farmers would not be able to sell their crop.

When Hermand and I arrived in Stockton, we did not have a place to stay because the Filipino camp had already filled up. There was only an old tent nearby. The tent had torn sides and no rooftop to cover us. Inside the tent, we found what looked like an old bed frame without any sign of a mattress. However, we had no choice, so we stayed there. The supervisor told us that when there were workers leaving, we had first chance to move inside the camp housing.

Thus, in that old tent we made the bed by spreading a blanket atop the old frame. Actually the bed and its frame were held together only by rusty springs. These were not strong enough to hold both Hermand and myself. Therefore, the springs creaked loudly with every slight move we made, disturbing any real attempt of rest. When we lay down and tried going to sleep, our bodies automatically rolled toward the center of the springs. We tried to get more comfortable by putting our backsides against each other, and facing opposite sides. Since it was cold outside the old tent at night, it was somewhat nice, lying in this position. At least it kept us both a little warmer. Facing situations such as this together, we soon knew each other's worst habits. Waking up during the middle of the night, we would prepare to start work quickly. Cutting asparagus was exhausting and back breaking to say the least.

When we finished working by ten o'clock in the morning, we would all gather by the housing barracks for a good meal. Then, Hermand and I would return to the old tent and try to rest. We repeatedly awakened to goats inside the tent coming extra close. But, we were young and could tolerate such discomforts.

Fortunately, for us, some of the Filipino work force moved to other camps not too long after our arrival. Hermand and I were then able to move into the camp housing. About fifty other laborers occupied the barrack-like rooming quarters with us. Both of us were thankful to be inside

Soon after our move into the camp, we received work at the packinghouse. Our job was to bundle and package the asparagus, preparing it for marketing. Our salary was not as big as while we harvested, but I felt grateful. At least, I did not have to work as hard nor begin during the night.

Because there were many Filipino's working with us, we were getting along very well with them. I was very impressed because they owned beautiful cars. On our day off, it was with these newfound friends we could catch rides into town. I learned that the US government brought the majority of these workers from the Philippines during the 1920's. They worked jobs as laborers by contract specifically for the agricultural fields in America.

After the asparagus season ended in Stockton, one of our Indonesian friends asked Hermand and I to go along to Fresno with him, and pick grapes. The vineyards were near to town, and the camp was nicer. Having arrived there we again gathered with numerous friends from Indonesia. Charles Sa'id was one of them who owned a car and always gave us rides to places. I still remember our two Filipino bosses who were brothers at the Fresno farm. They were Johnny Hayagan and his younger brother Maning Hayagan.

Here, I also again met with Ishak Dasaan who by then attended UCLA (University of California Los Angeles). Ishak and I had been good friends while we were in the Indonesian army together. He was a son of wealthy parents, but also wanted to be familiar with what it would be like, working as a farm laborer. He shared with me that as part of life experience, he was interested in knowing how it felt to undergo the hard work in the farm fields. Ishak later told me that with the money he earned from picking grapes, he would be able to buy new tires for his car and appreciate its value.

When the season was over in Fresno, Hermand and I left for Delano, located about fifty miles south of Fresno. This farm area was not too far from Bakersfield. Hired immediately we were grateful and the two of us settled in the camp there.

It was in the city of Bakersfield that the Indonesian Government had sent sixty Air Force pilot candidates for training at the TALOA Flight Academy. Here, specialized navigation training programs helped instruct those selected by our new government in Indonesia. Since this place was not too far from Delano, I was able to visit with the candidates. To my great delight, I met my close friend Nursan Iskandar, the son of Mr. Nur Sutan Iskandar, a well-known Indonesian author. There were other friends I made whom I still remember through the years. I often went to see them in Bakersfield, or they came to Delano to visit us for leisure during their free time.

Usually during their summer vacation, many Indonesian students from all over California worked on the farms. For entertainment, we usually went bowling at night. Almost every Saturday evening we went dancing at events organized by the Filipino community.

After the summer season, workers usually left to look for different jobs in other farm areas or went back to the city. Hermand and I decided it was best to return to San Francisco and there look for work. However, we had an opportunity to work for a short while in Half Moon Bay on a farm growing Brussels sprouts (which looked like miniature cabbages on stalks). I began liking Brussels sprouts after getting used to its strong flavor. While we worked in Half Moon Bay it was planting season, but Hermand and I stayed as long as possible to earn extra cash.

At that time, the two of us already saved some money to buy a car. In 1950, a 1936 Plymouth cost $200.00. That was the car Hermand and I chose, and used it to go everywhere. I was able to acquire my first "legal" driver's license by buying it for twenty-five dollars without having to take any tests. Since Half Moon Bay was not far from San Francisco, we did not stay there too long after having bought the car. We were able to go in to the city often and I soon found work at a restaurant in San Francisco washing dishes, earning one dollar per hour.

My desire to go back to school remained strong inside me. Once back in San Francisco, I immediately registered and attended Heald's Engineering College located in the city. Here I was taking courses in Civil Engineering. With my earnings from working at the restaurant with a one dollar per hour wage, I could afford to pay my tuition and rent a room with another friend Peter Ananda, a Business student attending the same school. I would eat dinner at the restaurant where I worked, which helped me save more money.

When Hermand met Dalin, they married soon after first meeting. Although life changed for us and we no longer lived or spent as much time together, Hermie (as I had started calling him), remained being one of my closest friends through many years.

# 11

# PIECES OF WHO WE ARE

You don't choose your family.
They are God's gift to you,
As you are to them.
Desmond Tutu

Upon invitation of the US Government, my older brother Abdul Malik (Hamka), "Uo Aji" to me, came to visit the United States in 1952. He had gained popularity in Indonesia as an author and his leadership in religious Islamic organizations. The purpose of the US invitation was for Uo Aji to tour the United States and lecture at various American universities about the Development of Islam in Indonesia.

*Note: In my brother's book "Empat Bulan di Amerika" (Jilid I dan Jilid II) [Jakarta: Tintamas 1953 Hal. 45) ("Four Months in America" Volumes I and II) [Jakarta: Tintamas 1953 p. 45] Hamka, wrote at length about his visit and experiences while touring the United States. (From: Author)*

During his four-month stay, I had not started working yet at the Indonesian *Consulate*. Since Consul Abdul Hamid knew I was Hamka's younger brother, he appointed me to accompany my brother to the different lecture venues as his translator while he was in California.

My brother stayed at my apartment in San Francisco, which I shared with friends. His visit with me was a real personal enjoyment. We constantly joked and shared just like when I was younger.

Although many years later, there would be question raised about our relationship; regarding the time spent with me in San Francisco, Hamka wrote:

*"Empat Bulan di Amerika,"* (Four Months in America) *"My thirteen days in San Francisco were the highlight of time spent traveling and beautiful memories. At that time, I again met my younger brother who had settled there, but whom I had not seen for almost ten years, since our parting. He left to travel to foreign countries after our father's death. He is my youngest brother Abdul Wadud Karim Amrullah, who in America uses the western name 'Willy Amrull.'"* (Quote is direct translation from Indonesian language)

I was fortunate for the opportunity to meet my older brother again during this visit in America, since we had not seen each other for ten years. That is one thing I did not imagine would happen and only two years after my own arrival in the US. Wherever we went, we took time taking pictures together just like tourists. On one occasion, we took a photo at the scenic beach of San Francisco.

*Note: Because the print I own is no longer clear, this specific "moment in time" of the two of us, is unavailable for use in this book. This photo does appear in the original Indonesian version of Hamka's book. In caption below the photo my brother wrote the following: "At the beach in San Francisco. In front is the author's younger brother A. Wadud Amrullah" (From: Author)*

Actually, among all my older brothers and sisters, my relationship with Malik (Hamka) was closest. As mentioned previously, when I was a little boy all of my other brothers and sisters being much older than me, had already left the village. They very seldom returned home, but Malik, who was living in Medan, North Sumatra, would from time to time come visit our father when he too was home in Sungai Batang. In those early days, Malik (Hamka) was already Chief Editor of a popular magazine *Pedoman Masyarakat*, Community Guidance.

Even though he came to Sungai Batang more often than the others did, circumstances in Indonesia would not allow us regular contact with him. This was especially so during the time of our father's exile in Sukabumi, Java, where I lived with Ayah. It was only when Uo Aji later moved to Jakarta that we often wrote letters to each other. Therefore, to have my brother visit California in 1952 and be able to have some personal time and rest with me, was an unexpected and fantastic experience.

On one occasion, I accompanied my brother to Sacramento where he lectured at a mosque. On our way back to San Francisco, the US Immigration stopped the car we were driving. An officer asked each of us for personal identification. Inspections such as this, especially along California agricultural areas, were common then and checks often performed to prevent illegal entry to America. Fortunately, I had the letter from the Indonesian Consul with me stating the nature of our travel and that the Indonesian Consulate appointed me as guide and translator for the visiting speaker from Indonesia. Not aware inspections like these were common; my brother became worried. He thought for sure US Immigration would detain his little brother. Since we had proper documentation, there was no problem.

During those thirteen days in San Francisco, Hamka also saw that I was working hard washing dishes in a restaurant while also attending college. I know that Uo Aji admired my diligence with the goals for my life. Seeing my enthusiasm and determination touched him; but he expressed concerns regarding my well-being during one of our more serious conversations.

While in New York and Washington DC, my brother met former Indonesian independence fighters who had also chosen to jump ship. Learning that these men received employment at the Indonesian Embassy and Consulate General in New York, my brother asked officials if they could possibly also help me. Before leaving San Francisco, he encouraged me to go to Washington DC although I was already attending Heald's Engineering College. Shortly thereafter, I decided to follow Hamka's advice.

# 12

# TIMES TO REMEMBER

We do not remember days,
we remember moments.
Cesare Pavese

SAWITRI… Thus, on counsel from my brother, I left San Francisco by the end of 1952. Heading for Washington DC, the journey took three days and three nights traveling by Greyhound bus.

After arriving, I stayed with my friend Ardi Sutono who already worked at the Indonesian Embassy. Waiting patiently for three weeks, there was no prospect of a position for me. By that time, I was running short of funds.

During the first three weeks in Washington DC, I had joined friends in their activities. Many were also former fighters like me, but were by then employed at the Indonesian Embassy. The center for our gatherings was usually in the recreation room of the embassy's basement, known as The Chancery.

At a choir practice there, I saw a girl busy arranging a group of singers and then joining them. To me she was very attractive, but I did not have opportunity to introduce myself.

On a Saturday morning, I attended a soccer practice at a field nearby the Embassy. There I saw the girl again. This time she was playing soccer as goalkeeper. She looked very cheerful and seemed to get along with everyone, even willing to be the goalkeeper for the game.

I asked my friend Ardi Sutono, who she was. He told me she was the daughter of the Indonesian Ambassador Pak Ali Sastroamidjojo and that her name was Sawitri. After another player substituted, I approached her and introduced myself. She asked me if I also liked playing soccer. I answered that I did, but did not have soccer shoes.

Fortunately, I remembered that a tennis court was located next to the soccer field. Thinking quickly, (since I wore tennis shoes) I asked if she enjoyed playing tennis. Replying she did, then added, "In that case, let us go to my house to get two tennis rackets and balls." We later played tennis.

That evening, Sawitri unexpectantly telephoned, inviting me to go to George Washington University where she attended school. Explaining there was a folk dance practice, she said, I would also have a chance to learn if I came along.

Her brother, Karnarajasa ("Yaya" for short) later dropped us off at the university. Going home, we preferred walking rather than taking a taxi. We chatted while leisurely making our way toward the embassy. Not realizing how quickly time had passed, we finally arrived at Sawitri's house several hours later. Following that evening, without my expecting it, my relationship with Sawitri developed quickly and was very sweet.

I received a telephone call from Consul Basri Haznam in New York, advising me to come for a position at the Consulate General office there. Since receiving the news about the job opening for me, I told Sawitri that I was going to New York. She let me know that she would love coming along to take me. Giving reasons that she wanted to visit her relatives, she added that I did not have to worry about her. At that time, her father the Ambassador was away, but her mother gave permission. Immediately, I left for New York. My friend Ardi Sutono drove me, and Sawitri was with us. This became one of the experiences in my life filled with affectionate love.

We arrived in New York on Friday with intent that I would see the Consul on Monday morning. We first took Sawitri to her relative, also an official with the Indonesian Representatives to the United Nations. She spent the night there. I stayed with another friend Pak Madin who had an apartment in Brooklyn. A former sailor, he had been living in New York for many years. Another friend, Eddy Suroyo, lived with Pak Madin.

On Monday morning while having breakfast with friends who were already working at different Indonesian government offices, the doorbell rang. When the door opened, we heard a loud voice shout from downstairs, "US Immigration!" Two of the immigration officers came up to the third floor where we were all seated.

My friends had their paperwork checked first. All of them had their identification documents in order. Only Pak Madin and I did not have proper papers. That instance I already felt that Immigration would surely detain me.

When asked how long I had been in the US, I answered "almost three years." I tried explaining to the officers that I had an appointment on that same day with the Indonesian Consul for a position to work. When I asked permission to call the Consulate they refused my request, saying that it would be best to call from my place of detention.

The officers took both Pak Madin and I to the Ellis Island Immigration Detention Center. We were brought across by ferry, and while looking out toward the center, I thought to myself I was going to the place which was full of history. Many ships, bringing immigrants from all over the world passed Ellis Island. Not so long ago, I myself had sailed by it and the Statue of Liberty while working on the MS Japara.

The officers were friendly with us and did not handcuff us either. They were amazed hearing my story, how I fought in the Indonesian independence revolution, worked on a ship and then jumped ship because I wanted to find a better life in this America, which was beautiful, free and rich. I told the officers, their country was free and limitless with opportunities. Listening to my story, they seemed sympathetic, and said in a friendly manner that they hoped release would come quickly after the court hearing.

After we arrived at Ellis Island, questioning happened separately for Pak Madin and me. Following this, officers escorted us to a large hall with bunk beds. At that time, there were many detainees from all over the world. Among them were those from Latin America, Europe, and Asia.

Actually, I liked staying on Ellis Island very much. Especially, if compared to the jail period I experienced in Indonesia with the Dutch. Through windows of the detainee quarters, I could see the city of New York, which looked very close. I even imagined that if there were a swimming competition from Ellis Island to New York, with a prize of release from detention and permission to stay in the US, I most certainly would participate and try my best to win.

We received fair treatment and food was enough. We were also free to exercise, move around and use the library. All kinds of interesting books filled the spacious reading room. Since I loved reading, it daily was a place of treasures and adventures for me.

On Fridays, the day of religious worship for the Muslims, an *ustad*, Muslim teacher, came to lead us from the Quran. However, to pray five times a day was very difficult. It was almost impossible because of the noisy surroundings with the many other detainees close by. Nevertheless, with every possible opportunity, I tried to do the prayers. However, while detained, I never saw among the other Muslims; their faith regularly put into practice.

On Sundays, a minister came to preach for two worship services. With nothing better to do, I attended both. Always curious, I wanted to know the differences between religions, including Christianity. I knew and believed that Islam considers *Isa Almasih,* Jesus Christ, as one of twenty-five great prophets honored by Muslims. This I learned since childhood.

During my detention, I received letters daily from Sawitri giving encouragement. I had sent a letter to my brother Malik (Hamka) telling him about my situation. He contacted Mr. S. Muhammad Rasyid in Indonesia, who then was the Secretary General of the Indonesian Foreign Affairs Department. Mr. Rasyid immediately requested that Ambassador Ali Sastroamidjojo have me released from Ellis Island. The ambassador then appointed Consul Basri Haznam to arrange it. At that time, the ambassador did not know yet about my relationship with his daughter.

After more than one month in custody, Consul Basri Haznam, accompanied by an attorney, came to Ellis Island. Release arrived for me with help of the Indonesian government; affirming that not only was I an Indonesian war veteran, but also a student wanting to continue my education. Once freed from the detention center, a position was open for me at the Indonesian Supply Mission in New York, located on the sixty-second floor of the Empire State Building. My status granted by the US State Department, was "Foreign Official" as an employee of the Indonesian government.

I fully realized that when I originally entered the US as a ship-jumper, how great the risk had been then. I also knew that it was utterly wrong to have done so. However, I also came to appreciate how much greater the opportunity was that I had been given. In my recitation of prayers, I gave honor to Allah and was grateful to the US government. Deportation back to Indonesia did not come for me, as it did for many of my friends.

After release from Ellis Island, my relationship with Sawitri became closer and we met almost every weekend. Sometimes she came to New

York or I went by train to Washington DC. News about our relationship eventually spread among the Indonesian community in both New York and Washington DC.

Of course when her parents learned about us, they did not permit their daughter to have a relationship with a former *pelaut*, sailor, especially one who was a ship-jumper. I heard about this from Mr. Max Maramis, who at that time was First Secretary of the Embassy in Washington DC.

Sent by the Ambassador to persuade me to stop the relationship with Sawitri, he came to New York a few times. He always invited me to have dinner with him at a restaurant. Each time we talked, he understood and sympathized with the situation. Making it clear, he felt it was not his business; he also reassured me that he did not intend to tell me what to do about Sawitri, but that he was only relaying the Ambassador's message. I respected and appreciated his wisdom.

One day, when I again was in Washington DC to meet Sawitri, the Ambassador telephoned me at Ardi Sutono's house. Of course, I was surprised, to receive a personal telephone call from the Ambassador. When I answered, he immediately asked me in a harsh voice what my purpose was coming to Washington DC. He then asked me, did I not know there was a regulation mandated by him, that no employees of the Indonesian government offices in New York could go to Washington DC without permission from their superiors.

I replied that I was not aware of any such regulation. The Ambassador then asked even more sternly "In that case, what are you doing here?" I answered, "I want to see your daughter and if you have time, I would also like to meet with you." For a moment he was silent, then suddenly said, "You may see me now." Since Sawitri was with me at Ardi's house, she already knew about the telephone conversation with her father. She came along with me to the embassy.

Coming to his office it was the first time I had opportunity to meet and talk with our Ambassador. Before meeting her father, Sawitri told me about his mannerisms. She let me know that when he was angry or annoyed, his voice usually became high-pitched.

After entering the Ambassador's office, he told me to sit in a chair in front of his desk. I watched his manner and attitude as he spoke, which was not at all, what Sawitri had described. He expressed his burden and feelings if I continued a relationship with his daughter. I listened carefully and calmly kept looking at his eyes. I could understand his concerns. It must be disappointing as a parent, to realize, that the hope for their child's future would perhaps not be what he and his wife expected.

Listening until he finished, I asked permission to talk. Sensing the moment had arrived for me to introduce myself; I hoped that the Ambassador would consider me mature as an adult. I then first shared about my own experiences and about my family background. I also made known what I had lived through during the Indonesian revolution and my desire to stay in the US to continue my studies. His expression suddenly changed, and it appeared he was very interested in what I was saying. After listening more, the Ambassador apologized and then suggested I go and meet his wife.

I did not know that during my conversation with her father, Sawitri was hiding and listening behind a thick curtain. When I came out from the office, she immediately hugged and kissed me. She was very proud seeing that my attitude did not seem to have the slightest fear. After that, we went out to lunch.

The following day I returned to New York. Soon after my meeting with the Ambassador, the city of New York no longer held any real interest for me. I had become quite restless and bored with what had been happening.

Mr. Max Maramis came to New York once more. This time, it was to ask me if I would like to transfer to San Francisco. If I agreed, he would immediately arrange for my reassignment to the Consulate of Indonesia there. Hearing this, I knew it was a last attempt from the Ambassador, to separate Sawitri and me. Because I did not want this matter to continue, I agreed to the transfer and returning to San Francisco.

Thinking back, I admit I felt very offended by the treatment I received by Sawitri's parents from the start. Therefore, I thought that if I did not live in New York any longer, Sawitri's parents would be satisfied.

Actually, I also wanted to return to San Francisco. After living in New York more than six months, I missed the appeal that the city held. San Francisco was not only clean and beautiful; but unlike New York, the weather was cool and fresh even during the summer. Besides, it was my intention to continue school after I returned.

When I let Sawitri know I was transferring to San Francisco, she was very upset and sad. I told her that if our relationship was still to continue,

I believed she would definitely like living in San Francisco with me; even if it meant being far from her parents. After I explained this, she was quiet and cried. I already knew however, that my returning to San Francisco would change the direction for our relationship.

During September 1953, I left New York by train. Traveling economy class without extra accommodations, this trip was not like my ship transfer from Lake Charles to San Francisco. The journey from east coast New York to west coast San Francisco again took three days and three nights.

Once I was back in San Francisco, I felt relieved and free. I immediately began working at the Indonesian Consulate (when it was still located in the SF Ferry Building), under the leadership of Consul Abdoel Hamid. He had immediately accepted me, and told me that from the beginning when he arrived in San Francisco and looked for local staff, he wanted very much to hire me. However, he was hesitant then, lest people think that because we were both *orang Padang*, Minang from West Sumatra, he showed favoritism. He informed me that was the reason why he hired Peter Ananda and other friends of mine.

I was very happy after returning to San Francisco. Meeting my friends again was good and I immediately returned to school at Heald's Engineering College. In San Francisco, I really felt free to move around and with whomever I wanted. The San Francisco lifestyle agreed with my personality, which was easily *resah*, restless and *petualangan*, adventurous. I liked to move fast. It seemed that whoever did not move quickly along with me, I left behind. Years later, I realized about my attitude.

After I was in San Francisco a few weeks, I heard from Consul Hamid that Sawitri had run away from Washington DC, and was on her way to San Francisco by bus. When the Consul called me to explain the situation, he asked what I was going to do about this. I told him this problem was my responsibility. Consul Hamid had received information from the Indonesian Embassy in Washington DC about Sawitri's arrival on the west coast.

When Sawitri reached San Francisco, I went to meet her at the bus station. It saddened me, how tired she looked having been in the bus long. She got up from her seat when she saw me. We immediately tearfully embraced each other. I was relieved she was unharmed while traveling alone.

While in San Francisco, Sawitri stayed at the residence of Consul Abdoel Hamid for the week. During that time, President Sukarno appointed her father Ambassador Ali Sastroamijoyo as Prime Minister. Information reached me that the Ambassador hoped we could persuade Sawitri to return to Washington DC.

Since her father had to leave for Indonesia, I told Sawitri that she should consider the pressure he faced. I also said that I did not want our problem to become a hindrance for her father's new position. I pointed out that it was better for her to return to Washington DC and think things over. Lastly, I mentioned I would wait for her decision whether she chose returning to Indonesia with her parents or stay with me in the US. With help from my good friend Sudharmo Martonegoro, who was studying at Berkeley (and still related to Sawitri's family), we persuaded her to return to her parents.

*After New York working at Indonesian Consulate in San Francisco 1954*

Looking back to events then, I had to admit that I actually was not ready for marriage. After Sawitri left for Washington DC, we still communicated via telephone, but only a short time. She had told me that President Sukarno and his wife Ibu Fatmawati already sent presents and advised her father to allow us to get married. The fact that no official engagement happened between Sawitri and I, made me feel even more pressured.

When the Ambassador and family returned to Indonesia, Sawitri also decided to go with them. Since that time, I no longer received any news from her. Therefore, our relationship was automatically broken off. A few years later, I learned that she married Abdul Majid, who was the Governor of Aceh Province at that time.

In this case, I realized my mistake. I also admit certainly feeling very offended by the ambassador's attitude toward me before we met, even though his opinion of me later changed. I am aware that any hurt caused was because of my pride and selfishness. Yet, the victim was Sawitri.

During 1958, I received news that Sawitri after a period of illness had passed away in Indonesia. Shocked by the information, I only hoped that within her soul she had forgiven me. I prayed that Allah would also forgive me for what I felt was my wrongdoing. Later, after I thought about Sawitri's life, it seemed like she was always in a hurry to reach something. Perhaps she already sensed that she would not have much opportunity to experience happiness in the corridor of her own lifetime.

LIFE'S VALUABLE LESSONS... I continued working at the Indonesian Consulate General in San Francisco for the Information Department. I had also returned to school, intending to complete my studies at Heald's Engineering College.

Four years after the break-up with Sawitri, I met Lorraine. She had many relatives including younger sisters she told me were in her care. In 1957, I was thirty years old and single. It was here, that the lure, causing me to make wrong choices, became destruction meant to break my spirit for life. At first, I did not see it; but at that point, dark paths lead into even darker tunnels.

The actual relationship was not long. Only five years – that being short, compared to the length of years I would live. During this involvement, life for me became alleyways to lies. The unhappiness such as I experienced then, was not at all, what I imagined would ever happen to me in America, but it did.

This was especially so regarding four children, each in time, making their appearance into my life. First was a little girl approximately one year old. Initially seeing her, Lorraine told me she was my child. I then, already should have removed myself.

Trying to make the best out of very questionable events, I accepted the little girl as my own. One year later, an almost identical situation repeated. Then it was a small boy. When I asked to see Birth Certificates of the children, I never saw them; but I still took responsibility. Eventually, pressures and severe disappointments, robbed me of any hope to finish my education, thus I stopped school.

Another girl and boy also made their entrances. In thinking back, it was absurd that within a period of five years and the four children, I never once saw Lorraine pregnant. During a portion of this time, I still lived in San Francisco and she in Salinas. A web of dishonesty widened, and within this, I loathed her emotionally unstable behavior. Nevertheless, I accepted what I deemed were my responsibilities starting with the first child, and was why I stayed.

To maintain stability in my own daily life, I continued my Muslim prayers. This gave me strength to cope with the assaults lashed out at me. It also taught me more self-control, so I would not retaliate to what I was experiencing. I believed that by remaining devout to my faith, I could somehow also do penance for previous mistakes. It became a true testing period of my personal endurance.

These living conditions also created a separation from my close friends. Those caring about me since my arrival in the US, felt helpless coming to my aid.

In 1962, after five years of relentless confrontations, I thought life was over for me. This forced me to make a decision. Because I chose to live, I also chose to leave, but still uphold what I then believed, were my responsibilities as a father.

The day I left, with only the clothes I was wearing; my Indonesian friends helped me break away from what they considered the *penjara penderitaan*, prison of anguish, to restart my life.

Following my decision, I continued giving of myself to the four children during whatever Saturdays allotted me. Nevertheless, through time, unspoken questions remained. Answers to these finally arrived for me many years later.

<u>Note</u>: *Although out of sequence with my story, the following information is in this section for purpose of reader's clarification. (From Author)*

In 2007 an Obituary printed in a Salinas newspaper ((May 17, 2007) became the beginning of final release for me.

Lorraine died. According to the obituary, family members I had believed (for fifty years) were her sisters; were in fact Lorraine's daughters.

During early November of 2007, I received heart-wrenching truth by way of a telephone call. After fifty years, revelation had at long last arrived. I was not the biological father of any of the four children. Stunned as I was, I felt incredible relief at the same time. After more than half a century, I finally experienced freedom from lies and secrets created around me long ago.

Further confession came at the end of that same November. The four children knew that I was not their biological father (but they remained silent). Lorraine was in fact their grandmother and the birth mother of all four, actually is one of Lorraine's own daughters. Finally, answers arrived to the questions that I had kept for more than five decades.

In 2007, (at my age of eighty), this experience was for me yet another valuable life lesson. God had specific purpose through this. I knew that year; I once again had a choice. This taught me even more about consequences to actions of our past, personal endurance, and opportunity to forgive each of those involved in this bizarre episode of my life. In choosing to forgive them, total ultimate release came for me… It is from this point, that I will return to sharing my journey.

THE ISLAMIC CENTER… During the 1950's to 1960's many Muslim immigrants arrived in America from Pakistan, the Middle East, Yugoslavia and other countries. Muslims in San Francisco formed an Islamic Center after purchasing an old church building for use as a mosque. Before buying the church, we rented and sometimes borrowed sites like the YMCA or school auditoriums, for celebration of *Idulfitri* after the

*Ramadhan* fasting month or *Iduladha*, which Muslims take part in after the pilgrimages to Mecca.

I became a member of the *San Francisco Islamic Center* and often spoke at the mosque during Friday prayers. I did this during my lunch at the Indonesian Consulate and was happy to have opportunity to address those attending.

One day, when I was speaking, the head of an Egyptian Islamic mission attended the Friday prayers. He had come to San Francisco to observe developments of Islam in California. After I gave my talk, he approached me and introduced himself because he was surprised that when I was reading verses of the Quran, (according to him) I expressed my Arabic well. When I said my name was Amrullah, he immediately asked if Prof. Hamka was my relation. He pointed out to me that as I was speaking, he already thought about my possible connection to Prof. Hamka having met with him each time my brother was in Malaysia.

Later that year for the celebration of *Idulfitri*, I again received an invitation to speak. Although I had already lived in the US for several years, I devoutly continued all the daily-required Islamic prayers and followed the mandatory month of fasting.

Each year when the Indonesian Consulate celebrated the Indonesian Independence Day on August 17, some of the Consulate staff had to say prayers according to each one's religious belief in a ceremony commemorating our freedom. Usually assigned to represent Islam by praying in Arabic, I did this through recitation of memorized prayers and verses. I was used to this since receiving teaching of the Quran from the time I was little.

Although I was Muslim, the Consul General requested I also say the prayer in Indonesian. Because I was not used to praying that way, I was somewhat confused and felt rather anxious, especially having to do so publicly.

Fortunately, there was Pastor Pohan from the Seventh Day Adventist church, the father in-law of Peter Ananda, one of my close friends. I went to see Pastor Pohan and asked if he would help write a prayer for me in Indonesian that I could read. He was pleased I had come to him and said he was more than happy to do that for me. At the celebration, my friends and other guests were very surprised that I also prayed aloud in the Indonesian language instead of only in Arabic.

In looking back, I enjoyed it, whenever I had opportunity to listen to Christians praying, because it seemed that whatever they expressed came from deep within and not repeated from memorization. Not until years later, would I learn about my own spiritual future in a plan not of my own.

INDONESIAN COMMUNITY CENTER – IMI 1962… During the 1960's, work duties consumed my time. With continued political events still taking place in Indonesia, the struggle for total independence was not over yet. We were still fighting to free the West Irian region from the Dutch. During that period, there were also many articles written by Dutch-Indonesian's who preferred going to the Netherlands (Holland), rather than becoming *warga negara Indonesia,* Indonesian citizens. Yet they had never been to Holland before.

*Note: Indo people also known as Indos, Indo-Europeans, Dutch-Indonesians, Indo-Dutch, or Dutch-Indos consists of Europeans, Asians, and persons of mixed European-Asian blood, and people who associated themselves with and experienced the colonial culture of the former Dutch East Indies, a Dutch colony in Southeast Asia that became Indonesia after World War II.*

*In 1949, 300,000 Eurasians who had been socialized into many Dutch customs were repatriated. The Dutch established a repatriation program, which lasted until 1967. Over a period of 15 years after the Republic of Indonesia became an independent state, virtually the entire Dutch population, of Indische Nederlanders (Dutch-Indonesians) – estimated at between 250,000 and 300,000 – left the former Dutch East Indies. Most of them moved to the Netherlands. In 1959 Dutch people who did not embrace Indonesian citizenship were expelled. An estimated 60,000 immigrated to the United States in the 1960's. The Indos are disappearing as a group. (From: Indo People – Immigration from the Dutch East Indies (1945-1965) Wikepedia, the free encyclopedia)*

Many Dutch-Indonesians faced disappointment after arriving in Holland. Dutch people's attitudes toward them were different from what they had experienced while living in Indonesia (prior to the Japanese occupation and Indonesian independence revolution).

Because of disagreeable conditions in Holland, many Dutch-Indonesians preferred immigrating to the US.

There were also Indo's in the United States who had participated in the revolution and effort for Indonesian independence. These people, who became my very good friends, like Ferdinand Pfaff, Al Roza, Albert v/d Berg and others belonged to the social association called Perhimpunan Indonesia. With their help, I began looking for Indo's (in the SF Bay area), who still loved Indonesia. I gathered other Indonesian friends living in both San Francisco and Los Angeles, to establish a new organization since the majority of original Perhimpunan Indonesia members had returned to Indonesia.

In Los Angeles, I contacted Dewi Dja whom I knew since 1950. (I called her *Mbakyu*, a term for Javanese women.) We had met on the farms where I worked when I first arrived in America. Even then, she used to be very active in the Perhimpunan Indonesia. This non-political social organization, aimed at introducing Indonesia to the American community.

I established the *IMI* or *Ikatan Masyarakat Indonesia* – Indonesian Community Center during 1962, while we still looked out for the pro-Indonesia Indo people. My reason for naming the organization *Ikatan Masyarakat Indonesia*, and using the Indonesian language was with the hope of attracting Indo's who still appreciated the land of their birth and wanted to join with us by becoming members of the IMI.

When we originally formed the IMI, one of our main activities was sports and the founding of a soccer team we called *Garuda* (King of Birds). The team quickly became a member of San Francisco Soccer League. Another team started, *Banteng* (Bull), which became a member of the Bay Area Soccer League.

The IMI also organized social events in the SF Bay area with our own band called *Orkes Merdu* (Melodious Orchestra) made up of community members who regularly performed for our activities. From the beginning, the IMI often organized Indonesian Community activities in northern California. These also included fund-raising events when natural disasters struck in Indonesia. We likewise participated in the annual celebration of Indonesian Independence Day on August 17th, with the Indonesian Consulate.

Through the IMI Community activities, we purposed to preserve our identity and promote respect of diverse backgrounds. Our motto *Bhineka Tunngal Ika*, Unity in Diversity, birthed from that objective. We also presented to the public, Indonesian music and dance, performed by students attending Universities and Cultural Arts Schools in the Bay area. Dewi Dja with her students from Los Angeles also supported these efforts. Since the IMI began, we organized many activities for the Indonesian arts. It was part of who we were and some IMI members enjoyed being part of our SF dance group. Activities such as these kept our spirits up and united. Thus from 1962 on, I represented our country in the US as my prime focus.

Although I was no longer a student, I remained active with the *PERMIAS* – Indonesian Student Association in the US. Other friends like Janner Sinaga, Alwi Dahlan, and Emil Salim (future leaders in the Indonesian government), were then part of the leadership. Since my objectives with starting the IMI were non-political, I did not see any need to discuss IMI organization plans with the students.

While forming the IMI, my hoping to find more Dutch-Indonesians who were interested, caused a major misunderstanding. The students immediately considered me a traitor. They opposed me because they believed while I was gathering Dutch-Indonesians; some were former soldiers of the NICA (Dutch Armed Forces) during our revolution. The students refused accepting the fact, that Indo people could also still love Indonesia. This eventually became a serious conflict.

During 1964, Indonesian Ambassador Zairin Zain visited San Francisco. At a meeting, held at the residence of the Consul General, all involved in the dispute (which had escalated in a period of two years) attended. Students expressed strong opposition that the IMI existed, claiming not even knowing who formed it. I immediately answered in a loud voice that I was the one.

The Ambassador became concerned about the obviously severe differences, and invited me to meet with him privately. In our discussion, I mentioned that because I formed the IMI as a community organization, I also encouraged Dutch-Indonesians who had participated on our side of the independence struggle, to be included. I said that I respected their loyalty to our country during the hard days of the revolution. Therefore, I expressed that the Indonesian Community Center (IMI) began with my friends who had willingly fought for the Indonesian right of independence in the same way I had.

When I shared these thoughts with Ambassador Zain, he understood my explanations. My willingness to risk criticism, especially pleased him; expressing also that my thinking, was "too advanced" for the students to fully understand or appreciate.

I felt happy knowing the ambassador understood my view for IMI's aim of uniting people, those originating from Indonesia living in the US, who also still loved Indonesia. I told Ambassador Zain my thoughts were also especially about the children born from Indonesian descent in the US. I believed they should know their identity in order to be proud of their heritage. It would take this private meeting to bring solution to the conflict. After the ambassador considered my explanations, he also conveyed to me, he would wholeheartedly support our IMI activities.

After my talk with the ambassador, the IMI Board met again with the students. I informed them about our discussion and stated that during our revolution I was active in the struggle for a free Indonesia. If any of them considered me a traitor, I allowed myself to be hung or shot. Asking where they had been during the revolution, the majority remained silent.

I would not only experience such situations with Indonesian students, but later also from other Indonesians recently arrived (1970's) in the United States. These people immediately opposed our IMI activities, staunchly disagreeing about Dutch-Indonesians introducing Indonesia's culture to the American public. I nonetheless kept expressing that we should realize Indo people were victims of history just like the Indonesians.

# SECTION THREE

## *1965 – 1980*

# 13

# ONE MORE CHANCE AT LOVE

*Do not fear taking chances, especially falling in love.*
*Live by the moment, as new hope for true happiness*
*can fill your heart again.*
Unknown

VERA... It could be said that between the years of 1962 through 1965, I was extremely busy establishing the IMI – Indonesian Community Center. All my attention I focused on the organization's activities and my work at the Consulate as Public Relations Information Officer.

Because of the previous unhappy experiences, I remained cautious and did not consider beginning any relationship with women that could possibly lead to something serious – especially marriage.

During this period, a branch of IMI also started in Los Angeles. Membership in LA consisted of a mix between Indonesians and Dutch-Indonesians under the leadership of Mustapha Amir.

I was thirty-seven years old in May of 1965, and had gone to Los Angeles with other IMI San Francisco Board members. We were to meet with Dewi Dja and invite her to come with her dance group to perform in SF. I never expected, that introduction to one of her students would possibly become a chance at love again for me.

Dewi Dja invited me to come along to Perry Studio in Hollywood where she taught Indonesian dance. Among Dja's students (mostly of international heritage), I saw one Dutch-Indonesian girl named Vera Ellen. Though seemingly very young, I noticed she gave serious attention to their practice.

That same day, I also met Fred George (Vera's father). Dja mentioned he was one of few Indo's she knew with a special love for Indonesian music.

She also said he shared his talents as a musician and singer for Indonesian *Keroncong*, folk style music. Thus, it was not surprising he also brought his daughter to learn Indonesian dance.

During the practice, Fred shared with me about his family. Vera he said was born in Surabaya, Indonesia. In 1955 at age three, she went to Holland when their family left Indonesia during the mass Indo diaspora. After living in Holland for almost seven years, the family immigrated to the United States in 1962. We exchanged stories about our beginnings in this new country.

After rehearsal, Dja invited our IMI group for sightseeing at Los Angeles's Olvera Street. Some of her students came along, including Dja's daughter Ratna and Vera who looked polite and friendly. She was pleasant and soft spoken with a gentle voice. I thought her English still had a cute Dutch accent. On that day in May of 1965 and first meeting her, it never occurred to me what my future held.

That same year on New Year's Eve, a tragic incident happened which deeply affected and saddened me. During the IMI's Celebration, my close friend Max Cosem (Kasim from our sailing days on the SS Japara and MS Limburg) suffered a major heart attack after performing an Indonesian dance with our SF group. Not only was Max my friend who left the ship together with me, we also had been roommates after I returned from New York in 1953.

*Willy Amrull (center front) with Max Cosem (left, second row)*

Max and I worked together at the Indonesian Consulate while he also studied at Heald's Engineering College. Recently graduated with a Bachelor of Science Degree that year, he planned a career as an engineer in the US. Max was only thirty-five years old.

When he collapsed, before paramedics arrived, all attempts at reviving him was in vain. Max died in front of me. I was so shocked I fainted into unconsciousness. Max was my closest and most faithful friend whom I knew truly cared about me. I grieved his death a long time. This provided another lesson about the meaning of life for me.

GETTING AQUAINTED... It would be more than two years later, before I saw Vera again. Toward the end of 1967, Dja came to San Francisco again with some of her dancers. The Consulate and Indonesia Tourism Board together hosted a special *Indonesia Night*. Asked to meet the group at San Francisco's International Airport, I was there to greet them. Although I did not say anything upon their arrival, the quiet Dutch-Indonesian girl whom I met almost three years earlier clearly caught my attention that day.

I was program MC for that event and all involved stayed busy. While I was in fact more aware of Vera during that weekend, there was no real opportunity of becoming better acquainted. The following months remained full with activities for me in San Francisco and the next year arrived quickly.

I received an invitation from IMI Los Angeles to attend a special event during April of 1968. There I met Vera again, and after seeing her, a sense of genuinely wishing to know her better moved within me.

As the evening progressed, I first took time to greet friends. Seeing where Vera was, even from a distance I had concerns. Besides there being a considerable age difference, I incessantly remained guarded about relationships, worrying that things would turn out like before.

For six years, I had made sure to be very careful, holding back with anyone from the opposite sex on anything, other than casual friendship. I persistently told myself, "It's okay to be friendly with everyone; but not be in a serious relationship with one." Even while keeping all this in mind, that evening I somehow felt different.

I went over to where Vera was. Inviting her to dance, she smiled taking the hand I offered. At first, we just made polite conversation. Her replies were friendly but with reserve. Looking at her, I thought she was too young. Yet something was nice as we chatted. Whatever words we spoke that night made me aware that even at such young age she was quite mature. In a pleasant way, it affected me.

To my own amazement, while we danced I suddenly glimpsed something of our perhaps having a relationship with time. This caught me completely off guard, but in looking back, I know that Vera then already embraced my life. I kept asking myself, "Is this really happening? After all I had been through – another chance?"

The following day, there was an IMI leadership gathering at Ali Assan and Dja's home. Again, I noticed Vera as she greeted people. In observing her, something drew me more. As I led the discussion, I saw she was quietly watching nearby.

When our group was leaving later that day, Vera was among those gathered outside the house. While saying good-bye to everyone I also quietly hugged her, smiling, as unspoken words lingered. My friends and I then drove off.

After returning to San Francisco, our contact with one another began. Yet again, much to my surprise, I kept sensing promptings to further a relationship with Vera. I soon discovered the attraction was mutual. Nonetheless, awareness of our age differences clearly remained with me. While she was in Los Angeles and I in San Francisco, phone calls and letters eventually kept us connected.

During conversation, what happened through the darkest period of my life emerged. Vera's understanding made me really see her heart even then already. Touching me at a level hard to explain, more appreciation awakened on my part.

Somehow, she aligned herself with me in a short period, and my naturally restless spirit was finding contentment. I kept thinking however, she was too young, especially for someone like me, with my kind of problems.

During late summer of 1968, Dja and her family including Vera came up to the Bay area. It was during this time, that we experienced a wonderful turning point together before they all returned to Los Angeles.

However, like a revolving door without stopping, Lorraine's absurd demands continued coming. Since I strongly felt I needed to first care for the children (assuming then that I was their father), I carried this responsibility.

After a while, some situations also arose about Vera, which I kept to myself. Sadly, I allowed these to influence me. I then convinced myself, that she really wanted better things in life. At that time, knowing I could not offer what I thought she really hoped for, I decided it was best that I stepped back and let go.

Everything between us came to an abrupt halt. I immediately felt the weight of my decision and action. Afterwards I realized that by being overly cautious; cost me what I finally hoped to keep.

Weeks, months and eventually an entire year went by. I had not directly heard anything from Vera anymore. However, despite the long silence, I would later learn about her true steadfastness.

When the person you love is by your side, every challenge is easier to face, every dream more attainable... every belief more grounded.

Anonymous

UNBREAKABLE BOND... During early December of 1969, the Consulate assigned me to go to Los Angeles. Union Oil Company sponsored a float representing Indonesia in the *Tournament of Roses Parade* on January 1, 1970 in Pasadena, California. Dja's daughter, plus other Indonesian instructors from UCLA would all appear on the float. Therefore, I went to Los Angeles again to stay with Dja and family.

After arriving from San Francisco, I suddenly on impulse decided to call Vera. Since the long year of silence, I hoped to talk with her and was relieved hearing her voice on the other end. She was very surprised and sounded happy to hear from me. As we spoke for a while, I tried keeping the suddenness of my call easy-going.

She mentioned it was remarkable; the timing of my calling, exactly as she was writing a Christmas card to me. Vera was elated with the coincidence, while I was too. After we chatted some more, realizing how much I really wanted to see her, I suggested that if it were okay I wanted to come by that same day. Vera's response was not hesitant, replying agreeably.

That evening I went to her parent's home. All of us enjoyed part of the evening together. Once the two of us were alone however, I felt uncertain of what to say or do next. Sitting across from each other at the table, we briefly did not say anything but neither could expression of our feelings stay back.

I reached over, took Vera's hand placing it in mine. We silently held on to each other that way. Soon, while still looking at me she began voicing her thoughts about the decision of the year before. She mentioned her disappointment. I could hardly believe I caused that kind of letdown. In those moments even doubts I had held, did not matter. Whatever the circumstances were, I realized her affection for me had been sincere the entire time.

Watching Vera as she spoke, I was thinking how much I enjoyed our conversations from the start. When I talked, I tried explaining, but also telling her what really led me to wonder if her feelings for me were only infatuation. As we sat with my hand still holding hers, I did not want to let go of it because of what I realized.

That night, I nevertheless needed to be sure of what she really wanted. I understood there were other possible paths for her to follow. Yet, that evening I felt I still could not assure her of certain things, I believed she hoped for in her future.

As she listened, I could see from the look on her face that this situation did not need to be made more complicated. Without any doubt, we both clearly knew enough time, was already wasted.

Before I left that evening, Vera reminded me about the card. Handing it to me, she remarked again that she just never expected to hear from me right in the midst of writing it. Saying goodnight we held each other close. Although we were not aware of it then, something much bigger covered us.

Even many years later, the mention and memory of that night would always bring us smiles. The reminder of our *beautiful moments* never forgotten, we were *sudah jodoh* – already matched, soul mates. I never expected; that meeting Vera in 1965 would eventually change my life to the extent it would.

Returning to San Francisco the following week, I went back again to Los Angeles by the end of December and celebrated the New Year with Vera and her family. The following morning we all went to Pasadena. To our great delight, the Union Oil Company float was awarded the Grand Prize in that 1970 Tournament of Roses parade; themed Holidays Around The World.

After the year began, our relationship quickly flourished. Essentially continuing where we had left of in 1968, everything moved rapidly forward, almost instantly reaching beyond my expectations. During that time, I was seeing that Vera really had a mature outlook. I was discovering even more that she understood my energy for life. I was forty-two years old.

Time arrived for me to speak with Vera's parents. In first asking for the hand of marriage of their daughter, Fred and Sonja George received me kindly. Although they accepted my love for their eldest child, Fred spoke to me in private, expressing his concerns regarding the big difference in our ages. In knowing me however, he did not view it as a problem but just wanted to be sure that I understood all the risks involved. He trusted I would take good care of his daughter. In looking back, considering both our personalities, I already sensed even then, that Vera and I could walk together through this *new corridor of our time.*

During 1970, Indonesia's President Suharto planned a visit to the US. Before his arrival, which included stops in San Francisco and Los Angeles, the Indonesian Ambassador in Washington DC had sent the military attaché to California for preparation in measures of security. The Consulate appointed me to assist because of my good relations with different groups within the Dutch-Indonesian community. I was to meet with the leaders I was acquainted with to explain matters of the presidential visit.

To finalize arrangements for community participation, I led a meeting at the San Pedro home of IMI leaders Djoko and Ruby Soejoto. I also announced at end of the meeting, that after President Suharto's visit, Vera and I planned to be married.

When I returned to San Francisco, I also made announcement of our upcoming wedding. Everyone was surprised. They all knew about my horrible experiences of the past and did not expect that I would marry Vera or anyone. Those of my closest friends understood and wished me real happiness.

Vera and I were married in Los Angeles on June 6, 1970. Because I was Muslim and Vera of Catholic background, we did not marry in a Catholic Church or with Muslim ceremony. Our vows were officiated in a Wedding

Chapel. My dear friend Henri Pohan was my Best Man and Vera's friend Ingrid Aliet her Maid of Honor.

On our wedding day, I was certain *God meant for us to be one.* During the ceremony, speaking our promises to each other, neither age nor religious difference mattered. These were our personal vows to God. The words we said became our commitment for life, sealing us permanently in this journey. A reception celebrating our happy day followed.

*Our wedding day very happy moments, 1970*

After our wedding, Vera immediately moved with me to San Francisco to begin our new life. The IMI-SF community honored our marriage by hosting a reception. The occasion also introduced Vera as my wife to friends and acquaintances who never met her before. Officials and co-workers from the Consulate, including Indonesian Consul General B. Nitidiwirya and his wife, were all present at the special celebration.

We had begun walking through our first passage of life together. I felt this was a new journey originally planned by the Almighty. Eleven years later, we would come to know God's incredible plan for our lives.

CHILDREN GOD'S GIFT... While Vera was pregnant, I was the happiest man imaginable. This was the first time I really enjoyed this new experience. I was finally able to watch a new life from God forming. For the first time I also watched the change of natural beauty during pregnancy. I wanted to enjoy taking care of Vera. This would also include taking care of our baby after birth. I had never known this simple kind of pleasure that I was living. After all that had happened before, I knew this was a special gift to me. I could hardly contain myself with the love already in me for the baby that God was giving us.

The evening Vera went into labor, I tried staying calm as I had to take her quickly to San Francisco Children's Hospital. With much anticipation, I kept a close watch on my wife sitting beside me in the car. We thought for sure the baby would arrive during that night or early morning.

Night became morning and by early afternoon of that second day problems developed regarding the delivery. Our baby girl, Rehana Soetidja was born at 1:02 am December 21, 1970 via C-Section surgery. I was the first one to see my new daughter after she came into this world.

Due to complications from the operation, Vera did not get to see the baby until the third day, which was Christmas Eve. I however, was in the Neonate Unit at all hours permitted by the hospital, looking at my daughter inside her incubator. Ultimate joy and happiness had met me.

With the baby's birth, Vera and I were *betul-betul bahagia,* very, very happy. Each day, we focused on our daughter's growth. During times when she was fidgety, I would hold Rehana until she fell asleep on my shoulder or in my arms.

I felt Vera had already done much during the pregnancy and delivery, so I wanted to help as much as possible. This particular responsibility of being a father I enjoyed very much. I had found contentment beyond what I thought life could hold. Never had I experienced this kind of happiness before.

STEPPING FORWARD... I can say that from the beginning of our life together, it was about daring to take risks. When we married, Vera had been willing to follow me immediately to San Francisco. I had made some major decisions about career changes and resigned my position at the Indonesian Consulate General. Having worked there for almost twenty years, I was ready for a new direction. I prepared for these steps by completing additional courses at the International School of Travel.

Before leaving the Consulate, I travelled extensively throughout the US and Canada speaking at seminars to promote Indonesia's Tourism. I had replaced Joop Ave a good friend of mine, when he returned to Indonesia to be Chief of Staff at the Presidential Palace. At that time, the Indonesian government had engaged the expertise of the US public relations firm Bell and Stanton of New York, which arranged all seminars and interviews where I was to appear. I felt everything was just right regarding the outlook of my career.

I had decided to resign from the Consulate, when a friend, Jasmuddin Dewan, asked me to join with him in establishing a US Branch of the Indonesian Natrabu Travel Bureau. We knew each other from working together at the Consulate before he opened an Indonesian restaurant that became quite successful. In beginning this new venture, I was very aware of the risk; but had confidence to open the travel agency in partnership.

Because of my years' experience at the Consulate in Public Relations, and with the Indonesian Tourism Board, we planned that I would assume General Management and Marketing of the business. Jasmuddin agreed to responsibilities of the Finances. We believed our venture could be successful. While finishing obligations with Bell and Stanton for the Consulate, I was able to arrange the acceptance and official recognition of Natrabu in the United States with the IATA (International Association of Travel Agents).

My legal status in the US changed once I had resigned from the Indonesian Consulate. Vera and I agreed that one of us should apply for US citizenship. Since already having Permanent Resident status, Vera applied in San Francisco. Having attended High School in the US, she passed the US Immigration examination and interview phase without any difficulty. I however, was still not ready to release my Indonesian citizenship even though I had lived in the US for twenty-one years.

Through this period, extreme problems arose from Lorraine. A tremendous force of setbacks hit me hard, all meant to destroy the happiness I had found. The compilation of everything forced me to decide that as much as I cared for the children, enjoyed my work and loved San Francisco; I refused losing the new happiness I had been given.

After Vera became a US Citizen, I made the final decision for us to move to Los Angeles. It was very tough for me to leave, but I had no other option and told Vera, I did not want, what we had, to be ruined.

After our move, with my career unexpectedly disrupted and frustration settling in, I experienced a short period of self-doubt and blame. I sometimes even began thinking about Vera and me; concerning different aspects of our relationship before we married. This was mainly due to matters (from my past) that I should have taken care of but left undone. Consequently, I also felt I was a disappointment to my wife, and that she really should have considered other choices.

Fortunately, this phase did not last long. I thought about all my years at the Indonesian Consulate. My documents status as Foreign Government Official only permitted me to work for the Consulate General in San Francisco. I still however, had a Social Security number and card (from the fifties).

I was Travel Consultant with an LA based agency specializing in Far East and Indonesia travel. I also began teaching Indonesian language at Berlitz School of Languages and translating legal documents. This led to additional part-time language instruction at Hughes Aircraft Company for engineers and technicians going to Indonesia (for the Palapa Satellite Program). Since one of my favorite sports was soccer, I also refereed games on weekends. This I enjoyed very much (sometimes three assignments in one day). All were part of my busy schedule, and somehow had physical stamina for all the different undertakings.

Even with facing many difficulties during those days, I realized how very happy I was for the first time in my life. Besides having a beautiful and faithful wife, the birth of our daughter Rehana also was a special gift to me.

The IMI–LA Community Center elected me as President the year after we moved. Vera began helping me with this as well. This sometimes included sharing about Indonesia with organizations. She also taught Indonesian dances to teens and children, most of Indo descent. We also hosted a weekly radio broadcast in Southern California, "The Voice of Indonesia," sponsored by the IMI.

Before the Indonesian Consulate General opened their office in Los Angeles, the IMI organized annual observances of Indonesian Independence Day and other events related to this. Members accomplished all these activities with the spirit of *gotong royong*, by working-together in family style. Vera and I constantly served for the purpose of the IMI community. While living in Southern California, these activities occupied us until 1977.

# 14

# RETURN TO INDONESIA

*"I must go after my dreams eagerly.*
*Even with many risks,*
*I will step toward the future God planned for me."*
Abdul Wadud Karim Amrullah
(From: Willy Amrull's Personal Journal)

FROM RISK TO FAITH… I had already learned the meaning of taking risks during early days in Indonesia. Losing both my parents before the age of eighteen forced me to grow up quickly. To survive in my country during the periods of occupation, revolution and change; I daily took risks.

I believe, that the way my parents raised me during early childhood; although followed by those teenage years of uncertainty, shaped who I became. Each of these measures in my life nurtured my desire that much more, to go and really see the world. I wanted to see my dreams come true because my enthusiasm for life had no limit.

My fateful arrival in the United States was part of that dream and one big dare. Thus for me, life was drenched in risks. No matter what challenges of life intended to intimidate me, I was not afraid. In later years, I understood that all things experienced in my past, had been molding me particularly for what still lay ahead, especially from 1970 onwards.

I received a new chance at starting life again. Even though I was at the beginning of mid-life, I had finally found someone willing to risk with me whatever it took. I enjoyed telling Vera my thoughts because I knew she listened with maturity. She encouraged me, willing also to climb to heights I had not yet reached.

Looking back, from all I previously learned and would still experience in the future, my spirit discovered more fully the meaning that *"faith without risk is not faith."* This faith eventually carved itself deeply into my soul.

For me, another special gift arrived on the morning of June 14, 1974, when our second child was born. A healthy baby boy; we named him Sutan Ibrahim Karim. By giving him this particular name, I actually gave Sutan my *gelar*, traditional title, would I have married within *adat Minangkabau*, custom. Once our baby was home, each time I held him it made me feel as if life's biggest problems faded.

Sutan's birth brought me more happiness. This began my longing to return home and take my family to Indonesia. Teaching them to be good Muslims – proud of their heritage; was something I absolutely hoped to achieve with my wife and children.

By 1977, many years had passed since my arrival in America. While spending much time representing my country abroad, I did not realize that twenty-seven years had gone by. I talked a lot with Vera about my desire of returning home. Even though she did not know what to expect, she agreed to this big change. Besides loving me, she wanted to learn more about Indonesia since she was born in Surabaya (East Java). Prepared to leave her family and our friends in the US, Vera later expressed that it was because she believed in our happiness, our future, and me.

My wife had been communicating with one of my brother's daughters through letters written in English. Because of this, Vera also was not afraid to live in Indonesia. She told me that she already had a friend who was waiting.

It took time to prepare, especially regarding employment. From my days at the Consulate, I had become acquainted with Indonesian executives coming to San Francisco and Los Angeles. Among them was Dr. Hasyim Ning who asked me to accompany him each time he came to the US. On one occasion, he mentioned that if I desired returning to Indonesia, he hoped I would consider working for him in one of his companies. He said, "Indonesians who had worked in the US were very diligent and smart."

After making the decision of going to Indonesia, I wrote a letter to Hasyim Ning whom I usually called Uda Hasyim. Notifying him of my desire to return home and reasons why, he immediately responded by reassuring me a position.

Because Uda Hasyim was familiar with my career background, he wanted me to remain in tourism. He owned a very successful travel agency called Pacto Tour and Travel with branches throughout Indonesia. Uda Hasyim offered me a position in Denpasar, Bali, which I accepted with pleasure. Having lived in the US for almost three decades, I was ready.

On May 13, 1977, I left Los Angeles for Jakarta. Vera and the kids stayed behind, since our initial plan was, that I arrange for their arrival once I settled down. In reaching Jakarta, I was like a stranger not familiar with many of the new streets, neighborhoods and areas developed after 1950. When I left Indonesia, the suburb of Kebayoran Baru did not yet exist. It was here I stayed, at the home of my brother Uo Aji (Malik), known publicly as Prof. Dr. Buya Hamka.

Six weeks later, my wife and children followed me. This was their first experience, with the humidity and a true test of enduring the climate without comfort of electric fans or air-conditioning. Indonesia's weather was not at all like that of Southern California. I was happy however that we were together again. Since we would be moving to Bali, my brother wanted us stay with him thru the orientation period of my new position at Pacto.

My brother looked very happy with my return. When I was still in America, I had notified him in a letter about my plans. He immediately replied that whatever facilities I needed for my family he would prepare for me. Once I finally returned in 1977, Uo Aji, true to his word, opened his home to us. While I was in Jakarta, my brother also made available to me the use of one of his cars. Orientation lasted for approximately five months; we waited at his home on Jl. Raden Patah I, no 2, in Kebayoran Baru before our move.

I registered Rehana in the kindergarten school at Al Azhar. Within a few weeks, she already memorized some verses of the Quran in Arabic. Sutan was still too small for school, but every morning he came with me to *Mesjid Agung*, the Great Mosque (located across the street from my brother's house) to pray with me and his *Pak Tuo Malik*, older father Malik. We also listened to the *Kulyah Subuh* – Morning Lecture, which my brother led. For me, all this was the beginning to fulfillment of wishes, which I had for our family to become good Muslims.

Vera immediately began learning the language and joined in with my brother's children, hoping it would help her communicate in Indonesian more quickly. Within a few months, she was somewhat confident using the Indonesian language, *Bahasa Indonesia*. She did this with the same determination like when learning to speak English after arrival in America as a child.

During those first months in Indonesia, although things were difficult for my wife, I saw her trying to adapt herself in all circumstances. She handled things calmly with peace of mind. What did however disappoint her initially, was realizing that in the country where she was born, people considered her a foreigner, *orang asing*, or *orang Barat*, a Western person. Although she was married to me (and was half Indonesian), she experienced not being accepted. Having come with me, I knew my wife had idealistic beliefs that were too naïve.

One day returning from work, Vera greeted me with news I did not expect. She told me that she had become a Muslim that day in a ceremony led by my brother. She explained that after I had left in the morning, she was with him while he ate breakfast. After sharing about an unusual dream, she had the previous night; my brother's reply was that perhaps it was time for her to become a Muslim.

Vera thought that by following my brother's suggestion; in addition to receiving his approval, and pleasing me, it would be like an "official" acceptance into my family. She felt that one of the reasons they excluded her was because she was not a Muslim, also because she was not Minang. Since our arrival, I observed how my wife tried adjusting herself with my relatives.

Vera told me, that although she felt apprehensive (since I was not with her) but knowing my desire for our family, she decided to take the step. During the ceremony, she followed my brother in reciting the *kalimah syahadat*, the profession of faith three times, in Indonesian, English and Arabic.

Afterwards, Hamka's wife handed Vera a package containing a *sarung*, the material for covering lower part of body, a *mukena*, white covering for a woman's head and upper body during prayer, and a *tikar sembahyang*, prayer mat. Vera told me, that the same morning, one of Hamka's sons had given her several cassettes with instruction to listen and memorize reciting prayers in Arabic.

While explaining to me what had happened, I listened closely trying to make out what my wife was really saying. After some thought I realized how desperately, she wanted acceptance from my family. I was aware also how fully she hoped pleasing me. But as much as I wanted Vera to follow me and be Muslim, I already had concern about this sudden decision. I knew how isolated she had felt during the past months.

MOVE TO BALI – ISLAND OF DEMONS… Official appointment as Branch Manager of Pacto Tour and Travel in Bali came for me toward the end of 1977. Ready for the move we flew to Bali, and stayed at the Bali-Sanur Bungalows until leasing a house. For us, the bungalow-style hotel seemed like a tropical palace. This was the first time since arriving in Indonesia that we were by ourselves. The bungalows were comfortable, clean and cool, and we considered it home for the following months.

Uda Hasyim initially was concerned about our choice of accommodations; but these cottages had beautiful gardens and also two swimming pools for us to enjoy. Uda Hasyim however, said he considered it as if we were staying in a *gubuk*, a shack. For our family this was a refreshing new environment. Not only was this very close to my office, it was also walking distance from the beach. For Rehana and Sutan this was especially fun. Not far from the bungalows on the beach, was a *tukang sate*, barbeque vendor, who became acquainted with Rehana and Sutan and we quickly became his regular customers.

The month of December 1977 arrived while we stayed at the bungalows. For our children it would be the first Christmas away from their *Oma*, Vera's mother, and family in California. On Christmas Eve however, the kids had a happy surprise with the delivery of a very large package at the hotel from Vera's aunt and uncle in Holland. In the box were many goodies for their enjoyment.

Almost three months later, we found a suitable house to lease. This kept Vera happy and busy because she was finally able to prepare that house as a home for us. With help in the house, it did not take long for our new home to be ready.

After our arrival in Bali, my first responsibility was to replace Mr. Warwick Purser, who returned to Australia. I was then immediately very busy with my work, tending to foreign clients especially those from Europe, America, Australia and Japan. During the 1970's, Pacto was the largest tourist agency in Indonesia, especially the Bali Branch. During those years, Pacto also served the majority of cruise ships arriving in Bali. Because we brought in many foreign tourists, relationships with the hotels, restaurants and art shops were very good.

Pacto also operated under the company owned bus fleet. Employees were in the hundreds whether working in the branch office or as guides and drivers in the field. I felt at the time, that the company needed to pay more attention to the long-term wellbeing of Pacto employees. I tried creating good relations, by giving incentives for working with enthusiasm, integrity and loyalty.

Work occupied much of my time while Vera cared for the children at home. I could see that it was rather boring for her to do the same things every day especially while the kids attended school.

I thought that perhaps, she might be interested in doing something different to keep busy. When I spoke to her about my concerns, an acquaintance of mine who owned a small boutique at one of the large hotels was selling his business. This meant that space was available at the hotel if we wanted it. After discussion with Vera about these possibilities, she agreed with my suggestions. Soon after this, the hotel also accepted my bid.

Another friend (whom I knew from the US while he studied there) agreed to supply inventory of high quality Indonesian hand painted *batik* creations and artifacts. Vera quickly focused on daily development of the Desiree Boutique, which opened in late 1978 at the Bali Sanur Beach Hotel.

After more than a year, and the boutique doing well, we were also able to open two other stores in a partnership. One store was in Celuk, a tourist attraction outside of Denpasar then known as the silver works capital of Bali. On site, Balinese artisans created silver jewelry and other silver works for the tourists. Sometime later, together with other partners another boutique opened in Sanur near the Pacto branch office. My wife stayed very busy. When we opened these shops, we did not start with lots of capital. I based it on the Minang business philosophy that capital is your *tenju bulek*, rounded fist. It meant that a business is established based on capital of trust and integrity. When I reported these developments to Uda Hasyim, he was happy for us, giving me his approval and encouragement.

RETURN TO BEAUTIFUL MANINJAU... In the beginning of 1980, Pacto assigned me to evaluate business development of the Padang Branch in West Sumatra. I had opportunity to return to my childhood village in Maninjau, which I left about forty years earlier. Having passed through the corridor of life, I experienced many changes since those years. I knew this time, Allah brought me back to my beloved *kampuang*, the village, where I took my first breath on earth. Sungai Batang, where as a small boy I rushed through its narrow streets, hurrying to be on time for afternoon Quran classes and running hard when the sky was frightfully red, as I feared the world reached its end.

Driving on the *Kelok 44*, the road with forty-four hairpin curves riskily winding down the hillside slope, I knew I would soon be home. Accompanied by several co-workers, excitement grew within me as each turn brought me closer to tranquil scenic Lake Maninjau. That was also the time that I would once again see the Tumayo Bridge.

From early days, I remembered that when going by the Tumayo Bridge, we had only to pass by the *pasar*, open market a short distance to arrive at the house where my family still lived. However, throughout all the years of being away, in my memory, the bridge was the clear road mark indicating I was almost home. On that day, once we reached the village at the bottom of the hill, I could not find the bridge.

It was evening and already dark. Carefully we drove on the narrow road beside the lake and kept driving until finally, we had reached Muara Pauh where my father's library was located.

I was astonished since this meant we somehow had passed my house. Turning the car around, we drove back down the same road. A short distance away, we found the house where I had lived until I was fourteen years old.

Since I was a little boy, I thought the Tumayo Bridge, was the longest bridge I had ever seen. Through the years, I shared stories about its beauty with Vera. I compared it to the impressiveness of the Golden Gate Bridge in San Francisco. Therefore, as soon as we reached my village, of course I immediately looked out for a sizeable bridge.

Finally reaching the house that evening, I knocked on the front door of *rumah di baruah*, which was the home of my Uni Halimah and my aunt, Mak Etek Jamilah. I voiced out a greeting, *"Assalamu 'alaikum"* – "peace be unto you." There was an answer from inside *"Wa'alaikum salam, sia u, masueklah"* – "peace be with you also, who is it, please come in." When my Uni Halimah opened the door, she was shocked to see me, since I had not let her know about my intent to visit. Hugging each other, she repeatedly cried out, *"Adiek den, adiek den"* – "my little brother, my little brother." Then, my aunt Jamilah also came to the door greeting me and asking, *"Sia waang, lai 'ang basuo jo si Wadud? Dima inyo kini?"* – "who are you, did you see Wadud? Where is he now?" From appearance, she looked like she had become somewhat absent-minded and confused with age. After I told her that I was Wadud and that I am home, my aunt cried. But about ten minutes later, repeated the same questions again. According to Uni Halimah, my aunt always prayed for me after her five daily prayers.

The next morning, I walked to our old house located next to Uni Halimah's house. It was *rumah di atas* where I was born. The house was in state of partial collapse and no longer occupied.

Then I went to look for the bridge. I soon discovered the Tumayo River had become a mere creek. Soon I saw the Tumayo Bridge, which was surprisingly undersized from what I remembered. Compared to other bridges familiar to me like San Francisco's Golden Gate Bridge, or even bridges over the Ciliwung River in Jakarta (which I escaped across when Dutch military police hunted me), Tumayo Bridge seemed miniscule. For a while, I just stood there taking in the site spread-out before me.

I realized then, how different our thinking was as children. I thought about what my outlook on life would have been, had I never gone out to see the world. Standing there alone, I once again appreciated the opportunities allotted me.

While I was in my village, I slept in the room where I used to sleep when I was little if my father was not home. That morning I also went to my mother's grave behind Uni Halimah and Etek Jamilah's house. In my heart I told Amak, *"Mak, ambo lah pulang"* – "Mom, I am already home." During my quiet reflection, I saw Amak's face and she was very happy to see me again.

*At my Mother's grave site in my village of Sungai Batang, by Lake Maninjau*

During this visit, I also had opportunity to borrow a motorboat from one of my long ago friends. With my nephew Alizar (Cha) accompanying me, I was able to call on some of our relatives and friends living around the lake.

One example of my changed adult view happened when I had dinner at Uncu Juri's house (*uncu* is aunt, not a blood relative), our neighbor who still lived in a *rumah gadang*, the Minangkabau big house with pointed roofs where I used to play. In those days, I was able to run around inside that house and played soccer with a tennis ball. This time however, when I entered that same house again I realized how narrow it was even without furniture in it.

While in the kampuang, I soon began feeling over-stuffed from eating too much good food. As I visited other family and old friends, invitation came to join them for a meal. I ate at least five times a day during that short stay in Sungai Batang.

Reflecting on these things, it was difficult grasping how long I really had been away. For me, returning to Sungai Batang and Maninjau was like stepping back in time and good memories.

"Parental love begins when new life is created.
Before our baby was born, we already loved and after birth,
we willingly would give until our last breaths on earth."
Willy and Vera Amrull

NEW LIFE FROM GOD… Arriving back in Padang, I began fasting before returning to Bali. I called Vera, and how very happy I was, when she told me the news that she was pregnant for a few months already, with our third baby.

Even at the age of fifty-three, I felt young and energetic knowing I would soon be a father once more of our third child. Again, the joy that brought me was very special. Indeed, for me age was not at all an obstacle to raise a new baby.

Having been to my village and seeing family from both my mother's and father's side, I knew it was time for me to take the step for our children, and responsibility regarding Islam as our religion. It was my intention that my wife and children would learn to pray and read Islam's holy book, the Quran. I believed it was important for me to teach our children about religion.

As soon as I was home in Bali, although immediately busy with work, I did not forget to arrange for an *ustad*, a Muslim teacher, to come to our house and teach the children. I also saw how occupied Vera was, putting much of her attention on our business, the pregnancy and other activities. It seemed like she had no time to sit with the *ustad* to learn.

We received news one evening of a burglary at our store in Celuk. We quickly discovered that the local police could not do anything. Before the theft, we already sensed a threat. Our business partners in this venture were Balinese; however, within the realm of religion and culture in Bali, I was an outsider. Even though a Minang, I was not Balinese. Vera was an overall outsider since everyone considered her to be an American.

Because our store implemented using fixed (retail) prices, other storeowners in the area did not look favorably on this. The norm in Bali; then was, "flexible" prices with use of codes. This also meant that the nationality of tourists determined the prices. Our Balinese partners initially agreed using the fixed price method.

We lived in Bali a total of four years. During the months while expecting our baby and even with other pursuits, which kept Vera busy, she also joined the Bali International Women's Association BIWA. This became a weekly activity for her. Members of BIWA were wives of businesses owners, government officials, and representatives of tourism. Different international backgrounds brought the women together. Vera also participated with another group of women connected with domestic tourism. This was an *Arisan,* a social gathering, to which members regularly contributed financially and then held drawings. Vera was the only foreigner.

An announcement at one of the BIWA gatherings was for a Bible study in the home of one of the members. While talking about it with me, Vera mentioned, that since she had converted to Islam, she felt uneasy about attending. I do not really know what then led her to accept the invitation. My wife attended only once. While awaiting the birth of the baby, the business also occupied her.

On September 6, 1980, our baby was born at the *Klinik Bersalin Manuaba* – Manuaba Birthing Clinic in Denpasar, Bali. We named our new daughter Siti Hindun, which was my mother's name.

Allowed to wait in a small area very near the Operating Room, I again was very excited. At Siti's birth, I was the first to hear our baby's healthy cry. What a privilege it was, that immediately following her birth, I was the first one to see and hold our new baby daughter. I felt elating joy.

With the birth, Vera underwent the third Caesarean-Section surgery safely. Although advised by a doctor to deliver the baby in Singapore or America, it was very important to my wife that our baby would be born in Indonesia since it was the birthplace for both of us as well. I thought my wife was brave taking this risk.

When Siti was born, we had already lived in Bali three years and experienced many situations of life in Indonesia. Our life since 1977 was very different from when we were in the United States. Even though so much happened during those three years, watching my wife, I saw she refused to allow obstacles to become reasons for us to leave Indonesia.

Our relationship as husband and wife and of our family continued to be securely content and happy. Particularly between the two-of-us, the strong harmonious bond remained *tetap terjalin*, intimately connected. It was during this time however, we encountered different incidents from *kekuatan-kekuatan gaib,* the unseen forces. These clearly existed on Bali, since it was also a well-known fact; Bali is the *Pulau dewata*, Isle of gods.

Even though we did not fully recognize it then, the evil, intended for destruction of our family and us as husband and wife did not succeed. Somehow, Almighty God protected us.

"There is nothing I experienced in life that God did not take
and turn around for my good."
Abdul Wadud Karim Amrullah

LIKE A ROARING LION… As I was leaving Jakarta and moving to Bali in 1977, Uda Hasyim warned me to be very careful. He reminded me about the bizarre experiences of Warwick Purser when he was heading the Bali Pacto branch. At that time, I did not pay much attention to what Uda Hasyim was saying. In the first two years we lived there, I myself experienced some peculiar events.

At first, it was gradual, but with time, strange occurrences increased. Sometimes, I could feel it early in the day when my face swelled up, Vera said that maybe it was something I was allergic to and should see the doctor. However, my face would look like a *barong* – a Balinese mythical character with bulging eyes. On several occasions, this happened when I had scheduled important meetings with foreign clients.

One morning when I woke up, I felt fine at first, but suddenly there appeared a large lump in my throat. As the sensation increased, the lump grew larger and I had difficulty breathing. I remembered Uda Hasyim's warnings and already sensed that these influences meant to harm us in a deep personal way. A friend later mentioned that I was experiencing this because someone really despised me and wanted to use *guna-guna*, black magic on me.

These types of occurrences were common in Bali. One of the Pacto guides informed me that he knew the person "buying black magic power" per *ekor*, by the piece, in Banyuwangi, East Java, located across the waters from Bali. At first, I did not say anything to Vera thinking it might alarm her even more.

I then focused on reciting all the Islamic prayers taught me by my parents, specifically for this type of situation. With these prayers all the *penggoda-penggoda*, demonic teasers would flee. Even after my usual daily prayers, which I routinely did five times a day, I repeatedly used these memorized petitions.

On another occasion without warning I became very ill with *muntaber*, vomiting. More problems arose in the middle of the night when due to my symptoms, I could not be admitted at the hospital where I had been taken. Vera, the driver, and I were sent to *Rumah Sakit Wangaya*, a hospital on the other side of Denpasar which (we were informed), specialized in treatment of illnesses such as cholera.

Driving through the streets in the dark night, Vera held me up in the back seat of the car as I leaned against her. I was weak and could feel my body become weaker. Frantic because I was so sick and unable to receive immediate proper treatment, Vera out of desperation silently asked God for help.

When we reached the Wangaya Hospital, the conditions there were awful. I was assigned a bed in a large ward with about 12-14 beds. Proper sanitization precautions were sorely lacking considering the illnesses treated. When we saw what was happening with patients around us, each reacting in various stages of their illness, Vera did not wait and rushed out. However, fearing my condition and having left me inside, she returned to my bedside. The strained look on her face showed much concern for me.

Then, matters suddenly began changing. Amidst all the chaos, I suddenly felt a surge of energy, which I could not explain. No longer able to lie down, I sat up in the bed and called the nurse over. I told her I was not staying and that I felt better. Set on leaving, I tried to reassure her that I was fine. The nurse, taken aback by my insistence, quickly gave-up and helped me from the bed, saying that I at least had to wait for a doctor to release me. Once the doctor came, I reassured him I was fine and wanted discharge immediately.

As we drove home, early morning light was appearing across the island. Neither Vera nor I understood what had just taken place at the hospital. All I knew was that my symptoms had abruptly disappeared as mysteriously as they had come.

After everything was over, Vera later admitted to me that while we were driving to the hospital she had asked God to help us. She said, "Suddenly it was as if a soft blanket floated over us." Our eyes could not see the battle around us but we sensed it. In the best way I knew, I recited many Muslim prayers against the evil. It stopped and seemed to have disappeared.

Months later, the businesses did not seem to fulfill my wife any longer. Although Vera never mentioned it, I clearly recognized that there was something else absent in her life. At the same time, situations also arose for me so that I no longer felt satisfied working for Pacto.

Besides my own disappointments, it was clear that Vera was becoming discouraged. I understood that her disillusionment about Indonesia was very big since she had come with hopes that had been too idealistic.

I realized later, that during the six years we lived in Indonesia, my wife's disappointments did not only happen in Bali, but also already while we were in Jakarta. To Vera, all her efforts to gain acceptance seemed useless. All this gave me much concern.

VERA – NEW BEGINNING… In 1980 our long-time friend from the US, Rene Creutzburg came to visit a second time in Bali. We first knew Rene because of the Indo-Community Center *De Soos* and IMI activities years before. Rene's brother-in-law had been my colleague whom I worked with through the Indonesian Consulate when I replaced him in the Promoting Indonesia speaking tour.

While Rene was with us, he asked where he could attend an English language Sunday church service. Vera knew about one held at Bali Beach Hotel in Sanur, and accompanied Rene there with no intention of participating. However, out of respect for our friend, she stayed and quietly listened.

After the service, while leaving the hotel an acquaintance Joye Alit, wife of Indonesian pastor Rus Alit, informed Vera about a baptism the following Sunday in Kuta. At home, she mentioned to me that she did not have interest in attending.

A few days later Rene left Bali. During that week, a serious situation developed with the Balinese business partners. In looking back, this became the critical turning point in our life as to what was worldly and what was spiritual.

Saturday, December 6, 1980, Vera still attended the BIWA organized event where she had committed to help. She told me later that while there, suddenly the realization came that a specific portion of life had already passed her by. Next, a thought unexpectedly struck her, "You need to start your life over and you need to start it with Jesus." She knew in that moment, that she must go to Kuta to ask about the baptism.

When my wife came home that evening, coming into our room and perhaps fearing my reaction, she suddenly said to me, "Schat, I don't know what you think, but I need to start my life over and I need to do it with Jesus." She then added, "I hope you understand."

I think perhaps because she had said it so matter of fact, I did not pay much attention at first to what she was *really* saying. I thought, "This is not a big deal or will be a problem." I knew that while she followed Islam, she had experienced various negative things. Therefore, it was my hope that with this kind of decision she would be more at peace among the *ahlilkitab*, people of the Books, as we viewed Christians. The most important thing to me was her happiness.

On Sunday December 7, 1980 in Kuta, Bali, Vera stepped into newness of spiritual life, followed with her baptism. The place known in tourism as *isle of the gods* or *island of demons* is where my wife found her way. Although I was not aware of it then, fate had also led me there with our three children to witness this.

Watching my wife on that day was a new experience. I thought it must be good for *her* life. At the time, I did not know what this really meant. I later learned however, that it was her public declaration of being one with *Isa Almasih* – Jesus Christ, who to me was a prophet.

A few weeks after her baptism, I noticed changes happening in my wife. I also saw she became very diligent reading the Bible. Vera always enjoyed reading. Because of that, two stacks of books were usually by her bedside (easy for her to reach). One stack was books not yet read, and the other stack was books she already finished reading. I noticed the type of books in the stacks changed. She thoroughly read Christian books that Joye Alit lent her and books from other Christian friends including Indonesians.

Once a week Vera followed *discipleship* teaching, which I did not understand the meaning of then; but her friend Barbara Bush came to our house and spent time with her. I observed how my wife's life completely changed. Worries from before, left her, and even if our business was slow, she was just peaceful.

The transformation in Vera added to my own happiness. When I came home from work, Vera would tell me what she was learning from the Bible or what she had read that day. There was excitement in her voice, which I missed since our coming to Indonesia. I did not understand it, but wondered how it was possible she had such joy.

One evening while chatting with me as usual, Vera unexpectedly mentioned I should perhaps consider changing my views about religion. Her saying that immediately bothered me. I thought she was too bold although she expressed it quite subtly. It made me think how she herself had been about religion before, especially Christianity. Therefore, when suddenly voicing to me that I should maybe change my convictions about Islam, confused and upset me as to how she could alter her own views so quickly.

Then at another time, Vera told me it made her very sad that when she goes into eternal life, I will not be with her since I do not believe that Jesus is the Son of God. I immediately voiced what I thought, but still tried reassuring her by saying, "It's a matter of interpretation." I also told her, "I think God and Jesus know what I meant and He will be the Judge. The most important thing is to follow the teaching of Jesus and for us not to disagree about the word 'son.' We know that God sent Jesus. He can do the miracles." In those moments, it seemed she accepted what I expressed.

Vera asked if she could call Harry Bush, Barbara's husband; mentioning that perhaps he could explain better what she meant. I agreed to meet because I also regarded him a friend. Harry Bush came to our house soon after this happened. That was the first day he and I had our real discussion about religion. It became one of many such talks (sometimes debates), as I defended Islam and my belief as a Muslim.

One time, while discussing the Quran and Bible, Harry tried answering questions I needed clarified. At one point, (I think because of all my questions), Harry asked me, "Isn't it hard for you to balance between Islamic and Christian teachings?" I told him, "I'm not balancing, but trying to find truth and am sure God is still leading me to it."

Toward the end of February, I left for the US to attend the PATA Conference in Los Angeles and San Francisco. Vera and the children stayed in Bali, but I was able to see the rest of her family, including friends we had left behind four years earlier. I returned to Bali on March 14, 1981.

It was very important to me, that we always had time with our children. Since television did not have much variety of programs, this gave us more opportunities. At night after the children were asleep, Vera and I enjoyed playing the Scrabble word game. This also gave us time to tell each other about our daily activities.

Knowing I loved politics, Vera told me about one of the books that she had just finished reading. Titled "Born Again" and written by Chuck Colson, it impressed her a lot. She shared details regarding what she learned about Chuck Colson's involvement with the Watergate incident in the US and the investigation thereafter. She talked about the entire book, including how repentance and being born again spiritually, came into place for Chuck Colson although he went to prison for his connection in the Watergate disgrace.

Telling with passion what she had read encouraged me. In sharing about "Born Again" and others books like "Peace Child" by Don Richardson, she was excited about what God had done for these people. Watching what was happening touched me although many questions were constantly mounting in my mind.

Sometimes, before sleeping I would ask Vera what she had learned in the lessons, she called discipleship. With the spirit of enthusiasm, she explained about *Firman Tuhan*, God's Word and the promises written in the *Alkitab*, Bible.

I compared all this, to when my wife became a Muslim. There had not been follow-up or further guidance. For her to receive the *mukena,* and *sarung* to wear for praying, with the *tikar sembahyang*, prayer mat, plus cassettes to learn how to pray, was supposed to be enough.

One day, Vera asked me if she could invite friends for Bible study at our home. I was surprised, but thought to myself, "As long as they don't bother me or try evangelizing me, it is fine." At that point, it was still my intention to show Christians, that as a Muslim I had much tolerance toward them.

During those months, even with the additional outside trials, seeing my wife's growing optimism furthered my own happiness too. Considering how Vera's life kept moving raised questions in me. But these I kept to myself. It pleased me, sensing we had stepped into a new portion of our *koridor kehidupan dan waktu,* corridor of life and time.

Once You spoke in a vision,
to your faithful people You said:
"I have bestowed strength on a warrior;
…with my sacred oil I have anointed him.
My faithful love will be with him,
and through My name his horn will be exalted.
Psalm 89:19, 20, 24 NIV

# SECTION FOUR

## *1981 – 1991*

# 15

# SUMATRAN WARRIOR AWAKENING

*"For I know the plans I have for you," declares the Lord,*
*"plans to prosper you and not to harm you,*
*plans to give you hope and a future".*
Jeremiah 29:11 NIV

One morning, June 10, 1981 to be exact, before leaving for the office, Vera said she wanted to speak with me. I joined her and took the chair beside her. I assumed it would not take long since she usually came straight to the point. Looking at her, I thought she seemed somewhat uneasy. Wondering, I watched my wife's face while smiling at her reassuringly.

As Vera began talking, she suddenly told me that she loved me very much. She then expressed that especially since we just had another baby nine months earlier; it made our eleven-year marriage even better.

When she spoke those things, questions immediately jumped up inside me. "What was the real intent of what she was saying?" my thoughts rushed. I tried to appear calm, while still looking at my wife. We were sitting in separate chairs but close to each other.

She added that even though our life together was very intimate and happy, she desired that we not only enjoy our happiness in this world, but also in eternity. This was the second time she brought up this matter.

While she spoke, I heard nervousness in her voice. Knowing that this conversation was not easy for her, I also saw expectation in her eyes. Vera continued saying that she longed for us to be in heaven together when our life on this earth ended. Looking at her closely, I suddenly felt the need to take a long deep breath. I sensed unexplainable tension.

Within me, another question instantly leapt up. "Were the words she spoke, meant only as persuasion to attract me in becoming a Christian like her?" Turmoil then began running wild inside me. Struggling to keep my voice calm, I still tried reassuring her by saying that as long as we remained faithful in our worship and devotion to God, He would also give her the desire of her heart.

As stress intensified inside me I told her, "I am a good Muslim; I am obedient in what I do in my faith." Tension still kept rising. Even though we already sat close together, I still bent forward leaning into her as I said those things. My eyes never left her face.

With quiet assurance in her voice, Vera replied that according to the Bible, whoever did not believe and accept Jesus Christ as their Lord and Savior would not go to heaven. This was exasperating. Unlike me, I was becoming more impatient and upset with her.

Without hesitation however, Vera continued saying that because she loved me very much, her hope was that we together would choose eternal life. In those crucial moments, even though she did not quote verses from the Bible, she spoke with full conviction while her eyes held concern. Had she become defiant in her demeanor that would have made it easier for me to respond harshly.

On that morning when my wife again shared her opinion with me, my heart already started feeling very disturbed because she spoke with such assurance. My own voice shouted inside me, "You must not tolerate this!" I struggled keeping my temper in control, yet all she said seemed convincing.

I tried covering the overwhelming annoyance growing inside me. I insisted she listen to what I had to say. I wanted her to have some fear in her. More fear of where this was leading. Did she not understand what this was going to bring us to?

From that moment on, everything escalated fast. Because of my own deep conviction about my Muslim belief, everything intensified. Replying with a loud voice, which even to me sounded very harsh, I said, "I recognize and honor Jesus Christ! If any Muslim does not recognize and honor *Isa Almasih* then that person is not a good Muslim! Can you not accept that?"

The next thing my wife responded with shook me even more deeply as she unceasingly insisted that the Bible showed her, whoever did not recognize and accepted Jesus Christ as the *Son of God*, would not enter the Kingdom of Heaven.

I saw that my outburst shook Vera because she was not used to such unbending argument from me. Still looking at me, she went on to say, "You recognize Jesus Christ as a Prophet and Teacher, but not as the Son of God."

Her choice of words completely infuriated me. Not only was it her words that struck, but she had committed what to me, as a Muslim was the biggest sin of blatantly blaspheming God. To say that God had a son like Him who is human, was outrageous to the belief of Islam. The anger exploding from me then; was my own soul screaming within, that I must defend my Islamic belief. It was the core of who I was!

In those heated moments, my wife sat there with that unceasing faith and certainty. The anger I felt, I had never experienced toward her before. In disgust, I could only think how she had gone too far with her offensive and personally insulting words. Vera just sat in front of me with a mixed look of sadness and expectancy. I still attempted reasoning with her while trying not to raise my voice any further.

Would she have looked arrogant about what she was saying, or would she have quoted Bible verses, I would have had reason to strike back against her as a Christian and dispute her words. My anger by then was like a dark pit since she had challenged the core of my soul as none other ever dared or succeeded. In those horrible moments, I became like a volcano spewing out boiling hot lava.

I was defending the understanding of my own beliefs and traditions. These I had carried in my heart for fifty-four years. In my trying to express this, I instead heard erupting from inside me, the uproar of unbelievable anger.

"What was happening?" I thought. Everything was becoming more argumentative from my side. I wanted this to be a quarrel between us. Hearing the words coming from my wife was in absolute violation against beliefs that I had lived with my entire life.

From everything Vera had shared, her persistent claim that Jesus was the Son of God was the most blasphemous act of sin any human being could commit. However, this was now my wife speaking these words against me. I kept thinking within those moments how I disliked her quiet certainty. I needed her not to be so secure in the stance of who Jesus was and what He meant to her.

She said she loved me much, but another love had come between us. Of course, I wanted her to respond also in anger. Instead, she kept her gaze on me. I needed to see there was more fear in her face. Even so, her eyes showed affection. I also saw that she knew what her stand and words could mean to us, for our marriage, our intimacy as husband and wife.

Still my thoughts raced on. I refused to give in to what I now considered my biggest battle ever. "What is this?" I asked myself. Had some demonic power over taken her that would make her voice sound attractive and her words seemingly truth? What was happening that I was so furious with her at the same time? I kept asking myself, "How could she look at me with that quiet certainty? Was this to be the end of us?"

I could not deny she had spoken without any hesitation about her spiritual experience since her conversion. What disturbed me most was the way she explained with such broad understanding about her belief. I knew that was what I lacked in my own life.

We sat almost facing each other, while inside me anger fumed. Suddenly a challenge appeared in my thoughts, but also a reminder of the changes I saw in Vera during the past months.

In those critical moments however, a challenge to reject what I had seen about my wife, grew inside me. Yet, I knew the way that she accepted life, even with the many trials that came, was unquestionable. I could not possibly deny those changes I myself witnessed. At the same time, I also wondered how my wife could love Jesus and me in the ways she described.

I remembered what I had read in her personal journal. The way she wrote how God was moving in her new life, and how He worked within her prayers. When I looked through these private writings, I knew it was wrong; but in having done so, I recognized that what she experienced was real. Vera had also entered dates on opposite pages of noted prayer petitions. These were the times God answered her requests. As she spoke to me on that morning, my wife was completely unaware that I had already read her journal.

*<u>Note:</u> Several years later, while sharing my story at a Retreat outside of Jakarta, Vera first learned that I had read her Prayer Journal. (From: Author)*

I had seen during the last months that she was no longer a worrier as before. I felt peaceful at that thought. Deep in my heart, I knew that my wife's strong conviction was all-true. I never expected however, that this situation would ever happen between us.

Nevertheless, I was not ready to give in either to what her words really meant. As I struggled, I heard myself making accusatory remarks. The way she looked at me in those moments, I would never forget.

Still, my argument became more severe. As the battle grew worse inside me, what happened next jolted me even more about myself. By then, Vera sat before me with what seemed like a demeanor of "no fighting back." My emotions kept rising to a peak above all the battles ever fought in my existence.

Before I knew it, I stood up and loudly ordered Vera to get out of the house, to get out of my life, to leave immediately and separate from me. I told her repeatedly, "Get out now and leave me, go back to America and take all the children with you."

I then threatened to divorce her, since I apparently was no longer good for her. I knew she understood clearly how easily I could divorce her within Islam. But even as I shouted all those horrible things, none of it made sense to me any longer.

The one thing that bothered me most was my wife's unmovable conviction of her belief. I also understood somehow that she was not going to let go of what she expressed earlier, no matter how deep her love was for me.

Realizing, what I had just said and done, I needed this struggle to turn around. Instead, I heard myself, in a mocking voice shout at Vera, "I don't accept that your God is Love. If He is Love, why did He allow a husband and wife, who love each other and have been married for eleven years, be like this?" Then bending down above her, I glaringly argued, "We are now in opposition with one another because of Him – *Jesus,* who is said to be Love. Where is God who is said to be most loving and gracious?"

Stepping back, my own attitude panicked me. I could not believe I had voiced what came out of me. How could I have wanted her out of my life? How could I have said that? I loved my wife and children very much. I always showed that love to them. Where was my patience and tolerance?

Suddenly I remembered my uncle's words from the past. He advised that as men, we should never show affection to our wife and children.

Displaying our love would spoil them. Struggling that day however, everything burst forth from my deepest corners.

I realized later, that with all turmoil exploding, the eruption had been from me. Vera only voiced, she wanted us to choose eternal life and be together in heaven someday. The uncontainable argument reached its peak while our children Rehana and Sutan were in school. Our helper in the house cared for Siti the baby.

At that point, *I felt my life shaken like never before.* So much had happened in such short time that morning. All my usual forbearance was completely gone. When Vera spoke earlier, she seemed very sure about her newfound belief. During all these months however, in my mind I still just left the matter of her personal religious ideas up to her. All that time, whenever she had shared with me I had told myself, "As for me, I hold on to my own beliefs."

SUMATRAN WARRIOR – BIRTH LAMENTATIONS… I needed to be alone. Not saying anything anymore, I walked away from where my angry outburst happened. Going into the children's bedroom, after closing the door, I began complaining to God. I had fallen to my knees as tears came. I told God, "I have been doing all the prayers and fasting all this time, all these years, yet you never showed your love to me." I also expressed defiantly, "From now on I don't want to pray and fast anymore, where has your love been for me?"

Things I read in Vera's personal journal again jumped before me. What she wrote was private, yet would not go away from my thoughts as I cried out to Allah – God Almighty. I remembered things she enthusiastically shared with me regarding what she learned.

That morning, I was fighting the battle for my life. I already felt remorse for all the angry words I expressed. There had never been this kind of argument and difference between Vera and me. Why did I say I wished her away just like that? Being with my wife had been a comfort. In all the ups-and-downs through the years, we were one.

Afternoon came and I was still in the children's bedroom. I heard them arriving home from school. Opening the door, I immediately hugged them. Not understanding what had happened they looked at me questioningly.

I then took the kids into the room. Hugging them again, with Rehana on my right, Sutan on my left arm, I asked them while crying, to also kneel and pray. I realized suddenly how confused my children must be with my behavior. I assumed they heard the start of a disagreement between Vera and me, while leaving for school that morning.

Continuing my battle and struggle with God, I thought about how I obediently had begun reciting additional prayers, but I felt God did not care. While kneeling with Rehana and Sutan still beside me, I thought repeatedly that even though I prayed seventeen times a day, including – *wajib, sunnah, tahajjud, dhuha,* (which were more than the five mandatory times of daily prayers), I felt Allah seemed not to hear any of my prayers, but ignored my life. I also felt that He never accepted my prayers.

Questioning myself about a relationship with Allah, I suddenly realized there was none. Instead, there was a high wall between God and me. In reality, the wall was an obstacle between us. Although my age had already reached fifty-four years, I felt that none of the prayers I presented toward Allah through my entire life meant anything.

I remembered that when planning our move to Indonesia, the purpose was for my wife and children, also to become good Muslims. What was happening to all the plans, which I believed Allah had stirred?

> "You did not choose me, but I chose you..."
> John 15:16 NIV

SUMATRAN WARRIOR – SPIRITUAL BIRTH... During those crucial moments, feeling despair and discouragement simultaneously, I recalled something Vera read to me while sharing what she discovered from the Bible. She had told me that Jesus was always knocking on the door of every person's heart and waiting to be welcomed in. Also, that when Jesus knocks on the door of our heart, He is a gentleman, never forcing His way through that door. He waits politely, and if we hear His knock and welcome Him, He will always be in our lives. I would later learn that was the verse from Revelation 3:20 NIV (paraphrased).

In my critical state, I expressed to God, "If it really is the truth that I must open the door of my heart, because it is a requirement that I must go through; then, at this moment I am opening that door for the Lord to come into my heart and into my life." Suddenly, I felt very peaceful as if the storm had passed.

However, a few moments later I realized that according to Islamic law, I became *murtad*, an apostate, in other words a traitor. Being murtad could be punishable by death. I then told God again, "If that is the punishment, I ask you God who created human life to take my life at this moment if I am wrong." Still on my knees and bowed down, I waited…

If I was going to follow the same way Vera believed, I needed proof that God indeed was alive and truly loving and gracious. It would be of no use if after accepting Jesus as Savior, my life remained the same and nothing changed.

I wanted God to show me He was alive! I wanted Him to take away my life at that instant, if I had committed the most unforgivable and greatest of sins. Acknowledging and accepting that Jesus is the Son of God would be a decision of no return within Islam. I understood what it all meant, yet there was this deep sense of peace in my soul, as I remained kneeling before God.

The day was turning to dusk and it would soon be dark. I got up from my knees and went out from the room to meet my wife. As I opened the door, she looked at me with concern in her eyes. While I had been wrestling inside, it seemed Vera had remained in the same chair, where I had earlier angrily spewed my outburst. I went and stood by her, saying quietly, *"I have opened the door of my heart, to welcome God in."* I know I startled Vera who looked up at me questioningly. Immediately rising from where she sat, we then went to our bedroom.

There, my wife took both my hands and held them in hers on the Bible. Bowing her head, she began praying with me. First quietly thanking God and then asking God's Holy Spirit to help me. Following that, we prayed for me to open my heart, as she said with me the *doa pertobatan*, prayer of repentance. I then accepted Jesus Christ into my life as Lord and Savior.

Next, we prayed for our lives, asking God to always lead and bless us, which Vera said very beautifully. I was so amazed listening to her, since it was the first time I actually heard my wife pray.

Afterwards I asked Vera where she learned to pray like that. With a modest smile, she answered quietly, "The Holy Spirit of God taught me; He is going to teach you also, because He is in you." In that moment I did not understand what she was saying, but I was certain it was good.

After we finished, having experienced the greatest battle of my life that day, my entire body and mind were exhausted. In my heart however, I felt elated, sensing deep peace. Later that evening, I told my wife, "Today, I heard the most beautiful prayer." We both agreed that a new chapter had begun in the journey of our life ...


"The Lord is with you, mighty warrior."
Judges 6:12 NIV


SUMATRAN WARRIOR – SPIRITUAL BEGINNINGS... It was after I began studying the Bible for myself, that I discovered the scripture Vera mentioned the morning of my "wrestling with God." I found this written in the New Testament book of John.

"For God so loved the world that He gave His one and only Son,
that whoever believes in Him shall not perish but have eternal life.
For God did not send His Son to
condemn the world, but to save the world through Him.
Whoever believes in Him is not condemned,
but whoever does not believe stands condemned already
because he has not believed in the
name of God's one and only Son."
John 3: 16-18 NIV

*"Whoever believes in Him (Jesus Christ) shall not perish but have eternal life."* I thought that was exactly what my wife tried expressing to me the day of my surrender to God. Because of the teaching I received as a child, I feared death up until then. Now I understood the promise in John 3:16 that whoever believed Jesus Christ to be the Son of God would one day have eternal life.

After my repentance, I was even more diligent in reading and wanted to learn further about the Bible. I wanted also to know more deeply about being a Christian. I did this through following *pemuridan,* discipleship.

For this part of my new life, God already prepared someone to help me understand. This was my American friend, Harry Bush whom I knew as a *hamba Tuhan,* servant of the Lord, from earlier (sometimes heated) discussions about the Quran versus the Bible. What I respected most was that while I was still Muslim, he never tried *penginjilan,* evangelizing me in such manner that I felt pressured. Harry became my good friend first.

About two weeks after my prayer of repentance, during one of our study times, Harry explained an illustration to me called the *Bridge of Life.* He was able to show me clearly how a person can cross over that Bridge and be one with God, forgiven and be spiritually *born again.*

Before I was a Christian, what first impressed me about Harry Bush was a serious incident, when a Bali Beach Hotel security guard physically beat him. Riding his motorcycle with his son by the hotel, Harry never retaliated though his left cheekbone was shattered and he almost lost an eye.

Learning about this attack showed me Harry's true character. When he returned to Bali one month after hospitalization in Java, I went to visit him and expressed my frustration that he did not fight back although he was a former Vietnam veteran. He could easily have hit back but did not do so. I had then told him, "That is why I do not want to be a Christian, because according to the teaching of Christ, if we are hit on the right cheek, we then give the left cheek." Harry smiled and only said, "I have to obey the Lord's command."

At that time, adding to my annoyance, was hearing from the Bali Beach Hotel General Manager that Harry had asked him to re-hire the same security guard. Since I was not a Christian then, I did not yet understand that kind of attitude. But deep within me, I felt the strength of Harry's faith. Through all this, I saw the loyalty of a person towards God. For me, this was very impressive proof that moved my heart.

After accepting Christ and being a believer, I did not want baptism right away as Vera had done. In my mind, I had to first study more about the Bible as guidance for my life. For some time, even the way I prayed was still with the *rukuk dan sujud,* kneeling and bowing positions that I had used all my life. In my prayers however, I no longer used the memorized Arabic verses from the Quran but I could to talk to God from deep in my spirit. I really felt the role of the Holy Spirit within me, helping me pray; as well as giving strength for weaknesses I had.

A few months later, I began walking in new life, *hidup baru,* on the path of time for me. Most notable then was that as I was changing, I was also no longer much concerned about negative circumstances at my office. I also did not worry about our retail businesses.

A desire was gradually born in my heart to be a totally surrendered servant of God, whom I had called *Allah – Sabhanahu Wata'ala* – Exalted God. I had become a disciple of Jesus Christ who I knew as *Isa Al-Masih' Alaihissalam* – Jesus Christ, Peace Be upon Him.

I remembered advice from my father many years ago. It was that if we make a decision, not to do so half-heartedly. God had been proving many things to me, even more so than what I had asked during my spiritual wrestling with Him the day of my conversion. I whole-heartedly believed that He was indeed God who is *Pengasih dan Penyayang,* Loving and Compassionate.

In 1981, I began to understand, that while I had been stepping through many passageways my entire life thus far, the Shadow of the Almighty had already covered me ...

~~~~~~~~~~

# MEMORIAL ~ MARCH 2012

## In Memory

### Abdul Wadud Karim Amrullah
"Pastor Willy Amrull"

### Entered Heaven's Eternal Rest
March 24, 2012

A letter from Pastor Harry Bush
Friend and Mentor
(Used Verbatim With Permission)

March 31, 2012

Dear Vera;

I write with a heavy heart but yet also one full of joy. I actually said, "Praise the Lord" when Barbara and I received the message about Willy going on Home. He had fought long and hard and it was time to go to the arms of Jesus, his Blessed Savior and Lord, to be at complete rest with Him!

189

I did not know **Abdul Wadud Karim Amrullah** but got a few glimpses of him when I first met Willy in Bali. Soon after you had received Christ and Salvation, you called me to come over to your house and try to talk to Willy, as he had gone berserk and was like a wild man. He thought someone had cast a *satanic spell* on you. He wanted it removed and for you to "be normal again." O' boy, o' boy, did I ever want to say, absolutely, "No!" to your request, but I couldn't.

That first evening I came over in early 1981, I saw the **Sumatran Warrior** in all his glaring as I entered into your house. Willy was beside himself. He paced the floor, talked loudly, which was so unusual for him. We batted heads like a couple of billy goats. Willy could quote more verses from the Al Quran than I could read from my Bible. What a clash that became, which kept on for quite a while. He was certain Allah was stronger than any other god, but just wanted to know what happened to you. Thus, on that evening, Willy (like the Apostle Paul) from the deep recesses of his heart wanted to know truth. The more he looked at Jesus the more he liked what he saw. Vera, your courage and commitment to Christ, along with my hard-headedness were the keys for Willy to peel back the decades of tradition and unfulfilled promises by a system of belief that commanded and demanded, but gave little in response.

I tried to explain to him how Christ had forgiven you of your sins and He (through His Spirit) had entered into your heart. Willy was by then shouting. I was shouting. I thought for sure we were going to have a fistfight right there in your living room. I left before we got carried away, with a promise to come back in a day or two and try again to explain what had happened to you. Upon returning, things were calmer but the fire in his eyes was not any dimmer. The *Sumatran Warrior* was ever present. He apparently thought that his god and his book (Al Quran) would easily win out over any other and that once he proved that to me, then we could also get you "back to normal."

We had a pretty hot and fierce argument (debate was entirely too placid or easy going of a word to describe it), over Allah verses God the Father, the superiority of the Al Quran over the Bible and vice versa. We got nowhere. We did this for the next two or three meetings, which were coming about twice a week. Now it had been a few months after your conversion and

Willy finally said one day, "Why don't you just tell me about your book, I know what mine says, but let me hear what you think yours teaches."

I then suggested that we begin with the Gospel of John, reading one chapter at a time and discussing it together each time we met. We agreed to use English, as Willy's English was far better than my Indonesian was. However, for these discussion times we would read the *Alkitab* (Indonesian translation of the Bible) for clarity. An interesting combination, but which we felt would work well for the two of us.

I clearly remember that first meeting, where we were going to discuss the first chapter of John. Willy was animated before we even sat down at the dining table. He said loudly, "Why do you people (Christians, I assumed) always talk about 'the Son of God?' Why don't you talk more about *'Firman'* (the Word)?" Well, we did not get past John 1:1-14 that day. "We know *'Firman'* we (as Muslims) can understand *'Firman'* " he went on to say during that discussion. *Allah* does not have sex and never had a son, but *'Firman/the Word'* that is different," Willy had then expressed.

We continued to meet regularly twice a week, or at least weekly. Frankly, I don't remember how far we got in the book of John. I do remember that pretty soon, Willy's focus of trying to find the weaknesses in the Bible, thus debunking it, so you could return to "normal," seemed to fade. He genuinely began to absorb the powerful and magnificent truths in the Gospel of John. I knew that John 20:31 reveals John's purpose in writing the Gospel, which was to reveal Jesus as the Savior and provider of eternal life. Willy was absorbing these bite-size truths and they were changing him. I remember Willy telling me in the beginning that his book the Al Quran was superior, but the Bible was a good book and useful. Then one day, not too long into our sessions, he shocked me by saying that both books were equal. Finally, he admitted that the Bible was absolutely superior even though the Al Quran had a lot of good teaching also.

Vera, I truly do not know the exact moment when Willy moved across that line from being lost and a fervent enemy of Jesus Christ, to the day that he truly embraced Christ as his very own Savior. But I do know that during those following weeks and months in 1981 *Willy went through a powerful transformation.* The fire in his eyes went from antagonism toward Christ, to a fierce loyalty to Him. Willy saw Jesus more clearly step- by-step and then the Father through Jesus in crystal clearness. He saw LOVE, both in Truth and in your daily reality with him. He could do no more than anyone else that sees the same thing, but embrace the Lord with all of his heart. And Willy (Abdul Wadud Karim Amrullah) DID! Oh, how much – did he do that!!!

Willy's life then did take on much of the Pauline flavor. He lost so much as the apostle Paul did. Willy would often echo Paul's words to the Philippians, "Yes indeed, I count all things loss for the excellence of the knowledge of Christ Jesus my Lord… and count those other supposed important things as rubbish that I may gain Christ."

Willy knew well the losses that he suffered, but he was also so very aware of the great gains that he was blessed by. I can remember him saying just how satisfied he was with his decision to "press toward the upward call of God in Christ Jesus." Like the apostle Paul, Willy would not be deterred from serving his Lord and Friend, Jesus – in any capacity he could manage. We have all stood by, or even from afar; and marveled at just how much the Lord could do (and did) through that **Sumatran Warrior** for Christ. Only heaven will reveal the tally at the end of time – of what God accomplished through **Abdul Wadud Karim Amrullah**, or as I knew him, *"Willy."*

If my memory holds true, you, Willy and the children moved from Bali to Jakarta within a few months after all these events. Then our relationship went from disciple maker to prayer supporter and advisor, through letters and written communication. Our hearts however, have remained joined together, even though our hands had to part for a long season.

Vera, I just cannot be sad when I think of where Willy is right this minute. I can see the gleam in his eyes, the inexpressible joy on his face and the ever-widening smile, as he fellowships with Jesus and the Father; while he talks and shares with the apostle Paul and Timothy and others of the New Testament era. I can see him among many other saints who also suffered and paid huge prices to follow Jesus, as they share and swap stories. Oh yes, Willy is sooooo at Home now. And in a blink on the heavenly time clock, we all will be with him again, doing it all over and over and over again. What Victory!

For you all our hearts go out. I know that the Great God of compassion will send his Holy Spirit to you to come along side of you and be your absolute Comforter. Please be assured of our prayers for you during these first hard days of separation from Willy. As happy as we are for him, we already miss him a whole bunch. And we will continue to do so while we are heavy of heart for you and the family. God can and will be your greatest Helper during this time and days to come. Call on Him, lean on Him and Love on Him. He will meet your needs both in your heart and through His Word to you. He will bring healing later that is His promise. Until then…rejoice for Willy and lean on your Lord Jesus.

I know that your *labor of love* in this manuscript is a heavy one. I am certain that the Lord is going to use this labor of yours in an exciting way! Both Barbara and I love you all.

In Him…By Him…Through Him,
Harry Bush

~~~~~~~~~

WARRIOR'S UPWARD CALL… One and a half month after my repentance, I received a telephone call on July 24, 1981 from the Governor's office in Bali informing me that news from Mr. Amir Machmud (Indonesia's Minister of Interior) reached their office. They notified me, my beloved brother Abdul Malik (Hamka) had passed away. My brother did not have opportunity to learn I had become a Christian.

I immediately flew to Jakarta so I could give last respects to him and participate with the funeral service in Jakarta. It was an honor also, officially receiving his remains and be there to place him in his grave.

Many sweet memories I had with my older brother. I cannot forget he came to meet me at Halim Perdanakusumah Airport when I arrived in Indonesia after many years. I also remembered how my brother opened his home to my family and me when we arrived in 1977.

Realizing he was gone forever, I was thankful for the opportunity of bringing him to his final resting place at TPU Tanah Kusir Cemetery in Jakarta. The entire nation of Indonesia watched my brother's burial via television; within me however, countless recollections of our relationship passed through my mind. These memories will forever remain a part of me. On that day, no one present at the funeral knew I had become a follower of the Lord Jesus Christ.

Rumors of my conversion began spreading. Rather than be the cause of problems, I wanted to remain sensitive to the mindset of my Minang family. At that time, Vera and I thought that perhaps it would be best for us to return to the United States.

After a second theft at one of our shops, I discovered how God always meant well and that in everything He had a better purpose. Capture and arrest of the offender did not take long. The young man who became like a part of our family was the burglar. Eko (name changed) lived with us, and had responsibilities of overseeing our shops. He confessed to the crime. Although detained in the jail at Denpasar Police Headquarters, my driver Nyoman and I brought him daily meals. During one of those times, Eko asked if I might bring a Bible for him so he could learn. When the burglary occurred, I was already following discipleship study and Eko said that he had been watching.

I brought him the Bible, and only God knew the intent of his request. Whether attempting to attract my attention and gain sympathy, or if God was touching Eko's heart to better his life, I left all this up to God.

This young man was a son of the Kupang Police Chief. When the case was going to court, Eko's uncle (also a police officer) came to apologize on behalf of their family. He pleaded with me, not to let the case go any further because of the humiliation suffered by their entire family. Since Eko had already confessed, I did not press charges. I also gave him opportunity to realize I forgave him. Once released from jail, Eko immediately left the island.

While still living in Bali, we experienced many other trials one after the other. But it was through these that Vera and I grew spiritually. Although experiencing many difficulties, we later understood it enabled us to empathize with others. We were to pray with those facing problems as we underwent, and sometimes even for those who originally intended us harm. Through this, we looked for answers from God who always listened to our prayers.

Even though there were so many changes happening in my spiritual life, I still had to think about my career. After my brother's funeral, I immediately returned to Bali. A distant relative contacted me. The insurance company he was a Director with, had invested in a travel agency, and appointed him to lead this new venture.

Since I resigned my position with Pacto, he asked me to help him and that, I not return to the US yet. By that time, the situation in Bali was no longer safe for us either. I had focused on studying the Bible and following discipleship training. Throughout Indonesia, reports continued spreading that I became a follower of Jesus Christ.

I accepted the offer, but allowed leeway for decisions about our returning to the US. By the end of that year, we prepared to leave for Jakarta with full conviction of God's leading.

# 16

# RISE OF THE SUMATRAN WARRIOR

*"I raised you up for this very purpose,*
*that I might display my power in you and*
*that my name might be proclaimed in all the earth."*
Romans 9:17 NIV

*"For I know the plans I have for you,"* declares the Lord... Thus, with encouragement from God's Word and strong faith, we moved to Jakarta. Our original plan of returning to the US was to avoid adverse reactions from people. I knew these would keep coming from all directions should I stay in Indonesia. However, rather than leaving, God planned for us to return to Jakarta first.

Immediately after our move, members of my family and old acquaintances, having heard I was *murtad*, an apostate, were not only disappointed but also angry. Initially they expressed this to me through phone conversations or coming unannounced to my office. Among accusations was that I was weak because I allowed someone to evangelize and influence me.

I continued Discipleship study without any delay. Another friend, David Wigger was able to teach me more about Christian foundations and Spiritual life. Harry Bush had introduced him to me. Every Friday, instead of going to a mosque near the office, I used lunchtime to study at David's home in the Menteng area of Jakarta.

Family members and others hearing about my decision to follow the Lord Jesus began coming to our house in Ciputat day and night. These visits were to ask regarding rumors that were spreading about me.

Sometimes there were those arriving unexpectedly late at night, persuading me to return to Islam. In their thinking, not only was I the son, grandson and brother of well-known influential Islamic leaders; but I had been an active member of the Islamic Center while living in the US for almost three decades. Since my family background was solidly rooted in Islam, they did not want to believe what to them was a scandalous impossibility.

There were people pointing the finger at me, saying I became a Christian *for purpose of filling my stomach*, i.e. persuaded by money and so forth. Family messengers came, also telling me how I shamed them as my family and our identity as Minang. They insisted it was their responsibility to convince me and return to the right path. I was confronted with verses from the Quran to which I effortlessly and without any hesitancy responded. As they debated the Muslim scriptures with me, somehow each time, the Lord gave me wisdom. Most often, this was also, through what I had studied and memorized from the Bible.

I knew the ways of my people very well. At that time, even though I mostly faced opposition from the Minang, I also reminded them that although I may have lived in the US for twenty-seven years, I always remained Minang and devoutly Muslim. What they refused to grasp was how it was then possible, that I found the *Way of Truth* as I claimed – in Indonesia.

Another incident happened with an *utusan keluarga*, family messenger, sent to our home by other relatives when I was not there. The woman brought a very aggressive message that I should return to Islam. She also expressed that what I had done was disgraceful and embarrassing to her and the entire family. Vera was supposed to remind me, that as a Minang I have to be Muslim because the Minangkabau base their way of life on *'Adat basandi syara', syara' basandi kitabullah.* In other words, when claiming to be Minang, one MUST be Muslim. This tradition, is centered on *syariat'* – Islamic Law, and *syariat'* based on the Holy Book, the Quran.

She said, for me not to forget that a Minang who left Islam is *murtad*, a traitor; and for Vera to understand that by my becoming a Christian, I was no longer under the *pagayubannya*, traditional kinship. With this, I would be *di kucilkan*, expelled from clan relationship and *dibuang*, disposed of – be an outcast.

Learning about this, made me think how I knew my identity. I was a Minangkabau (of heritage), with Jesus Christ as Savior of my life, and living under the Shadow of Almighty God.

*Note: The word Minangkabau means "Winning Buffalo" a proud statement for my people. I had heard there was a saying, that becoming a Christian meant losing the minang, i.e. the "winning," and remaining (only) a karbau, buffalo. In other words, Minangkabau people who are Christians are no longer viewed as Winning Buffalo's, but deemed unintelligent animals. (From: Author)*

Different occurrences continued, like people arriving outside our house on Sunday mornings. Usually about an hour before our leaving for church, they supposedly came to talk to me, but it looked more as if they were preventing us from going.

A relative also contacted me, to prepare a written statement, denying my conversion. This was for publication in the Muslim magazine (connected with my brother). When I refused, reaction came with dramatic crying and cursing. This included constantly calling me *kafir*, infidel.

One time, after I shared my testimony in Jakarta, one young man, a Minang who became Christian and was a former member of the Muslim Al-Azhar Youth Group, explained that they cursed me, by using Muslim prayers and considered me as *kerak kutukan*, the crust of damnation.

During those days, God gave me patience and clarity to explain with respect about my decision. I was able to do this without becoming annoyed or exhausted. In fact, I was glad to use such opportunities to tell my story and speaking about the goodness of God who wants to set people free from sins.

SUMATRAN WARRIOR – LIFE WITHOUT REGRETS...
Eventually, I not only faced Muslims, but also Indonesian Christians repeatedly persuading (half forcing) me, to speak publicly about my background and decision to follow Christ. The basis of their expectations troubled me. Since we considered some as friends, this placed Vera in a difficult position because they expected her to convince me to agree with their requests.

I was a Christian less than two years, yet the demand kept coming. I kindly refused, because I did not want to hurt people (the Muslims), even though they too already condemned me. What I understood was that we should only speak about the Good News of God's love, who wants to forgive and save humanity. For me, speaking primarily about my family background would only have been for momentary sensationalism.

I was regarded *pengecut*, a coward because I did not fulfill desires of certain believers. In their opinion, since I did not want to stand before large crowds I was lying about my identity. Supposedly I was only creating sensation about being the son of Dr. Haji Abdul Karim Amrullah, and (at that time especially) being a younger brother of Buya Hamka. From both sides there were accusations I wanted to make my own name known.

I quickly learned that human beings can make plans, but God's plan is always beyond those ideas. Before I returned to Indonesia, I was away from my country for twenty- seven years. During those years, I could easily have become a Christian in the United States and never have returned. Instead, I brought Vera and our children to Indonesia with *my* objective that they become good Muslims. But God had His own plan for my life. His plan did not include me only talking about family history for purpose of sensationalism

From the beginning after my decision to accept Christ, I wanted to give witness about God's love and greatness so that other people could receive it too. I was also determined to make sure that the door of opportunity for my testimony would not close before it even opened. God placed in me the desire to share how He changed my way of life and future.

It took me until I was fifty-four years old, to finally realize *kebenaran dari firman-Nya*, the truth from His Word. I knew that God gave me another chance to pass through a new season. After experiencing what He had done for my life, I would then give my testimony.

To remain positive, I focused on scripture. I understood the meaning of these verses, and *did* acknowledge the Lord Jesus before men; just not in the manner expected of me.

"Whoever acknowledges me before men,
I will also acknowledge him before my Father in heaven.
But whoever disowns me before men,
I will disown him before my Father in heaven."
Matthew 10:32-33 NIV

During that exasperating time, a verse also giving me encouragement was from Galatians 1:10 NIV.

> Am I now trying to win the approval of men, or of God?
> Or am I trying to please men?
> If I were still trying to please men,
> I would not be a servant of Christ.

Had I followed the will of Christians, i.e. to *expose me* regarding my conversion (before crowds); I absolutely knew, understood and believed, that the door would have slammed shut for me to speak God's message for His glory. Becoming God's servant, the way God Himself chose for my life, and pleasing only Him was my desire. Agreeing to these (well-intentioned) demands that early, would have given reason to those who did not like the news about me, to prevent the sharing of my testimony.

I noticed that the expectations placed on former Muslims in Indonesia; was to have them immediately publicize their testimonies, especially those with family backgrounds similar to mine. Therefore (in my case), by creating sensationalism, the opposition would have blocked God's purpose for me to spread the good news in the future.

I considered it a waste of time to think only about plans of others. I believe that with all plans we make, seeking God's advice with inspiration from the Holy Spirit should be first. Everything should be according to God's will and plan. That meant for me not to step ahead of God, even if it might take years before getting results or satisfaction.

In this case, I remembered the teaching and example of Christ in His conversation with a Samaritan woman (book of John Chapter 4). Here, Christ's wisdom shows how we can reach people who do not yet understand God's love and compassion. I also felt that this example would be most effective in sharing the Good News, rather than through sensation.

I wanted to give credible testimony about what God had done in my life, and what He could do for others. What the Lord can do in our lives with forgiven sins is different in each person.

In my understanding, a testimony should make people hearing or reading it, feel peace. The Good News that needed sharing was how only through *Isa Almasih* – Jesus Christ, forgiveness comes for all humanity.

I later remembered advice from the older and wise people I respected. That also included my father, who had also always said, that we who are *arif bijaksana*, wise, should not follow blindly and just accept information without first searching for truth. We must closely examine everything because God gave us a brain for thinking to know the difference between good and bad.

In that same manner, I wanted to be sure how God taught me first before I stood in front of many people. More than anything however, I had to make certain that I remained obedient only to all He purposed, so that doors of opportunities to serve Him would open for me.

My attitude was disappointing to fellow believers (in Indonesia), whether they had been Christian from birth or changed from Islam to Christianity. I always prayed to God about all the expectations people put on me. Although I regretted disappointing them, I also knew what God wanted from me.

After our decision not to return to the US, we underwent another serious trial. During February of 1982, Vera became ill. Friends arranged for her to fly to Padang, West Sumatra, where two hospital staff members met her, and drove her to Bukittinggi. She remained at Immanuel Baptist Hospital for three weeks.

Dr. John Applewhite and Everly Hayes his nurse received Vera. The same day of her admittance to the hospital, the Indonesian government had taken back possession of the facility. I later learned that the religious organization connected with my brother was central in the final actions of the hospitals transfer to the Indonesian government. Dr. Applewhite, who was with the Baptist denomination, continued his medical practice at Immanuel Baptist Hospital, and administered Vera's medical care. We were not at all aware of the hospital's transfer process until after Vera's admission there.

I had sent a letter to Uni Halimah in Maninjau (daughter of my aunt Jamilah), notifying her about Vera's hospitalization in Bukittinggi. Uni Halimah immediately came from my village with her youngest son Alizar (nicknamed Cha) to visit Vera. The acceptance, which Uni Halimah greeted her with, moved my wife very much. Cha was also very friendly. It was during that visit; Vera told Uni Halimah that I had become a Christian. Uni Halimah's reaction at that time was not one of surprise.

Halimah herself told me later, it seemed more important to her upon receiving this news, to show her love toward us instead of any judgment. She was my *uni*, my big sister (in Minang culture), who loved me so much and was very happy to finally have met my wife.

At the hospital, Halimah had expressed to Vera how much she wanted me to come home to Sungai Batang and live there with my family. She kept repeating, *"suruh Wadud pulang ke kampuang"* – "have Wadud come home to the village." My Uni Halimah just wanted me to come home. To her it did not matter whether I was Christian or Muslim; I was her little brother and I needed to come home.

After they left the hospital, Vera cried. She thought that perhaps it was because she felt relieved and happy finally experiencing, that among my relatives there were those who were kind-hearted, even though Halimah and Cha received the shocking news about me.

Vera remained in Bukittinggi for three weeks, and met Uni Halimah and Cha one more time. It was just a short visit when Vera was ready to return to Jakarta. My wife did not have opportunity to visit Sungai Batang or see beautiful Lake Maninjau. Uni Halimah, very disappointed, had hoped Vera could stay with her in my village for a few days before leaving West Sumatra. Saying she needed to go home first to the children and me in Jakarta, Vera promised to return. Fulfillment of this promise came fourteen years later when I took both my wife and our youngest daughter Siti to my place of birth.

While still living in Ciputat, we experienced many trials. Every time Vera and I faced another challenge, God repeatedly showed how He remained with us. Through all these events I also learned how God granted us perfectly answered prayers according to His will. We believed that by focusing our lives on the Lord, He was building character and making our faith strong. We did not know it in 1982, but God would give me opportunity to serve Him for many years to come.

The Lord has spoken.
Proclaim this among the nations…
Rouse the warriors!
Joel 3:8, 9 NIV

PREPARATION OF THE WARRIOR... In the two years after accepting Christ as my Savior, I used this time to study the Bible more deeply. Since we moved to Jakarta, we joined Bible groups and church. I also continued discipleship training with my friend David Wigger, and was ready for my baptism in water.

Pastor Gerald Pinkston of the Kebayoran Baptist Church (English worship service) received my baptism request. He advised me to think seriously about this step, especially because of threats made at that time.

There was a threat circulating and information given me that I had better be careful because someone was always following my family and me. I was to consider it a warning and for me to be extra careful since there was chance that my children may be harmed or kidnapped.

Concerned about the danger I was going to face once this news spread more widely in Indonesia, the pastor really wanted me to consider, that the public would view my baptism as having officially become a Christian. He warned me that because of this, I might lose my Minang relatives, friends, and even my job among other things. I was very aware of what could possibly happen since the Muslims already considered me *murtad*, a betrayer to Islam.

When we met again, Pastor Pinkston thoroughly discussed with me the Bible scripture. He especially focused again on the fact that I may lose my relatives and friends. His warnings reminded me of the Word of God in the Gospel of Matthew which stated:

> "Anyone who loves his father or mother more than me is not
> worthy of me; anyone who loves his son or daughter
> more than me is not worthy of me; and anyone
> who does not take up his cross and follow me
> is not worthy of me."
> Matthew 10, 37-38 NIV

The fact that I most likely was going to lose my Minang relatives and friends was something he believed I must seriously think through and not take lightly. He wanted me to understand the consequences.

I said to Pastor Pinkston that I believed and was sure the Word written in the Bible was from God Himself. I was always ready to face any difficulties, and willing to obey the Word of God

Pastor Pinkston then told me that for security reasons, the congregation would not witness my baptism as usually performed at the church. For safety of all, it was better to baptize me in a hidden place. We had access to the swimming pool of a friend and invited only a few people we trusted. I wanted to be certain the location was secluded and safe, not giving opportunity to individuals intending to harm us.

At last, on February 6, 1983 my baptism happened in Jakarta. I was fifty-five years old when I made my public declaration of total submission to Christ. I desired that the Lord continue shaping me according to His will and plan.

The understanding of *surrender* I knew about in reference to *submission* while I was still a Muslim. The word Islam in itself means surrender and full submission to God. I understood even more that through rituals alone we cannot feel peace, but must obediently surrender to the teachings of the Lord in daily life.

I also realized that all humans are sinners, and that our rituals and performance of worship alone cannot redeem that sin. Because of sin, without help from God it is impossible for a person to receive redemption by performing good works and deeds. In God's Word the apostle Paul wrote,

"For all have sinned and fall short of the glory of God,
and are justified freely by His grace
through the redemption that came by Christ Jesus."
Romans 3:23-24 NIV

·The full surrender and sacrifice of Jesus Christ, *Isa Almasih* on the cross, was a most significant event in history for us not to ignore or deny. This was God's purpose in giving salvation to all of humanity.

That night through baptism in His name, I knew this was part of God's preparation for my destiny. I clearly understood this was the way of God and I desired becoming a *hamba Tuhan,* servant of the Lord.

# 17

# ENDURANCE OF THE WARRIOR

*My shield is God Most High, who saves the upright in heart*
*.....who searches minds and hearts.*
*Psalm 7:10, 9 NIV*

Without noticing it, one and a half year went by in Jakarta. Reports about my Christianity continued spreading. This resulted in me resigning from my position at the travel agency. The company placed pressure on my relative in charge. Although sympathetic, it was still perplexing to him that I was no longer Muslim. We came to the agreement that it was best for both of us that I resign. While circumstances did not appear good for us, Vera and I were not discouraged.

An American friend offered me to join him in partnership with his newly formed construction development business. Himself having converted to Islam, he was an admirer of my late brother Hamka. During those days, not only was there a photo of Indonesia's President Suharto displayed on the office wall, but also a photo of my brother. Both exhibited with equal importance.

Actually, I did not have any experience in the construction business, and believed my friend accepted me into the company because of my relation to Hamka. He hoped that business plans would be more achievable in Indonesia when known I was Hamka's younger brother. After he discovered that I became a Christian, he was very disappointed and immediately worried that my exposure would work against his projected business goals.

Change again came, as stories about my conversion kept unfolding. When I travelled to projects as far away as Natuna Island near Sulawesi and other places in Indonesia, it meant I was leaving Vera and the kids in

Ciputat for long periods. Since neighbors learned I was a Christian, the environment we lived in was not secure. Concern of their safety laid heavy on me. I tried remaining thankful and told myself to view the situation as a way I could be an example among others, and work through this for God's glory. I surrendered my wife and children for protection.

I experienced many different things in those areas. One incident happened on Natuna Island when one of the young workers from West Java fell ill. We were nowhere near a hospital. I had just returned from town with Arie my assistant who was also a Christian from Menado. Having heard what was happening, I immediately went to the barrack where the sick man lay. When I looked at him, he was burning with fever. Believing death was near all the other workers had gathered. They had already started reading the verses of *Yasin – chapter 37* of the Quran often read when someone was dying.

The doctor from the Puskesmas public health clinic was not in the area and his assistant said there was nothing they could do. Because the worker was in serious condition and no one there to really help him medically, both Arie and I began praying for the sick man in front of the others. We also asked the Lord to show a miracle, so all could witness that He is alive, loving and merciful. All those gathered in the room also bowed their heads and voiced *Amin,* Amen when Arie and I finished our prayer. After we asked God for healing, the assistant also returned and helped compress the young man's body until he fell asleep late that night.

How happy my heart was the following morning. I praised the Lord when I saw the young man sitting in front of the barrack. When he noticed me coming towards him he had a big smile on his face. He kept thanking me, expressing his gratitude for our help and prayers. He also said that he knew it was the prayers that helped him get well again so quickly. Arie had also joined us. We both told the young man it was not us bringing healing to him, but God – Allah Himself – who showed His miracle because of His love for us. After this situation, there were more incidents, which I was able to use to tell about Christ. All the workers were aware that I was Buya Hamka's younger brother, and through these events, they knew that I had become a Christian.

There was another strange occurrence after the *Idulfitri* holiday also known as *Lebaran,* celebrated by Muslims after the *Ramadhan* fasting period. Since everyone had gone home to their families, two of the barracks remained empty for two weeks.

The first night we returned, a bizarre incident took place. The building, which I shared with other workers, seemed occupied by evil spirits. When we had just fallen asleep, sounds of eerie howling suddenly awakened us. Looking around the barrack, I noticed different men nearby taking turns making loud noises. By then they had also awakened everyone else. At first, there was laughter at the ones making the strange howling sounds just like dogs staring at the full moon. It did not seem too alarming, so we returned to sleep.

Then, just as I had fallen asleep, I woke up to the sound of stomping feet like a marching army. This was causing our barrack, (built over water) to sway. I became annoyed and ready to find out what was causing this nonsense.

I immediately went outside; walking around the barrack, and began speaking with a loud voice, "In the Name of Jesus Christ," ordering away the evil spirits attempting to bother us with manifestations. I waited, and shortly the noises stopped. After that night, this type of disturbance did not happen again while we remained on Natuna Island.

Laborers, also having experienced the evil, believed there was a separate spiritual force helping me. With what happened that night and with other situations, they concluded I must have supernatural powers. I told them I was not a *dukun*, shaman, but the power came from *Isa Almasih*, Jesus Christ.

During the partnership with my American friend, I mostly worked on the Natuna Island project for one year. How heavy my heart was each time I had to leave my wife and children behind in Jakarta While I was away, people repeatedly came to the house looking for me, asking my wife where I was and what I was doing on these long trips. Saying to Vera that they would return, and to let me know they were prepared to debate Islam with me.

For me, discussing Islam or Christianity with anyone was not a problem, but constantly having to go to Natuna Island (for weeks at a time) was. I started thinking what the future held if I continued working this way.

WARRIOR'S TRIALS AND REALITY... When more threats reached us after my baptism, I felt it was unsafe for our family to remain in Indonesia. Nevertheless, it was through trials experienced, how God showed His power in my life.

Difficulties with my friend worsened, as my Christianity strained both the business relationship and friendship. While I was away, he had talked to Vera about my position, and expressing his personal view about religion and me. First, he said he believed I was out of my mind if I thought of ever returning to America (because of the job market and my age). But, also mentioned, *"Willy has been a fish out of water – he has now found that water and has the power to sway the mass, however he does not see it."* He went on to say that, my "power" in Indonesia was because of my background, but since becoming more exposed, it would create more troubles for us. From that conversation, it was clear that my connection to the business was too big a risk factor.

With all the challenges we faced in 1983, the heaviest trial I was yet to experience (since becoming Christ's follower) was during the attempt of our leaving Indonesia. Vera and the kids were American citizens and because of a mistake of my own doing with their required documents, God used this problem to grow my faith in Him even more.

Since I was an Indonesian citizen, and they were included on the *KTP-Keluarga* (Family Identity) card with me as head of household – I thought there was no need to continue notifying Immigration. Through the years we lived there, I had reported my wife and children to the Indonesian Immigration when they arrived in Jakarta during 1977. I saw my mistake when the time came for us to return to the United States.

We also had another problem because our daughter Siti Hindun, born in Bali in 1980 needed a US Birth Certificate. The birthing clinic where she was born, had issued an Indonesian Birth Certificate. Complicating matters was the fact that at the time of her birth, I was still a Muslim. This all had to be taken care of first, which could possibly take a long time.

In Indonesia, the identity of religion is very important in official documents; handled differently than in the US. With help from the Head of Bimas Kristen in Bali, (Dept. of Religion Christian Section), whom I personally knew, our case was rushed. Soon thereafter, as the daughter of a US citizen, the US Consulate in Surabaya granted a "Certificate of Birth Abroad" to Siti Hindun Amrull.

In order for Vera and the children to leave Indonesia, they also needed an official release and authorization document from the Indonesian Immigration. I understood the problem, and that this was a serious setback for my family. I needed help.

It so happened, that our house in Ciputat was located near the housing complex for the KOMPAS Newspaper personnel. I was able to ask help from a friend there, who was in charge of preparing documents for the newspapers journalists to travel outside Indonesia.

I soon received information from him that the Head of Travel Documents Department at the Jakarta Immigration office was my good friend Burmadewani. He had been my schoolmate and was a younger brother of my commander Captain Sofyan when I was in the army as a youth.

In 1977, Bur who was then head of the Immigration Section at the Consulate General of Indonesia in San Francisco, (upon my request) issued a visa for my wife and two children. I never thought that six years later in 1983, when I needed help with the Dept. of Immigration in Jakarta, Bur would be the one to contact. God's timing was another miracle. If He had not placed my old friend nearby to help me I would have faced more difficulties

After explaining the situation, Bur did not hesitate assisting me. Good-naturedly he warned not to do it again. I could possibly be detained he jokingly laughed. Again, I was very gratefully thanking God for giving me the way out.

While I worked for the Indonesian Consulate General in the US, I had held Foreign Official status issued by the US State Department. In order for me to return to the US permanently, I had to go through steps of immigrating; and enter the United States as a Legal Resident. When my wife and children had to leave, I would not be able to go with them. As *warga-negara Indonesia,* Indonesian citizen, I needed a sponsor in the US. By July 5, 1983, Vera and the children had to leave Jakarta.

By this time, relations with my business partner were very strained. Meeting with him, the earnings paid me was only enough to purchase airfare tickets to the US for Vera and our three kid's. According to agreement, I was due a percentage from total contract profits. The remaining portion would be paid later he told me.

With my family's departure drawing near, we continued trusting God to provide. Vera and I were never discouraged because we knew God always kept His promises as written in I Corinthians 10:13 (NIV). We had memorized this verse:

"No temptation has seized you except what is common to man.
And God is faithful; he will not let you be tempted beyond what you can bear.
But when you are tempted, he will also provide a way out
so that you can stand up under it."

*Provide a way out...* We both very much believed that this promise from God was above anything else, because He is not a liar. All God's promises were true and we followed His leading.

During those first few years, we learned from experiences to believe that God knew how far we could endure all trials and temptations. He was faithful to our family by showing us a way out. My life had always been adventurous, but while my wife and I, walked together through another unknown passageway, we believed God went before us.

A warrior is not about perfection, victory or invulnerability,
he is about absolute vulnerability.
That is the only true courage.
Dan Millman

WARRIOR'S VULNERABILITY... Re-starting life in America would be different from anything we ever experienced before. In 1983, our beginning of this new adventure would be with divine help from God. For me to fully appreciate, that no matter what standard I desired in the world; the trueness of who I really was lay in the plan God already had while I was still in my mother's womb.

As I had voyaged across oceans, I followed the edicts of Islam closely. Yet, even before becoming a believer, I had already grown quite weary trying to do things on my own. Never did I envision that going to Bali would eventually change my life with such magnitude when I finally found the deep relationship with God.

The afternoon we left our home in Ciputat, about thirty children gathered to say goodbye to us. They were all friends of Rehana and Sutan who lived in the *KOMPAS* Newspaper housing complex. Having to leave their friends behind was difficult for our two oldest kids. Siti was still too small, but I knew even she sensed something in those moments as the car drove away from our home.

Our friends James and Dolly had invited us to stay the night with them before Vera and the children's departure. James, who was British, was married to Dolly, a lovely spirited Korean woman. We knew them from the Bible group we attended in Jakarta. The next morning they would help take my family to the airport.

Dolly privately expressed to Vera her concerns about having to leave Indonesia without me, and then handed a gift to my wife. We realized later that it covered expenses of fiscal-taxes due at the airport on departure and more. God's help was never late and His Word reminded me,

> "Never will I leave you; never will I forsake you."
> Hebrews 13:5 NIV

God knew our needs and answered our prayers. I was very sad however, since I could not leave together with my family. Besides the fact that I was still an Indonesian citizen, I was also uncertain of how long US immigration procedures would take. I kept asking myself, "When, would I meet again with Vera and children in the United States?" In order not to make it harder on them, I held back the devastation I really felt. During our last night, even in the moments of our vulnerability, we may have seemed powerless to the world; yet we held the highest power of all within us.

July 5, 1983, was the day of parting. Morning had arrived too quickly. All of us quietly prepared, not saying too much. Just as we arrived at the airport, our Canadian friend Rod C. met us. His willingness to be there during these hard moments touched us.

The mood was overwhelmingly sad for us as a family. Keeping our focus on formalities, we almost silently passed through airport check-in procedures. Whatever our thoughts were in those last minutes we kept to ourselves. Vera told me later it was a relief for her knowing that when she had to walk away with the kids, I was not left standing alone.

When the actual moment came, that we had to say goodbye to each other, Siti who was then almost three years old began whimpering and crying while firmly holding onto me. She did not want to separate from me. With her arms wrapped tightly around my neck, she clung to me as I carried her all the way from the waiting room to the boarding area. Once I put her down, Siti never stopped crying. I had to release her, while she continued screaming, calling out to me louder and louder, "Daddy, Daddy, Daddy!" She extended her hands, reaching out toward me, while Vera was trying to lead her away. My child's cries not only saddened my heart even more deeply, but it also strengthened my plea to God. I tried holding back my tears until I could no longer see my wife and children going further away from me.

Once Vera and the children were out of sight, I let my tears come as my heart felt crushed. Although the pain of separating under our circumstances was intense, I had again surrendered my family to God. I believed He would help us by opening the way to be together again soon. In all my weakness, I was also stronger than any other time in my entire life. When my wife and children left Indonesia, this was one the heaviest trials I ever had to face.

I soon learned that my relatives in Jakarta assumed I too had already left for the US. What none of them knew was that in actuality, I was staying with another American friend Dr. Henry Mosley and his wife, in the Kebayoran Baru area of Jakarta. I would remain with them while awaiting news from my wife about a sponsor for me.

Those days of having to stay behind, I could only wait on God. During this time, I had opportunities to share my testimony with different groups. I was comfortable speaking in small settings and give glory to God. I wanted people to know, that all the trials I underwent and overcame in my life journey, made my love for God grow even deeper and stronger.

During this time, a bigger obstacle in the relationship with my American partner arose. As weeks went by, I was not hearing from him although he knew I was still in Indonesia. The Natuna Project was finished months before, but I had not received the agreed entirety of payment for my work. Thus, while waiting for news from Vera, I learned even more how to walk by faith.

> Endure hardship…like a good soldier of Christ Jesus.
> No one serving as a soldier gets involved in civilian affairs –
> he wants to please his commanding officer.
> II Timothy 2:3-4 NIV

WARRIOR'S WAY TO SERVING… Once Vera and the children arrived safely in the US, she immediately made effort to find a sponsor for my immigration. I could then apply for legal resident status to return to the United States.

Our good friend Rene Creutzburg who had visited us twice in Bali was the person prepared to do this for me and he met all legal qualifications to be my sponsor. Thus, I would be able to leave Indonesia soon and be with my wife and children again.

With my interview scheduled at the US Embassy, they later notified me that all documents Rene had sent to Indonesia (verifying his ability to sponsor me) disappeared. The only alternative was to resend another set by mail. These were still the days before faxes and internet, i.e. regular post would take a long time. I wondered if the paperwork would arrive in time for my appointment.

The new set did safely reach Jakarta for the interview date. Embassy personnel informed me that they also located the original paperwork. Following all this, my interview went very well and permission granted me to immigrate to the United States as a *Legal Resident*.

Before leaving Indonesia, I met one more time with my former business partner. I shared my thoughts, letting him know I understood his position. I told him that I assumed he would keep our agreement. He assured me my portion before I would leave Indonesia. However, since that day in 1983, I never heard from him again.

The verse of I Corinthians 10:13 became even more alive in its truth to me. This proved especially so, after God reunited our family more rapidly than we anticipated. God knew about all our trials and showed His faithfulness to us. Because a way out is always given by God, we must believe Him and all His plans for us. It was even clearer to me that we had to remain obedient.

After arriving in 1983, it was my intent to go to Liberty, Missouri so that I could attend seminary there in preparation for ministry. But God had a different plan. Talbot Theological Seminary of Biola University and Fuller Theological Seminary in Southern California were the places where I would study and deepen my theological understanding.

My friend Jeff Kerkhoff (from the Lord's Grace of Downey Church), during a conversation with another friend Esther Nasrani; mentioned about my intent to go to Missouri. She advised him that I should stay in California. Being from Indonesia, she understood, what it had meant for me becoming a Christian while in Indonesia.

Sometime later, Jeff and I went to the Talbot Theological Seminary campus in La Mirada, California. While speaking to an advisor at the Admissions office, I shared my testimony. We realized it was all an instance of God's timing. The advisor mentioned that the Admissions Team had a meeting that same afternoon and would not meet again for some time after that day. Leaving the campus, I knew we did not have the funds, and Talbot was a very expensive seminary. Nevertheless, I believed that God would provide when it was His will for me to study there.

I soon received information that the Talbot Seminary Board of Directors, after hearing about my testimony held a meeting regarding my acceptance. They based my admission evaluation on *Life Experience*. I understood this decision was definitely not the usual procedure. But Talbot Seminary was happy to accept me because of what I had been through in my life. God also provided me a partial scholarship. Since I was fifty-six years old by then I thought I most likely was the oldest student in the seminary. Most of the other students in my classes were ten to twenty years younger. Some were pastors, or already held full-time ministry positions.

The next step was for me to find employment. Students often received support from churches or organizations, which send them to attend seminary. For me however it was different.

I was able to obtain a part-time job on the Biola University campus. Evenings, I worked in the Maintenance-Janitorial Department. After attending daytime classes, I swept, mopped classroom floors, and cleaned restroom facilities. Completing these tasks, I did so with a heart full of enthusiasm and energy. I understood God was nurturing and reminding me to stay humble.

Sometimes I would not go home if my next day's class scheduled early in the morning. I would then freshen up on campus. To save time and gas, rather than driving through heavy traffic I would take a short rest in my car.

I attended classes with joy and gratitude that these doors had unexpectedly opened. Years later in thinking back, I realized that the Lord Jesus Christ became my ultimate *personal Seminary*, specifically for my circumstances.

By the last part of 1983, my studies kept me much occupied. Vera worked Monday to Friday with Child-Care at our home. While I attended seminary we became active serving in the first church we attended after arriving in the US

THE WARRIOR'S HOPES... I felt that 1984 through 1987 was a period of continued spiritual growth for both Vera and me. God also opened doors for us to serve Him outside the church in various ministries.

We began discipling people who wanted to learn. Even those who had been Christians for a long time came. I felt we had to do this in obedience because for me serving God meant serving people.

Together with Dr. Iman Santoso and his wife, Dr. Roger Dixon (who served in Indonesia for many years), and some others, I became involved in an Indonesian students' ministry known as PERKANTAS (Fellowship of Indonesian Christian University Students). In this ministry, Indonesian students attending fifty-two different universities throughout California merged and established fellowship groups at the universities they attended. As a foundation, we had already begun discipleship training with some of the local students at our home.

In the beginning of 1987, though I had not yet completed my studies at Talbot seminary my desire to spread the Good News constantly stirred in me. After talking about different possibilities with Vera, we prayed together about these things.

Being back in the United States for only three and a half years and just having re-settled our family, we would have to make important decisions to follow God's plan. At that time, our three children were attending high school, junior high and elementary school. Therefore, we were careful not to make unnecessary changes for our family.

We eventually agreed that I apply with a mission organization that focused on reaching Muslims. It was my hope we could go to Suriname, England, or any country in Europe where many Muslims resided. What I failed to see was that God's purpose for me was already very specific. His plan did not include just any country where Muslims lived. Through a very hard lesson, I would learn that as much as I wanted to serve God, this was still part of my carnal thinking, *pemikiran duniawi*.

Waiting for an answer, no doors opened. Meanwhile we continued our ministry where we were, praying that God would show direction for me. It was then I began to understand that *my plan*, related to *my* desires, did not align with God's plan for me. I kept praying that He would give me guidance with what He wanted me to do for His glory.

In my mind, I still avoided the idea of going back to Indonesia, because I did not want to create more problems with my relatives and Muslim acquaintances there. I decided to wait since I was still finishing courses in Missiology at Fuller Seminary in Pasadena. Through different circumstances, I realized that it was not time yet for me to minister outside of the US. During 1987, our family moved to the Lord's Grace of Downey Church (formerly Lord's Grace Assembly) and we began serving there.

Dutch-Indonesian believers living in Southern California had established the church during 1972. Pastor (Jim) George Preijers, was founder. Years ago, before we were believers, we learnt that Vera's mother had asked prayer for us there. Since I was still Muslim, I wondered why these people prayed for me because I never would become a Christian. Vera had been very upset, because she felt we did not need their prayers. Only God knew how years later He would use that particular church with the process of transforming Vera and me. Therefore, our journey toward Christ actually began years ago with those initial prayers.

In looking back, a comical thing had also happened in 1974. Later, this became an amusing testimony as to how tolerant God was with me. Because I hosted "The Voice of Indonesia" radio program, we received an invitation to attend the second anniversary celebration of the LGA Church. Even though I was a Muslim, I wanted to attend the occasion and demonstrate tolerance toward Christians.

The event took place during the Muslim fasting month of *Ramadhan*. I purposely wore a *peci*, (black rimless cap) often used by Indonesian men while Vera wore the *sarung kebaya*, national dress style. During Pastor Preijers preaching, I listened closely. However, once he spoke about those who did not believe in Christ would be *doomed* and not make it into heaven, I defiantly thought, "Really? Did this man really think only Christians will enter heaven?"

Immediately I became annoyed because by performing my prayers devoutly and fasting, I believed I was most likely even more spiritual and committed to my faith than they. Hearing, *what I thought the pastor said*, my annoyance quickly turned into becoming offended. In those moments, feeling I right away needed to leave; I suddenly got up from where we were sitting (already toward the back) and proceeded walking out. Surprised with my unexpected behavior, Vera hurried a few steps behind me.

Once we were outside, trying to contain my temper (because after all, I was fasting!) I irately expressed to my wife, "The rest of my life, I will never step foot in that church again!" We went home without joining the other celebration for that day.

I was very upset watching the actions of "these Christians." At that time, I considered them *munafik*, hypocrites, who were only showing off their self-righteous holiness. Here I was trying to show how tolerant Muslims could be and these Christians were so inconsiderate toward my religion. But God already knowing the greater picture, understood the direction that I had to travel first.

Years later, as I remembered that particular Sunday of October 1974, it still brought chuckles between Vera and me. We appreciated God's good humor with His children. Who would have thought what could possibly happen almost fifteen years later in that very same church.

True greatness does not lie with those
who strive for worldly fame;
it lies instead with those
who choose to serve in Jesus' Name.
(Anonymous)

From Willy Amrull's 1998 Personal Journal

SUMATRAN WARRIOR'S HEART... During 1988, I received information that there was a newly formed Indonesian Christian fellowship in Southern California. Narwastu Prayer Fellowship, led by an Indonesian couple invited me to attend.

Happy with the invitation, Vera and I went and began attending regularly. I learned that for two years the group struggled planning a Revival Event in the US. I enthusiastically joined in because I was glad being with believers from Indonesia. We organized the event specifically for the Indonesian Christian community living in the US.

The Narwastu Fellowship also had plans to establish a new church. Two other Indonesian friends, whom I met while attending classes together at Fuller Seminary, approached me. They asked if I would assist them in this ministry, and starting the new church. The YPPI Foundation (*Indonesian Evangelism Foundation and Fellowship*) had sent these two men.

Knowing they had to return to Indonesia after finishing their studies, and since I permanently lived in the US; they asked if I wanted to be ordained as Pastor of the Indonesian language church. If I was interested, they both committed to help lead the new church.

A few months later, Dr. Petrus Octavianus Chairman of the YPPI Foundation visited me and asked if I would assist their ministry in the US. Dr. Octavianus explained that it was his wish to ordain me as pastor of the GPII (Gereja Pekabaran Injil Indonesia) Indonesian Mission Church, and appoint me as representative of the YPPI Foundation, should I accept.

Vera and I prayed about the turn of events, especially because I had never pastored an Indonesian-language church. We asked God if this really was His will since we were also waiting for direction regarding the mission field. Vera initially had very strong reservations about these new plans. But after discussing everything she told me whatever my decision was, she supported me.

I accepted the offer from Dr. Octavianus with pleasure. I felt the Lord called me where He wanted, bringing opportunity for me to obey His will. Wholeheartedly I believed that through this way, God could also bring me closer to people in Indonesia who were not believers.

I soon received word, that some people after learning I was to be ordained were already critical of me. Although not having expected this kind of immediate opposition, I accepted the offer as a responsibility given by God. In hindsight, I most certainly was too naïve then.

The Revival Event and my Ordination were to be the official opening for the *GPII – Indonesian Mission Church*. Not only did many Indonesians living in Southern California attend the 3-day program, but also a group of thirty-nine guests from Indonesia.

On Sunday April 30, 1989 – I was ordained as pastor of the new church. Incredibly, fifteen years after people had begun praying for us, I was ordained in the same church building, which I had defiantly said I would never return to the morning I walked out. Pastor Jim Preijers, was also one of nine pastors participating in my ordination service.

That day, in my message I expressed how magnificent God was in transforming lives. I told the congregation about how many years prior to that day, as a Muslim, I objected strongly to the Lord's Grace of Downey Church and its pastor. But God, while watching me *in the large picture of life*, already knew what was to come with time. As I stood before the people, I could only bear witness to God's greatness and the works He began in me many years before.

After I was ordained, my wife and children immediately supported me by being involved with the ministry. Our children were in their teens, yet always came and helped us. Because Vera still led Worship Ministry at the LGD church on Sunday mornings, we left home early. She would then immediately be by my side for the afternoon service of the Indonesian GPII church.

Before my ordination, I was one of the Elders of LGD. In forming the new church, we needed a location for weekly services. Through arrangements with church leadership, the LGD Board approved for the new Indonesian church to use their facilities during Sunday afternoons.

Both churches made an agreement for maintenance responsibilities. Although I shared all this in leadership meetings of the new church, my family were the only ones helping uphold this task, especially my son Sutan Ibrahim.

But then quickly a reminder came to me (from one of the leaders) that pastors in Indonesia are honored, respected people; not only as leaders who direct church duties, but also as valued older persons who are served by others. That comment more than puzzled me. It seemed that God instructed differently in His Word.

Be shepherds of God's flock that is under your care,
serving as overseers – not because you must, but because you are willing,
as God wants you to be; not greedy for money, but eager to serve;
not lording it over those entrusted to you, but being examples to the flock.
I Peter 5:2-3 NIV

*Being examples to the flock...* I learned that a good leader *serves people.* It seemed to me then, that becoming a pastor in the US was not the same as being a pastor in Indonesia. Since there were no volunteers from the Indonesian church offering help, I trusted that God knew best how to train His servants. Through this way, He wanted me to remain humble and obedient.

Before my ordination, we hoped to go to the mission field. Vera wanted to make sure I did not have unnecessary legal difficulties when I eventually would reach Indonesia. We therefore agreed that I would not go there until I was in possession of a United States Passport. We both knew that the procedure for American citizenship could take months, sometimes even longer. Once I applied for US citizenship, notification for an interview with the US Department of Immigration arrived in only a few weeks. It had taken many years for me to reach this point od decision.

I officially became a naturalized United States Citizen in Los Angeles, California on December 13, 1989, thirty-nine years after first setting foot on American soil. This was another miracle from God in my lifetime.

The GPII – Indonesian Mission Church in the US and the YPPI Foundation in Indonesia were affiliated. Two years after launching, weekly activities continued without any unusual incidents. Then a situation suddenly arose which became the start of problems within the leadership concerning me.

Instructions had arrived for me (from the YPPI Headquarters in Batu East Java), which were confusing since I understood the US based church had autonomy, i.e. was independent and self-governing.

I was to leave for Indonesia immediately for a six-month period. When this happened, the young church was not growing as anticipated. Since its establishment, the GPPI Church was not prepared to provide me a monthly salary. Therefore, neither the church nor denomination in Indonesia supported my family with an income. Outside the church, I still maintained a full-time job.

There had never been any discussion with the leadership, about a church income for me, not then, or prior to the ordination two years earlier. Sudden departure for six months meant I would lose my job. I questioned what was to become of my family and the church.

The US church income was low, but expectancy from Indonesia for a certain amount of monthly financial support (regardless of US proceeds), led to further problems. It also became very clear that I did not fit the conventional way for a pastor of an Indonesian church. All these became a heavy burden for me.

From the beginning, I understood the GPII church to be mission focused, and I valued the church's vision of *reaching out*. But I raised objections to the sudden measures and limitations. At this same time, people who had pledged to help lead with the new church also were not keeping their commitments.

Since returning from Indonesia in 1983, my desire for outreach kept increasing. I thought that by first serving with the GPII denomination in Los Angeles, a way would come to further this, especially with my vision for the Minangkabau.

As leadership problems continued, I was very aware of my own shortcomings. I knew that I was not the typical image of an Indonesian pastor. Rude criticisms directed at me were puzzling, although I was the first to admit I lacked eloquence and manner expected of me.

Not wanting any more conflict and after having sought God in prayer, I had peace in the decision to resign. Because my friend who initially had approached me about ordination was staying in the US after all, I agreed that he would be the best person to replace me. He connected with both the YPPI Foundation and GPPI Denomination in Indonesia. Since his wife and children had already arrived in the US, it was best for him to further the ministry. In a short meeting, I resigned as GPPI Church pastor, but never as God's servant.

This experience showed me, that when making decisions, no matter how sincere our intentions; if we first do not completely consider God's perspective, it only created disaster. Knowing that I only needed to please God, I remained optimistic.

Thus, this was another valuable life lesson for me with razor-sharp edges. It would however, later prove to be a steppingstone in my journey for future ministry. This experience increased my desire to be *God's servant in the field*. With my fire for West Sumatra not dimmed, I needed to wait on God.

After this experience, Pastor Jeff Kerkhoff of the LGD church, offered me to be Missions Pastor. However, I was like a ship ready to depart its dock. While still waiting in holding stance, God opened gateways for me to minister through discipleship to people desiring to strengthen their spiritual foundations and maturing in obedience to Christ. This allowed me time to prepare, as the vision remained within me.

My heart extended towards my people in West Sumatra and with time saw Christ's command of the *"Great Commission"* becoming more real in my life. A fire ceaselessly burned within me. I knew without doubt what God's instruction was to me personally:

"... Therefore go and make disciples of all nations,
baptizing them in the name of the Father and of the Son and of the Holy Spirit,
and teaching them to obey everything I have commanded you.
And surely I am with you always, to the very end of the age."
Matthew 28:19, 20 NIV

I realized my calling was not to establish an Indonesian church in America. God commanded me to go and reach people outside of man-made church buildings. My longing was to share Good News in open fields, bringing opportunity to people willing to listen about God's redemption. The desire kept rising within me for those God would lead me to. I yearned for them to know also the Truth about the Lord Jesus Christ. As written in the Gospel of John:

"I am the way and the truth and the life.
No one comes to the Father, except through me."
John 14:6 NIV

In looking back, I felt I was not any different from the Prophet Jonah who God directed to go to Niniveh. Instead, he ran away to Tarshis. The Prophet Jonah rebelled against God's command by going to Tarshis, causing God to bring down a great wind on the sea. A violent storm rose-up, threatening to break up the ship Jonah was on.

I compared the struggle I experienced with the church, as being similar to the great wind that God allowed with the prophet Jonah. What I had faced was like an enormous storm intended to threaten me.

Previously I thought that my desire had been to go to England, Suriname or Europe. But I realized, that by specifying to God where He should send me, even Los Angeles, had all been my own doing. It was wrong and it was sin. Just like the prophet Jonah, I too avoided God's command. However, I was to return to where my own roots had grown, *Ranah Minang*, land of the Minangkabau.

However painful the experience had been, it was actually part of my preparation to move toward the field provided for me all along. This lesson with the Indonesian GPPI church was really God's jewel for me. It helped me uncover the radiance of truth and totally surrender my will in obedience, to my patient compassionate God.

As a Minang son – a son of Indonesia – and having become a son in the family of God, I longed for my place of birth. I yearned for West Sumatra, the land and the scenic diamond-like brilliance of beauty there. The splendor of Lake Maninjau often appropriately referred to as *"SAKAPIANG KETEK DARI SIRUGO"* – a piece from Heaven fallen to earth, an epithet truly fitting its description.

Spiritually, I had already experienced a piece of Heaven here on earth in *my new life*, knowing *Isa Almasih* – the Messiah, Jesus Christ and receiving Him as my Lord and Savior. My heart's desire was for the Minangkabau people to also know *Isa Almasih* as their Savior.

When the angel of the Lord appeared…
He said, "The Lord is with you mighty warrior."
…"Go in the strength you have…
Am I not sending you?"
"I will be with you"
Judges 6:12, 14, 16 NIV

# SECTION FIVE

## *1991 – 2011*

# 18

# SUMATRAN WARRIOR'S QUEST

The call of God cannot be stated explicitly; it is implicit.
The call of God is like the call of the sea:
no one hears it, but the person who has the nature of the sea in him.
Oswald Chambers

As long as I can remember, my spirit always had a keen awareness of time and life. The hunger for adventure within living had brought me to a myriad of places through many years, all as part of a quest to succeed. My father had encouraged me to broaden my view, not to fear anyone or anything, and always live with integrity as a constant companion. Besides doing good to others whenever possible, he wanted me to understand early that I needed to have a healthy reverence for Allah – Almighty God.

Having passed through the narrow passage of my 1988-1990 Jonah lesson, I was prepared to follow God back to Indonesia even though it was the season in my own life, that I could retire in America and still comfortably serve God in other interesting ways. I was sixty-four years old by then and ready to journey where God was willing to use me.

In looking back, *iblis,* the devil, attempted stopping me from going to Indonesia. Through believers there, I received information that I should not come since the risk was too high. I remembered words of the Lord Jesus that He would remain with us always. Thus, I had confidence that God would lead and protect me. It caused me to ignore the well-intended advice, since this was *dalam rangka tugas dan panggilan saya,* the matter of my task and calling. I still planned to leave, but also kept in mind the message of the Apostle Paul to the Corinthians…

"…a great door for effective work has opened to me,
and there are many who oppose me."
I Corinthians 16:9 NIV

*A door for effective work had opened to me…* because of this; I would not allow fear of risk or worries of opposition hinder my way.

In 1991, being certain that my calling indeed was to go into the field, I left for Indonesia. On that journey, the first of numerous trips, I wanted to learn more about conditions of Christianity in Indonesia. I also hoped to visit with some of my old friends.

Arriving in Jakarta, having been away from Indonesia for eight years, my old friend Janner Sinaga met me at the airport. I considered Janner as my *teman-seperjuangan*, compatriot friend, who was with me through the 1960's struggles with Indonesian students when we were together in the US. I planned staying at his home during the visit.

My intention was to use that first trip to meet with various Indonesian Christian leaders including Dr. Soeradi, from Christian Center Nehemia. He provided much positive information regarding the state of Christianity and believers in Indonesia.

After meeting these leaders, having listened and shared with them, I returned to the US with mounds of valuable information. This increased my enthusiasm even more. I was also excited because God well protected my first journey and I arrived home safely. I began receiving letters from members of the West Sumatra Christian Fellowship – *Persekutuan Kristen Sumatra Barat (PKSB)* from Padang and Jakarta.

In 1992, I returned to Indonesia, this time specifically for travel to West Sumatra. Communication with leaders from the Minang Fellowship had been steady. How amazed I was, reaching Padang and finally meeting the Minang believers. Not only hearing about them from afar, but actually listening and speaking with them brought more joy than I expected. God increased in me the desire of making Minang disciples and strengthening them as followers of Christ.

Seeing their longing to grow in faith moved my heart like that of a parent. Most families were not accepting of the Minang believers once they became *pengikut Tuhan Yesus*, followers of the Lord Jesus. Considered out of favor in their families and community was painfully overwhelming.

One by one, I listened to their stories, and it was my hope to help with their spiritual growth. I wanted to help, because I had received help immediately after becoming a believer. This only happened through my following *pemuridan*, discipleship instruction.

It became clear, that to help Minang believers, I was to begin by simply starting with discipling them. To accomplish this, would mean spending time *one-on-one* with them or in small groups. Strengthening the faith of His followers would in fact be a first step (of many) among the Minang.

The time spent in West Sumatra during this visit, was even more valuable than my previous trip the year before. Desire of returning soon to *Ranah Minang* increased. I expected to be back and stay among them as long as I possibly could.

I saw God opening the door for me with *penjangkauan*, outreach, and obey *the Great Commission*. I was determined that the spiritual children in West Sumatra could learn from the *Great Teacher*, Jesus Christ. It was my hope before meeting them, and my prayer after gathering with them, that for God's purpose they become confident in their faith.

This was also how the concept to *"let Minang reach the Minang"* slowly emerged. I saw the door open even wider. It was my vision that Minang believers also receive a heart of love, and by truly loving other Minang, reach them in simplicity and power of Christ's love.

Returning to Jakarta from West Sumatra, I was very encouraged and happy having met Minang people of the same faith. After arriving however, my friend Janner immediately began suggesting, that rather than my focusing only on the Minang, it was much better for me to share my testimony in churches around Jakarta and throughout Indonesia. It confused me when he said, *"Wil, do not only think about the little people,"* reminding me why it was better, I share testimony only among influential groups. Many people whom he mentioned I knew personally from the past.

He then strongly advised me, to first concentrate on writing my testimony. According to Janner, my story could benefit me in many ways, because books written by me would establish my name in important places. He mentioned that I should share testimonies everywhere while people still recognized my brother Hamka's name.

I just as strongly believed that my story would have ended there. By sharing within influential circles, would have based my testimony on family background, and not on what Christ had done in my life. In my mind, all the well-intended opinions and suggestions would only harm the bigger picture of what God already prepared for me. Janner also believed that I could *sway the mass,* the same like I already heard about many years ago. I could not see how any of these ways were glorifying God.

Hearing my friend, express such views astonished me. I understood the directness he spoke with, which I appreciated. However, God had not shown any of it to me. These opinions did not change my focus about outreach to West Sumatra. Doing what people wanted would only cause more opposition from the other side, including from those with prior judgments against me.

Through the years, even some Indonesian Christians in California had made assumptions with opinions like my friend Janner. To them, having heard I was ordained, they too could not understand that instead of retiring and staying in the US, I wanted to go to West Sumatra.

WARRIOR'S VISION REALIZED… After having been in West Sumatra for one and a half month, I returned to the US. Knowing I had to find a way for traveling back and forth to Indonesia, I constantly prayed about all this, especially since I would be retiring in 1994 with less income.

I also still needed clarity for other things. Like, was it possible for me to do God's work without any help for my vision? Moreover, would Vera really be willing to go back and live in Indonesia again? She had returned to school in 1989 studying Respiratory Therapy and served with me at church, plus more. Many questions still required answers.

I knew God had given me a huge vision. The second trip again confirmed what He wanted me to do. The time for the vision's realization had arrived.

> For the revelation awaits an appointed time;
> …Though it linger, wait for it;
> it will certainly come and will not delay.
> Habakkuk 2:3 NIV

Once I was back in California, I immediately asked prayer from our longtime friend Jeff Kerkhoff, the church family and other trusted friends. In personal prayer, I always said to the Lord, "If this is a real task and calling from You, I believe that you my God, will provide for all my needs protection."

Vera and I also continued praying together about the next steps. I would remind her, "We pray before planning." During August of 1992, we decided to go away for a few days. For our retreat, I took her to a favorite place by the beach to talk about what lay ahead. This also included praying about my wife's plans. She hoped to work in the medical field when I retired.

Our time by the beach was intimate with God and each other. Vera already understood the vision, but I needed to know any reservations she had about our returning to Indonesia. We both knew that when she left Indonesia nine years earlier, she really thought of never coming back.

In seeking the Lord's guidance, we focused our prayers and discussions on Jeremiah 29:11-14 our life scripture. I had patiently waited for timing because I wanted my wife to be certain also, how God was leading us.

Vera admitted that seeing my enthusiasm when I returned home from the last trip to West Sumatra, she already knew it meant we would be returning there to serve. God had recently also shown her John 14:15 NIV, which she shared with me, *"If you love me, you will obey what I command."* During those days, we both prayerfully committed to God the timing of our moving and living in Indonesia once again.

After our retreat, we felt energized and had decided Vera would first finish school. It would finally take another year for me to sort thru fulfilling the vision. I knew without doubt that God would control the rest because I trusted His promises.

Commit your way to the Lord; trust in Him and He will do this…
Be still before the Lord and wait patiently for Him.
Psalm 37:5, 7 NIV

One way of trying to reach Indonesia was our application and then candidate acceptance with another missions-sending organization based in Florida. Through them in 1993, we received word that I was *blacklisted* in Indonesia. The leadership wanted me to consider the risk I was taking and the fact, that our presence there could endanger others. Vera and I did not allow that news to hinder us, but kept praying.

After Candidate Orientation in the beginning of 1994, it was our intention to follow-up on all requirements, such as the deputation process. I found the time constraint for raising their required financial support pledges difficult. I kept sensing that my time in Indonesia needed to be soon. I shared this with Vera and those praying with us; making clear, that it was not impatience, but rather an inner urging for a sooner departure. We also knew we needed a financial accountability covering before leaving.

We accepted with assurance that since God gave the vision, He would then also provide for all our needs. We had faith, for a way from God how He wanted His plans furthered. My financial needs as an Indonesian were not the same as if I were not from there. Vera, with her background and having lived in Indonesia for six years, knew we could live on much less for daily and overall expenses than what the organization estimated. We believed God for the financial umbrella covering which He would use for realization of this vision.

I was ready to return to Indonesia during 1994 for a third trip by myself. Prayers continued on our behalf. Even while waiting, we remained involved in different ministries. People again prayed for my plans to visit Minang believers.

Vera in fact, wanted very much to go with me but still hoped to finish her studies. Therefore, she decided to remain behind. Additionally, we had enough money to purchase only one round-trip airfare ticket to Indonesia and back.

We kept praying about how to stay in West Sumatra for long periods. We thought that after I retired we could perhaps stay in Indonesia one year at a time, come back to the States for a short period, and then return to Indonesia. To avoid problems that could possibly arise from such a plan, we also wanted to make sure we remained sensitive to warnings given about security. Thus, we prayed and prepared carefully.

We also had to think about our youngest daughter, who was in the tenth grade of high school. Vera and I were no strangers to moving since we had moved often. But for Siti this would be the biggest change; especially because of her education. We prayed because we really needed to prepare her. It was not easy for Siti as a teenager to leave her brother, sister, and friends in the US. She was fifteen, and although born in Bali, had lived in the US since she was three years old. For her this change was just as if moving to a foreign country.

For me, it was going home to where I was born, and had lived my earlier life. We understood and wanted to look after our daughter's needs. As a family, going back to Indonesia long term meant the disruption of life and our home in the US for the second time.

Besides other ministry obligations, I still held a job outside the church. From during my seminary days, I worked for a decade with this company. When I retired in 1993, I considered that job a real blessing because it kept me conditioned with physical and mental strength.

I knew in advance that my retirement income would not be large. Since Almighty God was "sending me" at the age of sixty-seven, we knew He would provide for us. The years I worked for the Indonesian Consulate, did not count toward my US retirement, because my salary was from the Indonesian government. In addition, while living in Indonesia for six years from 1977-1983, I held positions with Indonesian businesses.

I had heard that in Indonesia, when anyone reached the age of fifty-five they were considered *lansia* or *lanjut usia*, elderly and already entitled to a pension. Retirement in America usually is the season in life people looked forward to, and seniors often still served God with additional available time, mainly within the US. However, I chose the opposite, and wanted returning to my West Sumatra roots instead.

Often, people thought that retirees probably would not want to perform heavy tasks anymore either. Asked sometimes, why I wanted to do what was more challenging at later age, I always replied that Moses began leading his people when he was eighty years old. I felt God would also give me that same strength. Besides, I never viewed reaching out to others as a heavy task, but one that energized me. I also thought having opportunity to reach out at my age, still gave me plenty of time to do the best I knew how with what God taught me.

On July 2, 1994, while preparing to leave LA for Indonesia, I did not like leaving Vera behind. It seemed this trip was different. Her uncertainties about it were apparent. I asked God's peace when we said our goodbyes at the airport.

A few days after I left, it was through an incident with our car, that Vera discovered the Lord had made a way for her to go to Indonesia too. Having called our friend Jeff Kerkhoff for help, while waiting for repairs, she shared with him how strongly she felt that she should have gone with me.

Jeff later explained that funds were available, should the need arise for her to be in Indonesia with me. After receiving a leave from school and with a confirmed reservation, Vera was on a flight to Jakarta on Friday, July 8, 1994.

PURPOSE UNITED… God answered my prayers, and opened the way for my wife to join me. This was again a lesson for us, as through the Word, He assured us that His thoughts and ways are much higher than ours are. (Isaiah 55:8, 9 paraphrased).

I was amazed at how God's power was at work in Vera. When she and our three children left Indonesia in 1983, she had vowed never to return to the country of her birth. Her struggle with this was also noticeable. However, with the calling I received from God, my wife who all this time had been by my side both in joy and in sorrow, wanted also to obey the Lord.

Previously, we thought we were ready to go anywhere Muslims resided… as long not to Indonesia and especially not West Sumatra. When I was ordained, even I had begun thinking that must be my only calling – being a pastor in the United States. That however, was human arrangement and not God's real plan for me at all. He let me go through the experience much like the prophet Jonah, so that I really learned and understood His true direction for my life. I had to keep moving forward under the Shadow of the Almighty.

> "You will seek me and find me
> when you seek me with all your heart.
> I will be found by you", declares the Lord, "and will bring
> you back from captivity. I will gather you from all the
> nations and places where I have banished you," declares
> the Lord, "and will bring you back to the place from
> which I carried you into exile."
> Jeremiah 29:13, 14 NIV

When we were both in Indonesia that July of 1994, we met a group of believers in Jakarta. I immediately sensed they loved the Lord very much and had a love for Minang people. Pak Timotius (name changed) and Wilma Pattinama would eventually assist with the work.

In Padang, we met with Bruce and Lynn Sidebotham who were living in the area. The same day we arrived, Vera and I went to a gathering of the PKSB fellowship. We came also bringing a generous gift from our LGD home church to help purchase property for a fellowship building.

I had shared at our church and other meetings about circumstances of the Minang believers. Hearing about this brave group touched hearts. The contribution we brought came with love and instructions from our home-church Board to deliver the gift directly to Padang.

We left for the mountain town of Bukittinggi a few days after meeting with the Minang fellowship members. Friends from the US, Roy and Louise van Broekhuizen joined us. The scenic 3-hour drive through villages and rice fields brought back memories. For me, best of all was briefly stopping in Padangpanjang where I had spent my elementary school days during the late 1930's. The four of us checked-in to the Pusako Hotel after reaching our destination.

This also reminded me of my father's prison days so many years ago. For Vera, it was the first time back since her stay at Immanuel Baptist Hospital during 1982. We did not yet realize how relevant Bukittinggi would become in our lives.

The prayer group in Jakarta had introduced us to a worship song, *"Mataku Tertuju PadaMu"* – "My Eyes Are Fixed on You." The Indonesian lyrics of this song somehow helped Vera focus on God's will.

Regarding my wife's struggles (about living in Indonesia again), no one knew or understood the true depth of them. She knew what God was saying through Jeremiah 29:11-14 and desired obeying. She also wished being together with me in the work and wanted to commit to God's plan for our life and future. Nevertheless, she needed healing from wounds suffered the first time we lived in Indonesia. Lyrics of the song touched her to forgive.

Listening to me that morning, I could see how it moved her. I also reminded Vera how *Love conquers all,* and that I trusted God to accomplish this through us. I said, "Even during this period of our life, God is waiting for us to accept this challenge."

After much prayer and many tears flowing from both of us in those moments, I saw Vera's struggle finally leaving her. Giving ourselves entirely to God for this new responsibility, we also vowed returning to West Sumatra to do the work of His calling.

That was how God showed Himself. Both of us simply wanted to be instruments for His love and power to flow through us. We realized that as long as we were totally committed to bringing the Good News, the Holy Spirit would bring understanding in those who heard. He would lead them to open their hearts for Jesus, *Isa Almasih*, to become Lord and Savior.

When we were back in Padang, I assured the Minang believers that we would return to West Sumatra after affairs in America were ready. I also mentioned that we would be bringing our youngest daughter Siti Hindun with us. We all prayed together that God would continue preparing Siti's heart.

One month later, we returned to the US. After our decision, it still took us another year to organize the move to Padang. This included preparations for Siti and making final arrangements with the high school about her going abroad. Our daughter's tenth grade curriculum would come through an accredited home-schooling provider. We took all these measures so that Siti could re-enter high school without difficulty when the time came for her to return to the US.

A miracle to us was Siti's willingness to go with her parents, and having to adjust herself to a completely new environment. There was also Vera's school program, which she finished within that year. Most important to me was that my wife and daughter, transitioned to Indonesia as easily as possible.

# 19

# SUMATRAN WARRIOR
# SET APART

"Before I formed you in the womb I knew you,
before you were born I set you apart; I appointed you..."
Jeremiah 1:5 NIV

'Set apart'... "I know for certain that Jeremiah 1:5 was for me.
I understood it was God speaking about the life He
prepared and appointed me for....."

(From: Abdul W. K. Amrullah – Personal Journal)

Because I would be retired by 1995, Vera originally hoped that after finishing her studies to work in a hospital. But just like in Jeremiah chapter twenty-nine, God had His plan. In this case, we were returning to Indonesia with faith that was very strong. We absolutely believed God was the source for our daily needs and trusted that when God gave a vision, He also brought provision.

After meeting with leadership of our church, we continued believing God for a decision by the Board. They unanimously agreed to be the *umbrella covering* for the vision. This meant that Vera and I were leaving the US with an accountability system in place. We were accountable to our home church the Lord's Grace of Downey regarding all financial matters of the West Sumatra work.

It was amazing how God prepared everything. I would turn sixty-eight in June of 1995. For me, even at this later age, my spirit was very energized and looking forward to this new adventure.

*Sharing with LGD Church congregation.*

We had decided that when I officially retired, I should travel to Indonesia one more time by myself. We saved enough funds for me to go for about seven to eight weeks, staying in West Sumatra most of the time.

Since we had already received the umbrella covering from our church, we both felt it would be good for me to meet once again with people in Indonesia. Before my departure on this trip, while praying God showed us a vision that became our personal *Victory Vision*. Through this, God revealed His protection over us. I left Los Angeles on March 23, 1995.

Returning to Indonesia with my family was indeed a huge risk. In preparation, we needed to follow God implicitly with every step, and had absolute faith that He would take care of us. I always believed and expressed *"Iman tanpa risiko bukan iman"* – "Faith without risk is not faith." My wife, daughter and I were going to my people with God's love. It was with this love and big faith in Him that we were setting out.

My purpose is that they may be encouraged in heart and united in love…
Colossians 2:2 NIV

LOVE CONNECTION… On September 3, 1995, with the go-ahead consent of our two oldest children (Rehana and Sutan both remaining in the US), we boarded a flight to Indonesia. As many saw us off at departure, prayers and support from our family and friends went with us.

While in Jakarta, invitations began arriving for me to share my testimony. I occasionally accepted speaking at a church service, as long as there were no special public announcements made. Unfortunately, after I agreed to share at one particular church, a large banner appeared announcing an upcoming testimony by *Pastor Willy Amrull, the younger brother of Buya Hamka etc.* I was disappointed and regretted that even after an agreement this happened. Therefore, I cancelled.

The Lord had finally opened doors for realization of His vision. Each step I took needed careful consideration as I went forward in this new portion of my life. Since receiving Christ in 1981, many assumptions existed about me in Indonesia. These, brought accusations from people who most often had never met me. There were also those doubting whether God had really given me salvation, or that He called me according to His plan.

My firm belief remained that when God opened a door, He could immediately shut that door; especially if anything I did caused unnecessary sensation. Even though by 1995, I had been a follower of Christ for fourteen years, it still did not mean it was time to expose me to the public. That was the will of people, even if with good intentions. Achieving momentary sensationalism only, would not benefit God's purpose, or the love I had for my relatives and Minang people. However, my views were often misunderstood. Regardless, I knew that I only needed to remain obedient to God's leading.

Before moving to West Sumatra, we stayed in a house provided by an acquaintance. During this period, we also had gatherings with other Minang believers living in surrounding areas of Jakarta.

A displeased Muslim neighbor, reported us by writing a letter to the *Lurah*, Neighborhood Head, the Police Department, Department of Religion, and one copy delivered to me. The letter stated that if we continued *unauthorized gatherings*, he (the Muslim neighbor) would not be responsible if it created a public *SARA* disturbance, i.e. riot. This neighbor played loud music or recitation of Muslim prayers from a very large sound system when guests parked cars outside or near our house.

One afternoon, three police officers arrived at the house to clear matters of the complaint letter. I remained friendly letting them enter. Their posture was rather superior, but I invited them to sit down. I sensed the need for expressing to them, that although I lived in the US, because of the personal sacrifice of my life during the revolution, I had a share in Indonesia. In a subtle but direct manner, I informed them that I had come back to the land where I was born to enjoy results of that sacrifice. I also stated that our sacrifices of so long ago was for the freedom that they now enjoyed. The three police officers watched me intently as I then sat before them.

Not knowing how to respond, they focused attention on the objection from our neighbor about the *unauthorized spiritual activities* we were hosting. According to the complaint, we disturbed the peace and calm of the surrounding neighborhood. I listened carefully and responded that since it was the month of *Ramadhan*, we in fact respected and honored our Muslims neighbors who were fasting, *puasa,* by meeting after the daily *buka puasa*, opening of the fast. I said that we had specifically moved our gathering time, so as not to disturb anyone. I expressed that there had never been any intention to create problems.

Speaking with the three police officers gave me opportunity to quote a verse about fasting that I remembered from the Quran in *Surat Albaqarah, verse 183*:

> *"Ya ayyuhalladzina amanu kutiba*
> *'alaikumussiamu kama kutiballadzina*
> *min qablikum la'allakum tattaqun",*

> "O ye who believe fasting is prescribed to you,
> as it was prescribed to those before you,
> that ye may (learn) self-restraint."
> (From Quran Translation)

I quoted the verse in Arabic. Seeing their surprised expressions, I explained that not only did Muslims fast, but also the religions that came before Islam, i.e. Judaism and Christianity. Sharing this on purpose, I wanted these men to know I also understood the duty, which God had given to both sides.

After hearing my explanation, their manner changed to respect and friendliness; a complete reversal from earlier. I never needed to mention I used to be Muslim, but the fact I spoke the words in Arabic made me appear in a different light to them. They soon politely excused themselves and left the house.

I had earlier told Vera and Siti to remain on the second floor. I knew they heard the interaction between the police and me. My wife, daughter, and Ibu Wilma, a friend who happened to be there, met me when I came upstairs. The three had been praying, asking the Lord to grant me wisdom and protection. Through this incident, God again showed that His power and presence was always with us.

> Therefore, as we have opportunity,
> let us do good to all people,
> especially to those who belong to the family of believers
> Galatians 6:10 NIV

OPPORTUNITIES… In early February 1996, my wife, our daughter Siti Hindun and I left Jakarta for Padang. After arriving at Tabing Airport, we went straight to the house where we were to live, located on Batang Lembang Street in the Padang Baru area.

With the first rains, we quickly discovered the house had leaks. Having previously lived in Indonesia for six years, this did not trouble us too much. We considered this, and the hot weather as part of life in Indonesia. At first, I thought it might be difficult for Vera and Siti to live in the Padang humidity. But neither rain nor heat could prevent us from following God's call with joy.

We were thankful for the provision of the house. Our friends Lynn and Bruce Sidebotham had lived in the house before returning to the United States.

We had invited Yanwardi Koto, a Minang graduate from ETSI Seminary in Jogja, Java to live with us in Padang. I met Yan in early 1995 before he spent six months with the YWAM Discipleship Training School in Switzerland. After returning, he stayed with us in Jakarta before our move to West Sumatra. We sent Yan on ahead to Padang so that the house would not be empty when Bruce and Lynn left.

I was grateful to God and amazed that my wife and daughter both adjusted well within the first month in West Sumatra and accepted *keadaan apa adanya*, i.e. whatever state of circumstances. During that time, living conditions for us were very different compared to others coming from abroad. It was less effort for me as an Indonesian, and Vera with Siti, to adapt to living modestly. We learned and stayed thankful through the situations faced.

We blended in easily and liked sharing with whoever came to the house. Our meals were usually very simple, even if just eating dishes cooked from salted dried fish, *ikan teri,* or from soy bean cakes, *tempe* and *tahu.* With plenty of rice prepared for all… *tidak ada masalah,* no problem.

During 1996, another servant Pak Timotius (name changed) joined us in Padang. He was the evangelist we met in 1994 and had the same vision with me. His theological background was solid; and he wanted to stay in West Sumatra to help. I had immediately recognized his willingness to care about the Minangkabau people.

Before my return to Indonesia, other Christians in the US would ask me what my approach was going to be with the Minang. I only replied, "All I want is to gather my people and encourage them with love, whether they are Muslim or non-Muslim. If they are believers, I want to share with them about living their lives in Christ well, and how they could touch the lives of others."

I could only describe it as the *"one-on-one and more"* approach. To some, this was perhaps not a broad enough theological clarification, but I knew how the Lord was leading me.

*Vision "One on One and More" West Sumatra – 1995*

I sensed God's direction as in the story of John Chapter Four, about Christ meeting the Samaritan woman. God wanted me to be sensitive first and understand *the felt need* of people. I was to view this with His compassion. Above all, I was to love my people, following steps of the Great Commission to prepare them.

After having met Minang believers during my trips, I recognized there were those among them not yet *born again* of the Spirit. I learned this as they told me their personal stories. It confirmed how I was to begin. I should love them above anything else, with *God's unconditional love*. They often experienced pain of rejection and sometimes-total expulsion from their Muslim families. I was to help prepare them, and by example first, demonstrate how to be more like Christ. For that, I was to use what I termed the *"one-on-one and more"* application

Between Yanwardi, Pak Timotius and me, we worked out different tasks for teaching the discipleship curriculum. Numerous *anak-anak rohani Minang*, Minang spiritual children, already believing in the Lord Jesus kept coming to our house eager to learn more.

It was my hope for them to really understand, that by first being born again they were *made new* in Christ. By showing them from the Bible, I wanted them to know the meaning of *spiritual birth* as God's Word describes.

"...Flesh gives birth to flesh, but the Spirit gives birth to spirit.
You should not be surprised at my saying, 'You must be born again.' ..."
John 3:6-7 NIV

Vera and I also prayed that other area churches would understand the reason for my presence in West Sumatra. Coming with a distinct purpose, it was not my aim to establish another church there. I desired to fill a need. This involved *Pemuridan*, Discipleship for new Minang believers. In the time left to me, I desired only to be obedient to God and create good relations with all people, including the local churches and denominations represented there.

We asked God to raise-up Indonesian workers willing to spread the Good News, specifically in West Sumatra. It was very important to me that anyone coming for outreach to this area with us do so with *LOVE-filled hearts* for Minang people. My vision for these young ones was that as they matured in that same way; they could and eventually would, reach out to their own people.

Before beginning with these efforts, I understood the risk of criticism. When we committed to this work in 1994, my specific focus was the Minang. This may have seemed very naïve to others, but I trusted God to do His will.

As things progressed, together with Pak Timotius and Yanwardi, we began forming discipleship groups whenever and wherever possible. During group times, we discussed basic truths, and then daily applying in their lives what they learned from God's Word.

Starting with first strengthening the believers, I saw them slowly receiving God's power. I knew this could only happen through their personal understanding and developing Fruit of the Spirit in their lives. I strongly believed that eventually, they could go among their own families and communities with confidence as a positive witness based on Christ's Love.

It would take time and much patience on our part. Sharing love and being patient did not mean *memanjakan*, spoiling them, but developing spiritual growth. We, as mentors needed to practice and live out these Fruit of the Spirit as an example. I strongly believed that the concept of *one-on-one and more* would evolve when *genuine transparent love*, first came from us.

Between Pak Timotius, Yanwardi and me, daily schedules filled quickly. As we went to different homes, teaching individuals at our house occurred simultaneously. Having Pak Timotius and Yanwardi living with us, was more convenient.

Through the years, I often told my wife "Minang people are curious people. If they ask questions, it is not because they want to challenge, but because they are seeking clarity and want to know more." I would also say, "The Minang respect Christians when they see them live their lives accordingly."

In faith I foresaw, that as we helped to spiritually strengthen Minang believers, then my statement of *"let Minang reach the Minang"* would eventually result. This simple but direct idea however, would in the course of time, be misunderstood.

"What's the use, if the quantity of those who believe is so big, but the quality of their faith remains shallow?"

From: Willy Amrull's Personal Journal

HEART MATTERS… Within the groups, we encouraged sharing of personal stories about changes in the lives of those participating. This then motivated others. Discussion usually followed about what we were learning. Six various topics were base for the teaching.

First, we introduced Who Jesus Christ Is *(memperkenalkan siapa itu Yesus Kristus)* whom they called *Isa Almasih*, and why He is the Lord and Savior. We explained that when someone accepted Him into their hearts, the Holy Spirit would be in that person and this eventually produced *Fruit of the Spirit* in their lives.

Second, was learning His Word *(mempelajari Firman-Nya)* and God's desire to talk directly to us and leading our lives. In addition, the importance of knowing God through His Word, *Firman-Nya,* and the Holy Spirit showing His purpose for our lives. This would happen only by reading His Word consistently and practice this daily.

Third, was Prayer *(bagaimana kita Berdoa sebagai orang percaya)*, how we pray as believers. Through the Word, they learned how to communicate with God. This did not mean talking to God only from our side, but together with the Word, we could enjoy an intimate *two-way relationship* with our Lord. This was a way for the Minang believers to know if their relationship with God was distant or close.

Fourth, regarding Fellowship *(mengenai Persekutuan)* with God and people – how to treat others. That God's Word shows us, how to carry each other's burdens and supporting one another. We also discussed the importance of spiritual growth, which then aids harmonious relationships and fellowship.

Fifth, was about Witnessing *(mengenai Kesaksian)*. After several months, we saw spiritual growth furthering in the believers. Those being discipled learned also how to "tell their stories" about knowing Christ, and what He had done in each life.

Sixth, we shared about Obeying God's Command *(Menaati perintah Tuhan)* as directed in His Word. We clarified how as believers in Christ we are able to reject all the evil spirits that had been within us, and how to make place for the Holy Spirit in our life.

Although we explained God's Word in the groups, they, who had risked by deciding to follow *Isa Almasih*, Jesus Christ the Messiah, also taught us. They dared paying the price for salvation, which they received free through the sacrifice of the Lord on the cross.

We met Minang people of all ages who believed and were spiritually growing. Whatever they experienced no longer made them afraid as before, even when openly rejected by their families.

At first, it seemed they were living crushed defeated lives and feeling the loss of identity due to exclusion from the community surrounding them. Concerned about the conditions they lived in we did our best encouraging them; that once they were spiritually born again, their identity also became "their identity in Christ"

Our doors were always open. That meant all who came were welcome, including those with special needs. We also counseled families facing difficulties, and couples having marital problems. But we also had to be careful. They had to understand that not all people from America were rich. Vera and I shared what we could.

Our plan was that when discipleship teaching finished, we would continue showing them how to handle their personal problems with using Spiritual Warfare, *Peperangan Rohani* as mentioned in God's Word. While we, continued working with the different groups, time arrived for introduction to this topic. I took that risk.

To avoid misunderstanding with anyone inclined to think that Minang Christians learned how to wage war, or were receiving false teachings; it is necessary for me to clarify that the lessons were from the Apostle Paul about Spiritual Warfare. In this case, it was using *the Armor of God* from Ephesians 6:14-18, which we daily needed to put on.

By standing firm with *truth* as a belt buckled around our waist,
putting the breast plate of *righteousness* in place,
having as our shoes, *readiness* to announce the Good News of Peace,
also taking up *faith* as a shield; for with it, we will be able to put out
all the burning arrows shot by the evil one,
take *salvation* as a helmet,
and *God's Word*, as the sword which the Spirit gives us.
But doing all this in *Prayer*, asking for God's help."

Author Paraphrased

Having awareness, and using the (spiritual) "weapons of war" provided by God, enabled fighting-off the enemy's attacks. The new Minang followers desperately needed to know what those weapons were from God's Word.

After another six-month stay in West Sumatra, Vera and I went home to California. During that time, I prepared material to share with groups. After returning to Padang, without any delay I began teaching this topic. I immediately recognized that it was also a new challenge for our team. I reminded them that this was part of growth and maturing for all believers. It took much patience and care teaching the groups how to resist the spiritual darkness. It was a heavy task, but we saw progress in those wanting to live with spiritual eyes opened.

Once *Peperangan Rohani,* Spiritual Warfare teaching was completed and they realized how these things affected their personal lives, numerous ones began asking for personal healing ministry, *pelayanan pribadi.* When they requested *Pelepasan,* Deliverance, it was to be a cleansing and release of past wrongdoing, so that God could bless them. I was pleased with these results and together with our team regularly did this part of the work.

What you leave behind
is not what is engraved in stone monuments,
but what is woven into the lives of others.
Pericles

WEAVING LIVES… There were constant developments. We saw this as a very positive moving of God. As our relations grew with participating believers, we saw them maturing in their spiritual walk and becoming more confident in whom they were in Christ. I also watched the vision God had given me take shape. With this progress, Vera and I eventually also came to pay a price.

As small groups progressed, the *one-on-one and more* approach thrived through a period of three years. I was aware that time for me among my people was limited. However, neither age nor health would deter me. Then again, had I not reflected on this, would have been foolish on my part.

We regularly met on Monday evenings with the PKSB (Padang) Fellowship. The location was where quilters of Pamato Minang Quilts worked during daytime hours. Marta N. not a Minang, but committed believer led the women. The quilt ministry initially began with help from Lynn Sidebotham (who with her husband Bruce lived in Padang until our arrival).

Vera also began reaching out to the younger women. Though perhaps unusual in Indonesia at that time, via Song Signing a way opened to build relationships informally. Seeing an example of this creative form immediately drew the women. With their own desire to worship, *"bahasa isyarat,"* sign language, was a beautiful expression of hand movements, *"ekpressi gerakan tangan yang indah,"* applied to Indonesian lyrics and melodies. Enthusiastic response from the women made this a lighthearted and regular activity with plenty of camaraderie.

As relationships with quilters grew, Vera joined with Marta N. to find ways for marketing the beautifully hand-stitched quilts. My wife wanted the quilters to know that people in the US and elsewhere valued their artistic creations.

Because we knew about people often living in dire conditions, we hoped to help families in need (among Minang believers). However, it was never my objective to help others as a way of enticing and then evangelizing them; or for us to personally profit from quilt sales. Those who did not understand my purpose then, or were not closely involved with the work in Padang made assumptions. This issue became fuel for later fire.

During this period, a request to assist with brick making also came from believers living in a village about forty kilometers outside the city.

There were twenty-five men and five women Minang believers from that village. We regularly met to disciple them, sometimes on the beach. *Proyek JALA Batu Bata* – Red Brick Project began this way.

Eventually this spread-out to various projects, all intended to help people become self-sustaining. With those willing to work out proposals, we were willing to assist. In other words, if a person showed responsibility for an idea, we did our best to help them launch it. We however remained cautious about the perimeter of assistance applied.

Several years later, aid progressed into our giving financial support to four Minang men and women we had discipled. This enabled them to attend SETIA Theological Seminary in Jakarta. Together with Rev. Matheus Mangentang, Rector of SETIA Seminary, we networked in preparing these Minang students to become future leaders for West Sumatra.

During what became a commitment for a five-year phase of studies, all four students received full financial support through our ministry of JMO (assuring them full tuition, books and supplies, monthly allowances, housing, plus provision for their families). Because I understood what it was like to focus on studies and still have to work, I wanted these first four to have opportunity of completely devoting themselves to their education and concentrate on the path set before them.

I knew this was the best way to help. JMO ministry committed to this project believing with faith, that after seminary graduation these new leaders would return to West Sumatra to serve God and their own people.

Part of my vision for West Sumatra was, that these men and women would be the first Minang team raised-up, to serve God together, specifically for the Minangkabau. It was for that period of five-years while they attended seminary, I based my prayers on Ecclesiastes 4:9-11, 12 NIV. I patiently waited to see them become strong messengers, *united in vision of reaching out* to our people beyond the scope of church buildings and walls.

But I also understood, that although God gave me a vision, after graduation they still had to make their own choices about where, how and with whom, they allowed the Lord to lead them. I hoped they would realize the strength that came when God's people *united as one team*. At this time, I remain encouraged by the Word and I know that in this, I have fulfilled what God asked of me.

Two are better than one,
because they have a good return for their work:
If one falls down, his friend can help him up.
But pity the man who falls and has no one to help him up!
...Though one may be overpowered, two can defend themselves.
A chord of three strands is not easily broken.

Ecclesiastes 4:9 -11, 12 NIV

# 20

# COURAGE OF THE WARRIOR

It…takes courage to follow Jesus Christ…
It takes courage to stand up for Jesus Christ wherever you are.
Greg Laurie

So that we could remain in Indonesia for longer periods, we went to Singapore every sixty days and then returned to Padang. According to Indonesian immigration regulations, tourists could obtain a Visitor's Visa at the airport upon arrival, valid for sixty days. To avoid mistakes, we made certain to leave Indonesia every fifty-seventh day. Because of freedom that came with my US retirement, we were able to do this. Since I wanted to stay in my homeland as long as possible, we travelled to the US every six months even though my retirement income was small.

We trusted for provision of all necessities in the vision, totally convinced that God would meet our needs on time. We kept on believing that "When God gives the vision, He prepares provision" and that He would enable me to accomplish everything expected of me in His time. The Word of God stated it clearly, and I followed this completely depending on Him.

"And my God will meet all your needs according to his
glorious riches in Christ Jesus."
Philippians 4:19 NIV

God proved to me later that although I had to leave the US to follow His calling; and even without many pledges of steady financial support, the Lord Himself repeatedly provided for our needs. God always made sure we had enough.

In the middle of 1996, we went back to the US and took our daughter home to California. Siti had finished her tenth-grade home schooling for the year, and it was best to bring her home for her final high school years. We had agreed that Siti would continue the eleventh and twelfth grades in California. Vera and I would come to the US every six months. Siti would remain in California with Rehana, who was then already teaching. I would miss the times, of helping my youngest daughter with her Geometry lessons. But Siti was almost sixteen years old and we knew it would be better for her to stay in the familiar environment of our home.

While Siti was living with us in Padang, she learned about the culture of Indonesia and her Minangkabau heritage. This also included learning some Minang folk dance from a teacher who came to the house to give lessons. Siti also learned to cook some special Minang dishes from Mul our helper.

One of the most memorable things Siti and I experienced in West Sumatra was when we took her to Maninjau to visit our relatives there. When we reached a portion of the impressive panoramic view and looked down from the high hill, I stood there with my youngest child where I used to stand as a young boy. From this spot, we could see the beauty of *Danau Maninjau,* Lake Maninjau. At that time of late morning, the water looked like a huge mirror facing upwards to the blue sky, its reflection gleaming heavenward bright and clear. Siti was amazed seeing how beautiful and magnificent it all was. She then pointed to the lake and told me, "That's mine!"

Standing with my youngest child high above my village of Sungai Batang looking down at the rice fields below us, we viewed the land on which I was born and walked with my mother. That was an experience beyond my imagination. Standing on that same spot with my daughter, where I stood with friends many years ago and had such fun during my childhood. But in those moments, I was standing there with Siti. This became one of the most important highlights of my lifetime. I was sixty-nine years old that day in 1996. My spirit seemed ageless soaring above the beautiful hills and water of the lake in that treasured moment. God had allowed me to bring my youngest child to the place never removed from my blood and identity.

After driving down the hill on *Kelok 44* – the narrow road leading into Maninjau with its forty-four very sharp hairpin turns – we came to the lakeside road heading towards my Uni Halimah's house, next to the old house where I was born. This visit was even more special compared to my other visits, because my soon-to-be sixteen year-old daughter was with me. When we reached the house, we could see my Uni Halimah from the car as she came out and began sweeping the cement foundation of what had been her home before a recent fire destroyed it.

*Siti and her Mak Tuo Halimah in Sungai Batang - 1996*

While Vera and I remained inside the car, we told Siti to go out and walk over to meet Halimah by herself. When she was near, Siti greeted her by softly calling out to her, *"Mak Tuo?"* – "Older Mother?" Halimah looked at Siti and answered, *"Sia kau?"* – "who are you?" Siti replied, *"Siti Hindun."* We could see from inside the car that Halimah in that moment was stunned. Dropping the broom, she immediately embraced and kissed Siti. While she was crying we could hear her repeating, *"Anak den, anak den,"* "my child, my child." After that, Vera and I stepped out of the car to greet my Uni Halimah. She was so overwhelmed and could not stop crying. Soon my nephew Cha also joined us, and he too was very surprised by our unexpected arrival.

Both our old houses had burned down. Where my Uni was temporarily living was actually a small storehouse beside the old family home site. This also was where the rice-grinding mill was located. The building of another house for Uni Halimah, Alizhar (Cha) his wife and two children was in progress.

In 1994 when Vera and I came to Sungai Batang on our first visit to West Sumatra, we were very touched when we entered the house. Welcoming us was Siti's photo placed by Uni Halimah on a small table facing the front door, a pleasing greeting to whoever came into the old house.

I remembered when I came home to Maninjau in 1980 after the thirty eight-year absence. That was also the time Vera found out we were expecting our third baby. Uni Halimah then wanted me to promise that if we had a girl I would give the baby to her. When we visited in 1994, my Uni was telling me that I had promised to give the baby girl to her. Her version was of course a little different from mine, because I actually never promised her that. I did not know it was Uni Halimah's true desire to have a daughter, since she had had four sons. According to tradition, *a daughter is the priceless pearl* in the home of the Minang household. For me, all our three children were like precious gems.

Finally, in 1996, Siti was the first of my children to come with me to my place of birth. Our oldest daughter Rehana would come with me in later years. I hope to fulfill my dream for our son Sutan to come to this special area of my heritage. I believed that God would have my children know their rich legacy through time. To have been able to make that visit with one of my children was a celebration. It meant more to me than anyone realized.

In Padang, Siti had had opportunity to see what God was doing in the lives of Minang believers, including also God's two servants who were living with us. Siti considered them as her older brothers and we regarded both Yanwardi and Pak Timotius as part of our family. But Vera and I, had noticed that Siti looked lonesome and was longing for her older brother, sister, and friends at home in the US. She never complained and did her home schooling studies faithfully. But, we wanted to be sensitive to our daughter's needs.

During July 1996, we took Siti back to our home in the US. Vera and I stayed only a few weeks. After Siti settled in at home, we quickly returned to Padang to continue our tasks. It had been an answer to our prayers, when Tante Helen De Blouwe, an elderly friend from our church, volunteered to stay with Siti and Rehana while we were away. For Rehana, who then had graduated from California State University, Fullerton, it was the first school year of her teaching career and included her activities as Youth Director at our home-church LGD.

RESILIENCE... One year later in 1997, Vera and I continued regular activities in Indonesia. Our team members continued the work during our absence. This included also Spiritual Warfare teaching.

As from the beginning, after a group finished learning about Spiritual Warfare and if needed, we gave the option of deliverance and personal healing ministry *(pelapasan or pelayanan pribadi)*. Because of past involvement with occult practices, some showed personal spiritual struggles. We learned that sometimes, believers had still gone to the *dukun-dukun*, shamans, even after attending church as Christians. In ministering *pelepasan*, deliverance, we often experienced clear manifestations of evil.

After two years, the lease of our house at Batang Lembang ended. We moved to a house in the Parak Gadang neighborhood of Padang. The fact that the house was smaller did not lessen our enthusiasm. Yanwardi had married in October of 1997 and was living nearby with his wife. Two of our other team members, Pak Wasyu and Pak Timotius, continued living with us. Even in Parak Gadang our home was always open.

It was during this year there was considerable spiritual growth among those being discipled. With the increase of small groups, some who demonstrated spiritual maturity began helping us disciple other Minang believers (most often with *one-on-one* process). This was especially evident among the women.

Along with all the progress, misguided views and criticism from others arose about our work. It began slowly, but then serious differences of opinion began rising up regarding the purpose of our activities. This came especially from people who did not agree with the approach I was using. Ironically, those who whispered in the shadows did not reside in West Sumatra.

I suddenly faced assumptions that I was in West Sumatra because I looked for personal financial gain; when in actuality, my reason for remaining there, was to assist the Padang PKSB fellowship. Some saw no logic in what I was doing.

All misunderstandings and accusations proved again that when a door was open; the enemy (Satan) would enter into any situation. What saddened us most was that attacks were not only from the outside. These became a heavy burden for Vera and me to carry.

While I continued discipling, I refused to let continued murmuring interfere, or allow negative circumstances to hinder my way. God gave me a vision, and I had already begun seeing part of it come to fruition.

The ultimate *Penipu*, Deceiver–Satan, wanted to a make an instrument out of anyone possible to create division. This was confirmation that the devil as *Pemusnah*, the Destroyer, detested spiritual growth and strength, especially among the Minang believers. He knew exactly who to use for purpose of destruction.

I repeated continuously, that we needed to make sure the Lord Jesus ruled our lives from the throne of our hearts; and not allow human ego to rule. The Accuser, *Penuduh* of lies, tried using that form of deceit as weapons against the ministry and us. I knew I needed to endure whatever battle we daily faced. When 1997 was coming to its end, I was seventy years old and still learning life's lessons about obedience, tolerance and endurance.

> Only a life lived for others is a life worthwhile."
> Albert Einstein – Physicist

ENDURANCE… With circumstances as they were by mid-1998, my objective was to concentrate on the *quality* of faith of Minang following the Lord. It was my desire that when Minang people were spiritually born-again and accepted Christ as Savior, that they come to know Him more deeply through a personal understanding of God's Word. It made no sense to me, when the *quantity* was many but the quality of their faith remained shallow. Quantity in itself is not the only significant factor. That is the work of God and not ours. What is important is the quality of spiritual life in Christ's followers, to become faithful examples and witnesses who can be trusted.

Bringing people into the Kingdom of God was most important to me. By helping them understand the Biblical meaning of being spiritually born-again, I looked forward for them to see the quality of their spiritual lives change as they developed Fruit of the Spirit.

How it disappointed me, seeing Minang believers have no clear understanding or certainty about these things, let alone practice it. Yet most of them I talked to believed that because of the label *Orang Kristen,* a Christian they would go to Heaven. It always reminded me of what Christ said,

"I tell you the truth; no one can see the Kingdom of God unless he is born again."
John 3:3 NIV

For me this meant that after opening of our hearts for Christ and repentance, we received eternal life. Growing stronger spiritually by maturing Fruit of the Spirit and following God's commands was crucial.

How could we know the will and promises of God written in the *Kitab Suci,* Holy Book, if we did not learn? To be a born again Christian was not just a label. If we did not first correct our relationship with God, how could we understand and feel His power in our lives and prayers?

Through His Word, God also gave me wisdom about the Fruit of the Spirit, a reminder…

"You did not choose me, but I chose you
and appointed you to go and bear fruit – fruit that will last.
Then the Father will give you whatever
you ask in My name."
John 15:16 NIV

According to my understanding, the Fruit that God intended are love, joy, peace, patience, kindness, goodness, faithfulness, gentleness, and self-control, as mentioned in Galatians 5:22, 23.

Fruit of the Spirit, we developed with the help of the Holy Spirit who lives in us after being spiritually born again. Thus, according to my understanding, being a Christian meant that we ultimately must have these traits evident in our lives. I was optimistic that the example of love and patience given those taught in the groups would grow and they become examples themselves.

Like a sounding *beduk* – the drum that awakened a new dawn for me during childhood days – God's voice repeatedly echoed this in my heart. I was to teach them and make disciples, so that God Himself would eventually *let the Minang reach the Minang* and do so *one-on-one and more* in His timing.

"The Lord will fight for you,
and you shall hold your peace and remain at rest."
Exodus 14:14 AMP

CONTENDING EVENTS ... During our years in West Sumatra, 1998 became the most challenging as more disturbing situations developed. Included, was one about a Muslim girl brought to our house during March 1998. What followed that same year were extremely bizarre events. Media in Indonesia later publicized ludicrous versions.

Before coming to us, the girl convinced people of a local church about her alleged difficulty. She claimed she was to be chained, *di pasung*, by her father, a lecturer at the Islamic University in Bengkulu, because he discovered she became a Christian. Her story began *an unrelenting saga* in the lives of those who at that time had been willing to help her. The eventual aid given her sadly turned into life-shattering misfortune for people.

Those who created a drama to benefit their own objectives later generated perverted facts of what actually happened. The results advanced into legal proceedings, causing incarceration for three men.

Alleged charges also turned into claims about evangelization i.e. *Christianization of Minang people in West Sumatra*. Public opinion and interpretation about this added fuel to the fire, even though the girl was not even a Minang. Allegations of evangelizing this girl by force surrounded all this, although the girl herself requested help (from us) as a persecuted Christian.

Versions reported by mass media in West Sumatra and throughout Indonesia were from fragments gathered here and there. From this conclusions were made by both the Christian and non-Christian community – Indonesian and foreign alike.

Marking me, "the mysterious *Pendeta Willy*," Pastor Willy and my involvement; will always in itself remain controversial because of contrasting media interpretations. I state here that before and throughout the ensuing court proceedings following this bizarre case, I had constant communication with those involved whom I needed to interact with throughout that period.

During court proceedings the girl who had introduced herself to us as Defi, acknowledged identity of three additional names.

In our first meeting, I repeatedly touched on basic Islamic beliefs. I reminded her that the decision to become a Christian was blasphemous to Muslims causing her to become an *apostate,* a traitor to Islam. This usually resulted in very heavy punishment. When I used verses from the Quran regarding Jesus Christ, she seemed tense, sometimes appearing to differ with me. From her reaction, I already wondered how well she really understood Islam or even Christianity.

I was also not sure how much this girl really knew about the meaning of *having become a Christian* (as she had originally stated). I emphasized to her that the requirement, *syarat*, was not easy. I mentioned that repentance of sins and acknowledgement of accepting Jesus Christ as Lord and Savior was of utmost importance. As I spoke, a slightly unsettled expression had appeared on her face. I asked her if she had already done this. If not, was she ready for that? She answered "yes."

Before praying with her, I also clarified the difference between baptism and repentance. She received what I explained without hesitation. Everyone present followed in prayer as I placed my hand on her head. The girl verbally agreed.

Considering the claims of her story, I knew it was an enormous risk to help her, but I believed *faith without risk is not faith*. Several months after initially meeting her, those helping, enrolled her at school again in Padang. During that time, Defi lived with a family who had opened their home and let her stay with them. I had agreed that we would assist if needed. This I based on God's Word.

"If anyone has material possessions and sees his brother in need
but has no pity on him how can the love of God be in him?
….let us not love with words or tongue but with actions and in truth."
1 John 3:17, 18 NIV

My question to those who doubted our sincerity was this, "If there had been any harmful intentions (on our part), would we have enrolled her in a Padang school?"

Perhaps all this still raised questions among those who did not understand why we were willing to help the girl. I always remembered however, a message from the Apostle Paul to "share with God's people who are in need." (Romans 12:13 NIV)

DOING GOOD… Through the years we remained in Padang, others from the fellowship sometimes also received assistance during illness or hospitalization. Occasionally, we helped families living in unbearable conditions. One family in particular looked as if they lived in a *tempat kandang kambing*, a goat pen. We helped relocate these people to somewhat better shelters.

In short, those we saw in need received attention in whatever way we could. This did not mean that I was a financially well-to-do person, but simply a retired Minang of advanced years who enjoyed the blessings from God by sharing with others. For that same reason, I believed we could show our *love in action* through providing help to the girl, Defi, who claimed she needed it.

Perhaps there are those who thought I was too naïve and unwise. Nevertheless, in the love of God, that was not at all foolishness or naiveté. He wanted to use us as instruments of His love. Through many years God had shown His love to me when I had faced all kinds of difficulties.

I have tried walking my life journey, with the aim of doing all the work in love as shown in the verse from I Corinthians 16:14 – *do everything in love.* For me that meant sharing God's love not only in word or tongue but also in deeds and God's truth. I wanted to return goodness from what God had given to me.

I knew that helping others, included the girl who came to us that day in March of 1998. With the story, she told from the start, I was certain that meant our surrendering her totally to Almighty God who is all-powerful and who knows all. I thought from the beginning, that if her story was false and used only to draw aid from us or for other reasons, God alone sees everything. *Wallahu-alam!* – God knows best!

In June 1998, Vera and I went home to the US. During the early part of August, we returned to Padang. After settling back, we continued our usual activities. Soon after our return, several more troubling incidents happened.

I had immediately sensed there was a big change, even in those who were very close to us. It bothered me, and I wondered what could have happened during our absence. This became a period of much sadness for Vera and me.

My wife, also, very restless about what was happening around us; believed that any issues about Defi could endanger not only us, but also everyone who had been helping with her. Since we did not know about the possible negative developments that occurred while we were away, Vera also strongly believed (from the beginning) that we should not take any more risks in this particular instance. Between the two of us, she was the one who usually had further discernment of what was to come. Therefore, she constantly warned me to be careful.

Things had taken a serious turn when police came looking for the girl at her new school. The following morning after that incident, Defi came to our house brought by others. After discovering that she carried a knife under her clothing while at school, we asked why she feared for her safety. She said that former classmates were looking for her and intended physical harm.

After discussion with Defi, she had opportunity to choose; remaining in Padang or moving away to continue school in Malang (East Java). Even the principal of her school had notified us, of available help in this situation. Therefore, with all possibilities very carefully and clearly explained to her about school and living arrangements in Malang, Defi did not hesitate; immediately answering *"ya"* "yes," that she wanted to go.

Through the entire discussion, I saw Vera's expression while she looked at Defi. My wife, who had been quiet during the conversation, suddenly asked the girl in Indonesian, "Can you tell us the truth? Who was the person who first came to our house, and who came three days later?

Taken aback, noticeably looking uneasy by the very directness of the questions, Defi suddenly confessed to all present that, it was not she who came the first time, but her older sister Lia. In other words, the girl sitting before us, was after all not the girl we prayed for on that first Friday she came to the house.

Defi's answers that morning, established a clear picture of how long and how deliberately, both these girls plotted the deception. It really burdened my heart about them. They had been lying to all of us the entire time. What ensued in the following days would only complicate matters.

In due course, the deceitfulness spiraled completely out of control. Months later, after the girl's return to Padang and to her parents, all well intended actions became fuel for the blaze of their falsehoods. Ultimately, those who had tried helping *"the girl with diverse names"* would pay a severe high price.

Do not be afraid of them;
the Lord your God himself will fight for you.
Deuteronomy 3:22 NIV

PATHS TURN DIRECTION... Other destructive situations intensified in the months after our return from the US (early August 1998). Issues concerning the girl (although she had been returned to her parents), plus other influences increased disputes within the fellowship. Even while passing through this challenging and sad period, I carried on with teaching those who remained faithful.

Our team consisting of four at that time never stopped bringing God's Word forth. I was thankful for Pak Timotius and the other two-team members, Pak Wasyu and Pak Sumar (names changed), both young men from Java, who kept walking with me during those heartrending days. I knew the vision I had would continue finding its way, regardless of the circumstances or opinions of others.

In returning to my roots, I never imagined, having to experience treatment in the manner, we ultimately received. Everything surfacing was like dross needing refining. I considered what happened throughout 1998 as a turn of direction in my own life path. This, I too had to pass.

I remembered a message from the Lord Jesus in the gospel of Mark that became clear to me.

"And if any place will not welcome you or listen to you,
shake the dust of your feet when you leave,
as a testimony against them."
Mark 6:11 NIV

Although misunderstandings became "like a very sharp knife continually being sliced into me," I refused to allow it to hinder the reason why I was in West Sumatra. Considering how the Lord Jesus experienced abandonment by the disciples He loved, we could only pray for my *saudara-saudara sedaerah*, people of my area, to receive God's wisdom and spiritual strength. We especially prayed for those who murmured a lot, causing division but not having courage to face me openly. All through this incredibly sad period, difficult as it was, I made sure Vera and I stayed in the path of forgiving.

We planned going to Singapore toward the end of November 1998. As was routine, to secure our visas, we would stay there a few days then return to Padang. Careful with our finances, instead of going home for Christmas in the US; we decided to remain in Padang that year and travel to California at the end of February 1999.

Longtime friends Mitch and Radna Kohn had placed a large order of quilts during 1998. Initially the plan was for Marta N. to send that order to Denver, Colorado in the US. We learned if sent via a shipping company, the quilts would not reach Denver in time. During a phone conversation, our friends asked if we would be willing to bring their quilts to California before Christmas. Knowing that we already planned for our routine Singapore trip, they wanted to provide airline tickets from Singapore to Los Angeles (as a Christmas gift) so we could see our family. Vera and I, grateful for the offer, thanked God that we could go home to the US after all.

On Sunday morning November 28, 1998 in a downpour of heavy rain, we left Padang; intending to return from California right after Christmas. Arriving in Singapore, we waited at Changi airport for a flight that same afternoon. This time our arrival at Los Angeles LAX was even more welcoming than our past homecomings.

Following a quiet Christmas day at home, a disturbing telephone call reached us from West Sumatra. The news was about the girl with the conflicting story. Since she returned to her family four months earlier, we had not heard any news about her. Shocking information emerged regarding accusations from her. Why she waited months before making the accusations public, will always remain a mystery to me

There were charges of kidnapping and rape. Allegedly, Christians committed this type of crime toward young Muslim girls in West Sumatra (i.e. gathering and then forcing them to become Christian).

I was told rumors had spread about *a pastor* (i.e. me) living in the Parak Gadang neighborhood who was responsible for all these actions. Reportedly, the Governor of West Sumatra had summoned local religious leaders, police, and even some from the armed forces to an emergency meeting to help with investigation of this case, and hoping to prevent a *SARA*, riot.

I was also warned that in an attempt to rouse the public, it was broadcast in mosques throughout West Sumatra that Christians were distributing money in the amounts of one million Rupiah's (equivalent to US $100.00 at that time) to people willing to leave the Muslim religion. I supposedly was the culprit pastor distributing this money.

I felt sad about the anguish experienced by those and their families, who months earlier, with kindness had agreed to help this girl. When news reached me later that the situation was worsening, I had already planned returning to Padang with Vera. But two of the men, personally expressed to me that I should not return to Padang. Trusting their judgment, I agreed to wait.

How shocked I was when an even wider range of allegations emerged. Since I supposedly was the mastermind, I then became the target of Muslim articles and gossip tabloids. These accused me of hiding in the US because I feared apprehension by authorities and a possible prison sentence.

My only response regarding the accusations was that I came from a family that never feared prison. In fact, we experienced imprisonment for the beliefs we held, like when arrest came for me during the Indonesian

Revolution. Incarceration by the Dutch was far worse than anything I would have faced in my older age. Therefore, to all who judged me, I would only express ...*"each of us will eventually give an account of himself to God."* (Romans 14:12 NIV)

# 21

# SUMATRAN WARRIOR'S HOPE

*The word hope I take for faith; and indeed,*
*hope is nothing else but the constancy of faith.*
John Calvin

Still advised to remain in the US, and awaiting word about (what became known as) "the Wawah Case," I knew I could no longer stay silent. As my first effort, I sent a personal letter to an old friend, Dorojatun Kuncoro Yakti, who during June of 1999 was Indonesian Ambassador to the United States in Washington D.C.

Vera and I continued *a writing campaign* to organizations worldwide we felt needed awareness about the case and the three men sentenced to prison. We contacted human rights and faith based organizations including also American officials whom we believed would give attention to this case. We were especially thankful to Congressman Joseph Pitts of Pennsylvania who sent a letter (to then) Indonesian President Bacharuddin Jusuf Habibie. Congressman Pitts' Washington DC office contacted me and then sent copies of that same letter to the Governor of West Sumatra, the Chief of Regional Police, the District Attorney, and Attorney General.

While the case was still in court, media tabloids continued a "sensationalism feast" by reporting exaggerations of events including about me. Many versions appeared about who I was, or was not.

When told, that the Indonesian authorities wanted to know my whereabouts, I immediately complied by providing all requested information. I waited for a reply, but there was no further development. I then wrote a formal letter to the Governor of West Sumatra, sending copies to other officials. There never were any follow-ups at all from any Indonesian authorities.

Having returned to my *tanah air*, land of birth, and seeing the suffering of those neglected; I helped people because I remembered the teaching of Christ, which instructed us to help, defend, and love those in need.

Having assisted the girl, I knew as Defi (who initially seemed sincere of heart and told that incredibly disturbing story); I was still glad that we showed our *love with action* to help her. I only know God sees and judges the heart.

Only God knows the depth of truth or deceit in this particularly sad saga. The girl with her own words of confession, revealed to us the deceit she committed.

I have wondered and prayed about the young woman who became the momentary star of this drama. How chained is her conscience today? How imprisoned are the souls of these two sisters Lia and Defi? Only eternity will tell.

I believe that all this that happened, was a personal challenge for me to keep my faith strengthened. I remembered what Christ said in the Word which encouraged me,

"If the world hates you, keep in mind that it hated me first."
John 15:18 NIV

I could only pray and forgive those with judgmental hearts against me. All who assumed I fled to America should first have investigated more about me. Had we intended not to return to Padang, we would have taken all our personal belongings with us.

Since my first trip in 1990 and all the ones in the following years, I returned to West Sumatra with hope of also going back to my village as often as possible. I wanted to enjoy the later portion of my life in my home country that I loved and fought for in my youth.

When I first left Indonesia in 1949, it was, to not only become a merchant marine and sail without limits. But I was very optimistic with high hopes for my life. Throughout my many years abroad, I had continually represented Indonesia. I never forgot the heritage I came from.

I also never forgot what I lived for during my younger years, as mentioned in earlier pages.

At this point, writing this memoir and being more than eighty years old, I cannot express any regret for the good we did for others.

Don't you know that day dawns after night,
showers displace drought,
and spring and summer follow winters?
Then, have hope!
Hope forever, for God will not fail you!
Charles Spurgeon

NEW DAY DAWNS… In 1999, I did not go to Padang. Instead, I waited for news from those initially telling me to stay away. I was thankful our daughter Rehana travelled to Padang. Together with our friends, Pastor Jeff Kerkhoff, his wife and Wilma Pattinama, Rehana visited with the three incarcerated men and witnessed their suffering. The day she saw them they were inside an enclosed cage-like area with other prisoners at the Padang police headquarters. A fire had destroyed a portion of Muara prison.

When Rehana came home, she immediately told us about her desire of returning to Indonesia. Since finally meeting with those whom she had heard much about from us, her heart opened. I think that having been in Padang, she understood why the people from my birthplace were so important to me.

Considering the circumstances, our response was that if it were in God's will for Rehana to return and stay in Indonesia, then God would secure good employment and a safe place for her there. We discussed the various possibilities. She insisted on looking for a job herself, reasoning that if God wanted her in Indonesia, He would open the door for her.

Rehana received a teaching position, as a foreign (American) instructor at *Sekolah Pelita Harapan*, SPH (Light of Hope School). Leaving her career in the US our daughter returned to Indonesia in time for the new school year.

After settling into her Karawaci apartment provided for foreign instructors by the school, she began teaching the 2000 school year. Through new doors opened by the Lord, Rehana with enthusiasm also took opportunity for ministry. She worked and stayed in Indonesia for three years from 2000 through 2003.

Until then, I had remained in the US only because of people involved in the case. God knew my desire to continue with what we established in West Sumatra. During this period of delays, He repeatedly demonstrated to us that He is God who never fails those who belong to Him and love Him with all their hearts and souls.

I received communication from two of the men sentenced and other friends in West Sumatra, informing me it was really best to remain in the US. Thus, I had also waited throughout the year of 1999. Attacks of criticism and blame came from the Muslim community receiving accounts of the case through media. Condemnation also landed through Christians who publicly distanced themselves from me; yet voiced opinions partly due to my silence.

> "The fear of human opinion disables;
> Trusting in God protects you from that.
> Proverbs 29:25 MSG

In 2000, our oldest daughter was already teaching in Indonesia. After many consultations with the people who were constantly praying with us, I left Los Angeles, arriving in Jakarta on August 15, 2000. In Indonesia, I only notified those who needed to know that I was there. I was also able to meet with friends and other close connections.

Time spent with our *anak-anak rohani*, spiritual children, (then attending SETIA Seminary) was a blessing for me. Travelling with me, Rehana was also finally meeting the other people close to us in Padang. Until then, she had only known their names.

While our daughter lived in Indonesia, she helped oversee progress of the students studying at SETIA and the work in Padang still carried on by our remaining team there.

*Note: Through what became a period of five years, the Minang students received full scholarship support from Jabez Minang Outreach. JMO is our non-profit (faith based) organization in the US, which we officially established for our West Sumatra outreach.*

For me this particular visit to Indonesia was also an opportunity to meet with a renowned attorney regarding the case and discuss with him steps I should be taking legally. Although we had given financially for attorney fees while the case was in court, this consultation gave me more personal encouragement because I finally had a chance to discuss the legal aspect (in Indonesia) binding me in this case.

This meeting took place on September 18, 2000 in Jakarta. The attorney told me he could hardly believe that a younger brother of Prof. Dr. Hamka would become a Christian. He admitted that upon first hearing about the case, he believed all fault and errors lay on our side. That day, after hearing from me, he understood and promised to support our efforts. I told him that whatever personal consequences there would be, I was prepared. He gave me advice to follow.

Even after this consultation, I knew it would not change any decisions made by the Indonesian court system but I knew I finally had opportunity to seek my own legal counsel. I stayed in Indonesia for six weeks and then left Rehana in Karawaci to return home to the US.

Vera and I stayed in California as her health also worsened. Suffering with severe Arthritis, she needed a right Hip Replacement surgery. Actually, my wife had physically suffered much while we were in West Sumatra. As her condition worsened, we prayed with others for a miracle regarding Vera's need for medical insurance. Then, God who always listened, answered us. Through a miracle of God using His people, Vera received the necessary approval and health insurance.

Although I had been in Indonesia during August and September of 2000, I returned to Jakarta six months later for our SETIA Seminary students. I landed there on March 6, 2001.

During this trip, I also planned returning to Padang because I wanted to meet again with the three incarcerated men and their families. Even two years later, provoking articles about the case still appeared in the media. This included also articles from my brother Hamka's children publicly denying any relation with me.

By ship, I travelled to Padang with one of our seminary students. We left Jakarta March 15th believing that everything would go smoothly while we were there. My being onboard brought back sad memories of last seeing my mother at Teluk Bayur Harbor when I went with my father into exile as a youth.

After our arrival, we were immediately able to go inside the prison and later spent time with the families. I made certain that any outsiders who did not need to know about my presence in West Sumatra remained uninformed.

By March 20th I returned to Jakarta, and three days later having accomplished what I needed to do, I quietly left Indonesia for Singapore to see my daughter on my way home. Rehana injured her knee at her school SPH and had surgery. We planned to meet after I went to West Sumatra. She was still in physical therapy but released from the hospital. I also met with the Singapore church supporting our work.

I went home to California on March 25th where Vera waited for me. She was ready for her Hip Replacement surgery, which was scheduled a week after my return. The surgery was successful. Although her recovery was not easy, it was a relief to see my wife improving. The excruciating pain she had suffered for too long was gone. Although the physical therapy she received took several months, I saw my wife get better and was encouraged.

A few months later, there were developments in Indonesia for which I needed to return on a third trip. Leaving Los Angeles once again on September 8, 2001, I stayed with Rehana while in Jakarta. She also was still healing from her surgery a few months earlier and would be starting with her second school year teaching at SPH. It was while I was in Karawaci, I learned about the horrific attack of the World Trade Center in New York on September 11th (9/11)

After meetings in Jakarta and being with our four SETIA Seminary students there, I was again also able to go to Padang. This time I went together with my daughter and some friends. Once in Padang, I received opportunity again to see the three incarcerated men. How grateful I was that God answered our prayers and plans for visiting each time. I was glad seeing them, as all three seemed in good health.

Although confined inside walls, a weekly worship service held at the prison raised their spirits. Inside the compound, the prison authorities provided a building for these services. The men shared with me also, how God was using them to minister to other prisoners. One of them worked as a carpenter making furniture.

Remains of the orchid nursery (project) which we planted at Parak Gadang during 1997, had somehow been moved to the prison and there replanted and looked after by other prisoners. This was my third time being back after the trial. Again, outsiders who did not need to know about my presence had no awareness I was there.

Rehana and I flew back to Jakarta, but before I returned to California, an American friend of mine, a pastor in the city asked me to meet a young Muslim man, already reached out to by a member of his church. Since my friend had difficulty explaining the Holy Trinity to the young Muslim, he hoped I could help explain from the viewpoint a Muslim could more easily grasp.

…See, I have placed before you an open door that no one can shut. I know that you have little strength, yet you have kept my word and not denied my name.
Revelation 3:8 NIV

OPEN DOOR… With my pastor friend, I went to a coffee shop to meet Andi (name changed) who wanted to know about Christianity. It did not take long for the young man to ask me about what was on his mind. I welcomed all his questions because I knew his desire to hear my explanations and receive some answers from me. While listening, I remembered how I also had the same type of questions before accepting Christ as my Lord and Savior.

I first explained to Andi that when God created the universe He used *Firman* – His Word. Thus, *Firman* – the Word – is God.

In the beginning was the Word, and the Word was with God, and the Word was God.
John 1:1 NIV

I told him that in my understanding the term *Firman Pencipta* – the Word, is God the Father, the *Creator*. With God the Father, (as His children) we did not have permission to come face to face with Him. An example was Moses (whom Andi as a Muslim understood to be one of the Prophets). When meeting with God at the burning bush, Moses could not come near to God to look at His face. The place where Moses was standing was holy ground because of God's presence. Therefore, Moses covered his face to show His fear of looking at God (Exodus 3:5, 6). After I explained this to Andi, his attention remained focused on every word I spoke.

I shared with him about the relationship of Jesus Christ, *Isa Almasih,* with God the Creator. I said that God is Love as is written in I John 4:9. So how could God show His Love when we were not allowed to even look at Him?

This is how God showed His love among us:
He sent his one and only Son into the world
that we might live through him.
I John 4:9 NIV

I told Andi that because of His Love for us God sent His Son. I then continued that as I understood it, Jesus Christ, *Isa Almasih,* is the WORD, *Firman,* who lives *with* us and that He (Jesus Christ) is also *one part* of the Creator and is always together with God the Father. He is the Savior sent by God the Father to show His Love to us. For this reason, He (Jesus Christ) sacrificed Himself on the cross as the Redeemer of sins, *Penebus dosa-dosa,* who saves us from our sins.

Andi and my pastor friend continued listening to my explanation regarding who the Holy Spirit, *Roh Kudus,* is. I said that before Christ was crucified, He told His disciples that He asked the Father to give us (mankind), a Helper that is the *Roh Kebenaran* -- Spirit of Truth -- who is always with us and lives within us, to continue applying the work of Christ's Salvation. This means that He, *Isa Almasih* (Jesus Christ), is the WORD who through *His Holy Spirit lives in us.*

When God was creating man He said, "Let *us* make man in *our* image, in *our* likeness (Genesis 1:26 NIV). God did not say the word *I* but expressed *us* or *our.* I continued, "That is the reason why, in my perception, when God created this universe, all three parts of this *Firman* – the Word – each had their own role."

In order to clarify things better to this young man, as to *why* it is that *we need* Christ in our lives, I thought it was better for me to show him an illustration. I took a napkin from the table and sketched a deep chasm, which I told Andi we needed to cross. That chasm I told him represented the separation between God and us. Trying to cross this chasm with only our faithfulness or just our goodness is not possible. We must have *a bridge to cross* in order to reach God waiting for us.

I continued drawing on the napkin, explaining that we needed a bridge to go across to the other side where God awaits us. This bridge is Christ, who sacrificed Himself to save us. I said to Andi, "This is what is called the *Jembatan Kehidupan*, Bridge of Life, and is *the way* we can reach across to *eternal life* promised by Christ by way of our crossing this bridge."

At this point Andi did not take his eyes from me while I explained how we all have sinned and that the payment of our sins is death. I paused for a moment and then told the young man, "But God showed His Love to us because of Christ's sacrifice on the cross when we were still in sin. Because of that, we should realize and repent so our sins are wiped away. I went on to say that because of God's grace, we are saved by faith.

I also told Andi that before I accepted Christ as my Lord and Savior, I wanted to learn about the Word of God in the Bible by myself. I told him also how I had tried to read the Bible when I was much younger and then tried to use just my intellect. However, at that time it was very difficult for me to concentrate on anything I read in those pages of the Bible. I only liked to read the stories in the Old Testament because there were many accounts about the prophets I knew about as mentioned also in the Quran as well. I shared with Andi that every time I attempted reading the Bible, especially the New Testament, *Injil*, it was very difficult for me to accept in my mind what was written. It just did not attract my heart and was not interesting to me. In fact, I thought it was boring. Then later I discovered the reason why I did not understand the Bible was that the Holy Spirit, who would teach me, was not yet inside me.

I went on to say that after I accepted Christ, I finally came to understand the deep purposes of God's promises in His Word. I became very diligent in reading and learning what was in the Bible until I desired to attend seminary.

Before we finished our conversation, Andi asked me if he could take the napkin with the chasm illustration drawn on it. I told him that I would give it to him with pleasure. Following this, the three of us quietly prayed together.

A few days after meeting with my young Muslim friend, I left Jakarta for home in the US. While I was in the plane, I thought about my discussion with Andi. I was remembering again, how difficult it was for me while still a Muslim to accept the concept of the Trinity.

While I was crossing the wide ocean, I had a lot of time to think and pray for Andi. It was my hope that the Holy Spirit would touch Andi's heart, and open the door for others like him, looking for answers from God.

Reflecting about the time I spent with this young man, I also had opportunity to think about attacks I received through the years from people who did not like me since I became a Christian. Only God could see into the hearts of all men; and only He knew their motivations, leading them to seek either a life of darkness or light.

Whatever public opinion was about me, especially regarding the (Defi) case, and even judgment from others who misunderstood the direction of my life since becoming a Christian in 1981, I would continue praying for them all.

God's Word had given me strength during all this. I really believed in the scriptures, that God Himself would eventually decide if I am guilty or not. No one should be too quick in judging if a person is wrong or not because the time is not here yet. We need to wait until the Lord comes. He will open all secrets hidden in the dark. He is the one to expose all motives in the hearts of men (from 1 Corinthians 4:3-5 paraphrased).

I had been very thankful for the Word of God. It reassured me that each person would receive from Him the praise deserved. This was the greatest comfort, because only God knew all my desires.

For this reason, my confidence remains in the Lord alone, since He has known the full plan for me. He is the one who always faithfully walked before me or beside me while I stepped through my passages of life…

# 22

# SUMATRAN WARRIOR
# EVENING SHADOWS

"At evening time, being thankful and enjoying God's blessings."
A.W.K. Amrullah ~ from personal journal

He has made everything beautiful in its time.
He has also set eternity in the hearts of men...
Ecclesiastes 3:11 NIV

Year after year, I have felt God's protection because that is the assurance He promised. I am thankful for all the challenges of unique experiences that came with each new day. Anytime God wants to call me to Himself and Heaven, I am prepared. I know I have already lived and done all that He requires from His people. I am grateful for all the warnings the Lord gave me from His Word, which have been the source of absolute guidance for me. I am content knowing that the Holy Spirit of God has had His way in me because all I desire is to hear the Lord Jesus say, *"Well done, good and faithful servant!"*

I hoped to teach all my *anak-anak Rohani,* Spiritual children, (who have known me personally, or even those who do not), that they too can grow to have a strong personal relationship with Christ and solid foundation with God who created them. With intercession through Christ as their Lord, they will bloom to become a light and blessing for the people around them.

As God's children, we do not have to memorize all kinds of human teachings. When we restore our relationship with God, the Holy Spirit will lead us in anything we pray about and have to do in pleasing God's heart.

But we personally must know the Lord Jesus Christ. Then we are able to prove, that He indeed is the Living God who listens to every prayer from deep within our hearts.

It is very important to me to remind God's children to be fully aware that God's love for humanity is great. In addition, because His love is great, He gave to us His one and only Son Jesus Christ, so that whoever believes in Him shall not ever perish but have eternal life. We must enjoy God's great love and spread it to everyone we meet.

RE-UNION WITH MY CLOSE FRIEND…Although I had traveled through oceans of time and roads of life for decades, my heart always longed knowing about new developments in Indonesia; even after all the years of living in the United States,

One day while reading an Indonesian magazine *Indonesia Media* (published in the US), an article caught my attention. Written by Sobron Aidit, he shared about his experiences abroad. After requesting and receiving contact information from the magazine, I immediately e-mailed Sobron (who had been living in France); asking about his older brother Murad Aidit, with whom I had been very close friends since we were fifteen years old.

As it turned out, Sobron responded immediately giving me his brother's address and telephone number in Indonesia. At first, because it had been such a long time since Murad and I had any contact, as well as knowing about his poor health condition from when he was young, I would not have been surprised if the reply was that my friend had already passed away. Therefore, I was very happy to receive the good news that Murad was still alive.

I immediately telephoned Murad in Jakarta. Hearing his voice, I was thrilled, since we had parted ways about fifty-eight years ago. It was unbelievable to both of us that God had given us opportunity to talk with each other again and that it seemed as if no time had passed. We were laughing so hard with each other, just as we had those many years ago when we were eighteen-year-old youths.

In our conversation, we were both also very amazed to think how God had still given us time to hear from each other after almost six decades. We laughed loudly, reminiscing about situations of before when we were still very young and mentioning our hilarious behavior along with it. We also talked about how our lives had experienced much tragedy that forced us since then to grow up faster and more daringly. After talking to my old friend for about an hour during that first phone call, I promised Murad that I would come visit him as soon as I went to Indonesia again. (Our last communication before this telephone conversation had been a letter from Murad, which I still held on to since receiving it in San Francisco during 1961).

In 2005, our daughter Rehana was ready to return to Indonesia. I entrusted a letter with her to bring to my friend Murad Aidit. I was not able to come along because of health issues with my heart; making it impossible for me to travel at that time. I later heard from Rehana that meeting with Murad was emotional. He was overjoyed finally meeting one of my children. His message to me was that before he dies he wished to see me first.

During March of 2006, I underwent a procedure for insertion of a Pacemaker for my heart. By December of that same year, I was able to go to Indonesia. I traveled to Jakarta on the same flight with Roy and Louise van Broekhuizen, who were with Vera and me during 1994 in West Sumatra. Even though the plan was for me to travel to Padang again, it was most important for me to meet with my old friend first whom I always remembered and loved.

My reunion with Murad was also very emotional as we realized how God had still given us long life to experience seeing each other again. When I arrived, we embraced each other for a long time. I later asked Murad to stay with me at my hotel so we could have more time to share together, especially the nostalgic stories we had lived through.

In our talking, Murad told me about his life and about his experience in prison while exiled to Buru Island for fourteen years. He also complained that we used our lives searching for the meaning of existence. Murad had also spent time in Russia to study the philosophy of Communism. He told me how through the years he learned a lot but never found what he really desired. Listening to Murad's complaints about life's disappointments, I felt for him. Hearing about the frustrations and letdowns he had experienced really touched me. Soon he began talking about religion and at that point, I knew, I was just to listen to him first.

That night at the hotel, Murad continued telling me about insights to life that he was still looking for. He mentioned how he also traveled the road of becoming a *Haji*, i.e. one who within Islam has made the pilgrimage to Mecca. Besides all the difficulties he underwent through the years, Murad also shared about the obstacles during 1996 in order for him to go on the pilgrimage as a Muslim, since he was actually not supposed to leave Indonesia. At the time, he also wanted to understand the philosophy and deeper meaning of being a *Haji*. Murad went on to say that once he reached Mecca, "I stared at the *Ka'bah*, (Muslim's shrine) for a long time. But I still did not get the answer to my questions that bothered my thoughts."

While I listened closely and silently prayed, Murad continued telling me, "As you know when I was in Jakarta during our younger days, I always liked following friends to attend the religious services at the Catholic Cathedral, or Protestant churches. But at that time I still had not received the answer to what I was searching for." Murad kept talking, "But life kept moving on, not waiting for us and what we hoped for; then we too followed the direction and path of aging." After that Murad said, "It was at this point I was thinking, what is the success of our lives?" He continued pouring out his sorrowful lamenting, "I can clearly answer, that my life is not a success like I wanted it to be. However, that does not mean we have not contributed anything in this world. We can let others evaluate that."

It was interesting for me to hear the mournful expressions of my dear friend and his views about his life. I realized in thinking back on my own life, that no matter what my plans might have been at one time (i.e. to be a rich man in many worldly ways), I too had been seeking contentment with God for many years. I appreciated that in His mercy, God had given me the greatest spiritual freedom and wealth possible in this world through the Lord Jesus Christ for all eternity.

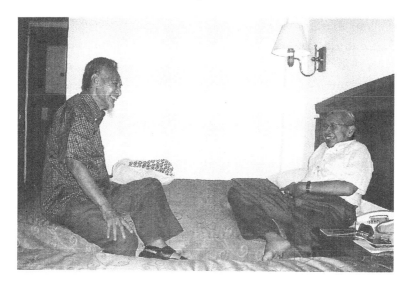

That night Murad and I continued for hours wandering through the hallways of times in our lives. We had a chance to laugh and cry together regarding the direction and turns of our paths, which each had followed. It was here at one of the turns of our stories I used the opportunity to tell my friend about the goodness of Christ, *Isa Almasih*, in my life. As I shared my testimony, Murad listened intently and then told me that he too wanted to experience that same encounter like me.

Before we rested that night, Murad and I prayed together first and I asked the Holy Spirit to touch the heart of my faithful friend so that he also would find what he had been searching for all his life.

"Even if we persuade only a few,
we shall obtain very great rewards,
for, like good laborers, we shall receive
recompense from the Master."
Justin Martyr

NOTHING HOPELESS... After our reunion of December 2006, I continued telephoning and writing Murad regularly. This I had already begun doing earlier that year. With each phone call, it was as if time never passed. We always laughed rowdily remembering our youth, even though some of our conversations turned rather serious. In the pages of this book, I included my last letter to Murad Aidit, which I sent on March 13, 2007. This was three months before I would come to Indonesia again. When I wrote this letter, Murad was in failing health and just released from the hospital.

*Note: For non-believer's reading my story, it is my hope at this time, that every person reading the contents of the letter will meditate upon its message while praying to God, for an open heart, wisdom, and that He shows Jalan yang Benar, the Way of Truth. (From: Author)*

(Translation from Indonesian language)

March 13, 2007


My beloved friend Murad,

How happy I was to hear your voice, especially because you have started to laugh again although your body is still weak. It means that your enthusiasm is still burning. I am so sure that we will meet again any place that God shows us. We will be together again to enjoy (eternal life) if we really believe in faith. The Bible expresses that "Faith is being sure of what we hope for and certain of what we do not see... And without faith it is impossible to please God, because anyone who comes to Him must believe that He exists and that He rewards those who earnestly seek him" Hebrews11:1, 6 NIV.

You also know how my life's journey has been. I was raised and taught to become a Godly person and followed the best I could. But I thought it over and asked myself the question, "Is it enough to apply only rituals, which were taught to us for gathering merits to go to heaven?" I used to be so worried that later on the last day, these things are weighed and the scale shows the weight of sin is heavier than the good deeds.

I especially wondered, how we have to cross the bridge that I have known about from before, called *siratalmustaqim*, which will be very narrow and thin; as thin as a single strand of hair split in seven parts. Then once we are buried, the angel of death will wake us up with a whip once the people attending our funeral will have left (seven steps away from our grave). When I was little, I was always afraid of death...

After I learned from the Bible, I realized that all humankind are sinners, none of us are holy. We cannot save ourselves. Because of God's grace, we are saved by faith and not because of the result of our works. So, nobody can boast about this. The wages of sin is death and hell, but God's gift is eternal life in Christ Jesus – *Isa Almasih*.

In other words Murad, we can receive what we do not deserve. God is Holy and just, and He must punish sin, yet He loves us and has provided forgiveness of our sin. Jesus said, "I am the way and the truth and the life... No one comes to the Father except through me."

Since we were small, we were taught to say, *"Bismillahirrahmanirrahim"* (In the name of Allah, most Gracious and Most Merciful) every time we do something. All those times we were still looking for God who is Gracious and Merciful. I found a Word of God (scripture) which said, *"You will seek me and find me when you seek me with all your heart"* Jeremiah 29:13 NIV.

At the beginning, I did not understand the purpose of God letting Jesus be crucified. The answer I found in the Gospel of John 3:16 NIV, *"For God so loved the world that he gave his one and only Son, that whoever believes in him shall not perish but have eternal life."*

Before, when I heard about the "son of God," I considered it was degrading God's name. But I learned that all who accepted Him, to them He gives the authority of becoming sons of God, those who believe in His Name, children born not of natural descent, nor of human decision or a husband's will, but born of God. If we think about it, what is wrong if we too are called "son of God," yet we were allowed to be called "son of Indonesia" or "son of America," etc.

Murad, for this we are never too late. I began to realize and repented after my age had reached fifty-four years old. Jesus Christ said, *"I tell you the truth, no one can see the kingdom of God unless he is born again"* John 3:3 NIV. The apostle Paul also said, in his epistle of Romans 10:9 NIV that if you confess with your mouth, "Jesus is Lord" and believe in your heart that God raised him from the dead you will be saved.

Perhaps, it seemed that I was trying to give you a sermon to persuade you to join the Christian "religion." My purpose is only to relay the message of the good news, which we can receive as a gift from God so that we can have a close relationship with Him.

What's more, I would be rejoicing if we could see each other again in heaven. If you are able to accept this and make it worthy of consideration… the requirement is only through personal repentance of sin with a prayer like this to God, "Lord Jesus, I believe that You are the Son of God and that You died on the cross, and were raised from the dead. I know I have sinned and need your forgiveness. I turn from my sins and receive you as my Savior and Lord. Thank You for saving me."

Murad, you are more than my own brother to me… that is the reason why I dare to give you this message. I would not be able to help with other things besides praying for you day and night. May God always bless you and your family.

From your faithful friend,
Wadud


I sent this letter through our fellow co-worker Pak Timotius to bring personally to Murad. I had prayed with Pak Timotius over the phone before he left for Depok to see my dear friend Murad. According to Pak Timotius, when he handed the letter to Murad, his condition was so weak that he could not raise himself up from his bed, nor could he read my letter. He asked Pak Timotius to read it to him. Murad listened intently and paid careful attention to my life testimony since he also knew my circumstances from the past.

After reading of my letter, Murad took the letter from Pak Timotius and put it to his chest, saying, "Wadud is my good friend from when we were small. But even though we had separated on different paths…now we met again." Murad went on speaking, "I want to also find, that which Wadud has found." He then informed Pak Timotius that he would also like to do same thing I did.

Murad told Pak Timotius, "I was looking for God everywhere, even to the center of Moscow and Mecca. I learned from many books comparing so many religions in the world, but I never found God. After I saw and listened to Wadud's life story I was moved by it, and it convinced me in my heart that God really exists and is living."

When asked by Pak Timotius if he realized that he was a sinner and was ready to open his heart to receive Jesus Christ as his Lord and Savior, Murad replied, *"saya sedia"* – "I am ready." Pak Timotius, representing me, led Murad in prayer asking God for forgiveness and opening his heart to accept the Lord Jesus as his Lord and Savior. At that moment, Murad's spiritual condition was changed and our friendship was not only to be on this earth.

As part of the follow-up, Pak Timotius and some other friends visited Murad, at least once a week in the months there after. They would share small bits of God's Word with him and let him reminisce about our years together as youths. Each visit, they saw my friend get stronger both physically and spiritually. Speaking over the phone, Murad told me he was very happy that God's servants often came to see him.

God's Word says there's no hopeless situation…
Our hope is the anchor of our soul,
…the confident hope of Jesus Christ's return!
Donald Baker and Emery Nester

SOUL'S ANCHOR OF HOPE… I planned returning to Indonesia in June of 2007, however, not alone. This became another witness of God hearing and answering our prayers. Vera was able to travel with me to Padang after again experiencing additional physical difficulties.

Three years earlier, in May of 2004, doctors were certain that because of declining health, my wife would not live much longer. Vera's prognosis then was bleak. Diagnosed with *Cardiomyopathy* (a weak left ventricle of the heart), she was informed that her life expectancy (statistically) would reach only two and a half more years *at most*. It was a shock to our family but especially to my wife. When this happened, she was very active with me, teaching small groups. We also continued the work in West Sumatra, and she had her own undertakings. Her cardiologist strongly suggested that she immediately stop all her activities.

At the beginning of 2007 after much prayer, Vera again asked her cardiologist (a believer), if she could travel to West Sumatra. He understood her hopes although previously having advised against this. However, after results of a variety of tests, Vera was told, "If you want to go to Indonesia, now is the time, but only shortly." With a supply of many medications and more prayers, she was able to leave with me.

I was thankful my wife had this opportunity and strength from God to visit her *anak-anak Rohani*, Spiritual children in Indonesia, especially those in West Sumatra. Rehana and a group of our friends from Los Angeles and Jakarta came with us to meet my beloved Minang people and see beautiful *Ranah Minang...* the one place on earth, always etched in my heart and never forgotten.

At that time, I did not think much about already having reached the age of eighty years. Although I realized that physically, I was not as strong like when I first returned to West Sumatra during 1980, I did not feel my own health would be a problem on this trip.

A week after seminar-style meetings with the SETIA graduates and others, plus ministering to individuals needing *pelayanan pribadi,* personal deliverance ministry, I became ill from exhaustion. By the end of July, following the three weeks stay in West Sumatra, we still had to return to Jakarta before traveling back to the US. At that point, I did not feel physically fit.

I especially had not wanted to miss meeting with Murad while in Jakarta. His wife and their youngest son brought him to our hotel so that Murad could again spend some time with me. Just like my previous visit in 2006, we spent hours talking about our nostalgic tales of youth. For us, it still seemed as if no years had passed by.

During that second re-union July of 2007, Murad had already become a follower of Jesus Christ. How happy we were having another chance to share our feelings with each other that last time. I did not forget expressing to Murad how thankful I was that God had given me another opportunity to see my old-time friend whom I loved. During the last night, knowing we would meet each other again in heaven, we both were especially joyful. I told Murad that between the two of us, whomever God called first *ke rahmat Allah,* to God's grace, would wait for the other in heaven.

We had arranged for Murad to return home in Depok the following afternoon. I lastly told my friend, "We will see each other in heaven." With certainty, I sensed this deep within my spirit.

*Note: That was the last time we saw each other here on earth. God called Murad Aidit home to heaven the following year, on March 29, 2008. He was over eighty years old. (From: Author)*

Although I knew, I was not well enough; we had to return to the US the following day. After praying with the group before leaving the hotel, Vera suddenly expressed to everyone her burden about our flying home. She said that as we prayed she knew that Rehana needed to go with us on the flight (rather than a later date as originally planned). Unwavering, my wife said that it was an urgent warning from God. So together with Rehana we made the last minute decision for her to leave with us.

While driving to the airport and arranging flight changes, seating for Rehana was available on our flights to Singapore and the US. Physically feeling worse, I thought that once we were on the final flight home I could relax and rest. When we left Singapore, I began feeling worse with nausea and weakness.

While experiencing the physical trauma in-flight, fortunately a doctor was onboard who examined me and then had communication with an American hospital. After administering oxygen and emergency care, they moved me to Business Class, where I could lie down while receiving help for remainder of the flight (without diverting).

Finally reaching LAX, an emergency medical team awaited us. Our other children and friends (notified by Rehana) were also at the airport. I felt very weak, but after landing, my blood pressure improved. Against

Vera's wishes, I chose to go home. A few days later however, I required hospitalization. I eventually recovered from the physical setback. Although I remained weak in body, the Lord very much strengthened my spirit.

That 2007 trip to Indonesia was to be the last time I met with our Minang spiritual children. During November of that same year, Satan blatantly attempted destroying our ministry's outreach in West Sumatra. However, God continued His own plan. I do know that in all this, I gave my very best effort in preparing His new servants in the time allotted me.

I knew that the portion of the task given me, i.e. make disciples and prepare Minang servant-leaders, had entered into completion phase. I foresaw that in coming years, my vision would abound. With this, I meant that a new harvest would flourish for God's Kingdom in Ranah Minang through countless others.

After returning from that last trip, I accepted the fact, that it was time to start preparing the draft of this memoir. I also realized, that would I have shared about my life journey too soon, I would not have been able to include my beloved friend Murad Aidit's, *victory story*. God indeed knew the "full scope" of my life's picture – to every smallest detail. I am glad I waited on His timing for the writing of this book.

# 23

# SUMATRAN WARRIOR
# LIFE REWARDED

*Ultimately, we shall spend eternity with God
in the place He has prepared for us.
And part of the exciting anticipation is His promise
to reward His servants for a job well done.*
Charles R. Swindoll

During the month of July 2008, there was another miracle. After much prayer and planning, Vera was strong enough to return to Indonesia and West Sumatra once more. She and Rehana brought a group from various church denominations in the US interested in visiting West Sumatra. While in the Bukittinggi area, the group witnessed the baptism of twenty-three new believers.

Vera arrived home safely in August. I saw her face beamed, having witnessed rapid growing faith of the spiritual children. At that time, God already blessed my wife with an additional one and a half years *beyond* life expectancy. She had received more grace from God as He extended her days for His purpose in her.

I felt very happy and grateful, that through the years of my calling, our efforts were not in vain. Even though we sometimes felt so exhausted and frustrated facing all kinds of obstacles… We overcame because God spoke to us from the Word,

"Come to me, all you who are weary and burdened,
and I will give you rest. Take my yoke upon you,
and learn from me, for I am gentle and humble in heart,
and you will find rest for your souls.
For my yoke is easy and my burden is light."
Matthew 11:28-30 NIV

We remain grateful to have been included in His work until surrendering to Him on the last day. None of our efforts in following His commands went wasted, although while doing this work, many tears have spilled from us.

In this case, I called out asking God for help, and each time I remembered His message in Ephesians…

"For it is by grace you have been saved, through faith—
and this not from yourselves, it is the gift of God—not by works,
so that no one can boast. For we are God's workmanship,
created in Christ Jesus to do good works,
which God prepared in advance for us to do."
Ephesians 2:8-10 NIV

I will always give thanks to God for all His answers to my prayers. He saved me and forgave my sins with the promise of eternal life. I am very thankful; God gave me opportunity to obey His commands. *My time is in His hands.* During the remainder of days granted me, it is my prayer, that God allows me to complete His plan and purpose.

To those who remained and endured with me through the years, whether in Indonesia or in America, I express gratitude. All, who during this portion of my life, have faithfully stood and survived as we went together in serving others, I am grateful that we walked side-by-side, holding hands as one.

We reached out with God's love, especially to the Minang people who are forever close to my heart. Together we went with the vision given to me by God. Now we can jointly also declare to Him just like Jabez in his prayer:

"Oh, that you would bless me and enlarge my territory!"
1 Chronicles 4:10 NIV

During 2009, God allowed me to finish writing this book. The story of what the unique life of an adventurous person has been like for eighty-two years. It is the account of my life journey, as God's shadow hovered above and His love encircled me.

For many years, I walked this road, and lived through countless devastating and heart-breaking experiences that shook me. Sometimes those particular portions of my life, especially from earlier years, were like an avalanche sliding down a hill losing its foundation. I also experienced crushing disappointments in and from my past, but all these fragments of suffering brought me to a straight path and discovery of Truth.

News reached us on September 30, 2009 of an earthquake that struck Padang with a measure of 7.6 on the Richter scale. The land of Minangkabau, its foundation shaken; resulted with heavy damage in the city and nearby areas.

Since our focus for outreach had been the Minang since 1994, I immediately notified US ministry supporters. Our co-workers kept us updated about most pressing needs of the people and what way to best directly assist them.

I prayed for all my close relatives still living there. I was thinking about my family in Maninjau, my nephew Alizar (Cha), his wife Ati, their children and grandchildren; hoping they were all safe. I also thought about our co-workers and those to whom I ministered. When this happened, I was only able to pray that God would provide for all their needs.

When I was first aware of the terrible situation, it reminded me of the assurance and promises from God. I have had these for a safe haven, especially during times of terrifying shocks in my own life. No matter how traumatic the destruction surrounding us has been, God always remains in control. I believe this because God ensured that He would never leave or forsake us. Therefore, I was certain that despite the unnerving shaking of Ranah Minang, God's presence remained there among the people.

At this point, and in closing of my story, I would like to express gratitude to God because *how uniquely intent He had been in achieving His purpose for my life*. He allowed me time for the daring adventures of youth, and teaching me through the years His wisdom. For this, I am thankful because along with it, He also gave me His grace to love others, especially during my latter seasons.

God also gave me many years of a wonderful marriage in the second half of my life. In this relationship, the Lord has been our solid Ark, our *Bahtera*. He has been the Compass to refuge and Anchor of security for Vera and me for forty-one years thus far.

I am very thankful to God that He gave me my wife as *my helpmate*, to stay by my side, the companion of my life. As Adam voiced when he received Eve, *"You are bone of my bones"* (Genesis 2:23 NIV) that too, is the expression from deep within my heart and token of love for Vera, *"my Schatje"* through our many years.

God gave us the gift of three beautiful children, an "early reward" for me during this lifetime. Indeed, He saw every part of my life, even if I did not. The Lord then gave to me, this treasured family for more than forty years already. Our daughter Rehana Soetidja and her husband Tyson Caparino Rodriguez, our son Sutan Ibrahim Karim Amrullah, and our youngest daughter Siti Hindun and husband Gerardo Villarreal.

God also gave Vera and I, the prized *"pearls of the Minang house,"* the gift of two granddaughters, our very sweet Ariani Eliese and Anaya Jolie (who call us *Babo* --"Nambo" i.e. grandfather in the Minang language and *Oma* for grandmother). They are all the greatest blessings of my entire lifespan.

Readers, who have walked with me through these pages, already know how my parents loved and educated me. Therefore, there is no reason for me to voice that I did not receive any affection during childhood. I feel that my parents have taught me, as is stated in God's Word with advice from King Solomon. From early childhood, they instilled within me, to have devotion and reverence for God. This they did through their example of love for me...

> Train a child in the way he should go,
> And when he is old he will not turn from it.
> Proverbs 22:6 NIV

I am very impressed with the instruction from King Solomon, which has been a message and guideline for me. Although all my children are grown up, as a parent and grandparent, I trust that in continuing their own life journey, they too come to rely only on the Lord; always remembering that I showed them the examples from my childhood and after receiving Christ.

At this point, I also must express regarding the traditions I originated from, "No one can take away my heritage. God gave each person He created a birthright. Who I am as a Minang, and the legacy that is for my children, is forever mine to leave for them."

As final words of this book, and having shared with readers within these pages about the "passages of life" which I voyaged through; some thoughts come to mind. My friend Murad (whom I mentioned throughout my story), before leaving this world, was given enough time by God to meet Him. Murad had told me about his struggle to regain his rights as an Indonesian citizen after his many years of exile on Buru Island. However, since Murad found his way to God (through Christ), we know from scripture that Murad has now already reached and received his complete right of citizenship, to eternally remain in God's Kingdom – Heaven.

It is my hope that everyone having read this memoir can take time to meditate and really-really pray, so that God can show the way and right path to Truth. I myself, after reaching the age of fifty-four found the Lord Jesus Christ. I also really understand in whose hands our time is, and the time that we journeyed through, has already become our past. Yes, time is in God's hands. If death comes, it is according to His will, because He can instantly take life. I know that God already planned every day in our life. That is, from the beginning until the very end of our last breathe on this earth. If we look back, at where we have already been on our journey, then, what we have experienced was God's will for our lives. *Therefore, whatever we have lived through, good or bad is according to God's will in His perfect timing.*

## "He has made everything beautiful in its time..."
### Ecclesiastes 3:11 NIV

I now clearly understand why it was time for me to write this testimony. Through the years, when asked to share my written story, I felt that I had not yet experienced necessary changes needed in my life. I could not yet speak; in addition, I also felt that I had not yet accomplished God's will and purpose for me.

At present however, I have already walked and run a long way through my later years. Now, there is only one thing I desire when I meet my Master later. I look forward to that moment, when I will rejoice to hear His words...

## "Well done good and faithful servant!"
### Matthew 25:21 (NIV)

In finishing, I can say that my life steadily moved forward because the Anchor of my soul, is the Lord Jesus Christ for all eternity. He stayed beside me; His shadow hovered over me, while protecting me through every season.

By openly having shared my story, it is my hope that examples given may become the catalyst to develop spiritual hearts and mobilize many others. All glory and praise be to God, who has called us into an intimate relationship with Him. I believe and I am sure that...

He who dwells in the shelter of the Most High
will rest in the shadow of the Almighty.
I will say to the Lord, "He is my refuge and my fortress,
My God, in whom I trust."
Psalm 91:1-2 (NIV)

*Author's Family*

*Sitting from left to right: Abdul Wadud Karim Amrullah (Pastor Willy Amrull),
Ariani Eliese, Vera Ellen Amrull, Siti Hindun Amrull-Villarreal, and Anaya
Jolie. Standing from left to right: Tyson Caparino-Rodriguez, Rehana Soetidja
Amrull- Rodriguez, Sutan Ibrahim Karim Amrull, and Gerardo Villarreal.*

# LAST WORDS

"The true legacy a man leaves behind
is not in personal possessions
but in the spirit within his family."
Anonymous

While my husband's Indonesian version of his autobiography DARI
SUBUH HINGGA MALAM ("From Dawn Until Dusk") was being
edited by the publisher in Indonesia; he already began translating and
revising that work into English. This was during July of 2011. It was then;
he also began adding bits of information, which for various reasons he did
not include in his Indonesian manuscript.

With release of the Indonesian book in 2011, neither he nor I could
travel to Indonesia. Our eldest daughter Rehana and her husband, Tyson
Rodriquez, went to represent us at the launch event. After their return,
Willy was finally able to hold in his hands a copy of his newly published
book. What joy it was for him, having accomplished this writing and
actually seeing result of his hard work.

During the thirty-one years after his salvation, the subject of when
to write his story would occasionally surface. Each time when pressed to
write, Willy expressed it was not yet time. Then one morning, my husband
suddenly said to me, "When the book is published, my task on earth is
done." He sounded so sure, it shook my heart.

We had already begun working for several months on the new
manuscript. As my husband translated his original Indonesian text into
English, literally *side by side* with him, I began facilitating the English
version.

In December 2011, we faced news that my husband's health was seriously declining and would continue doing so rapidly. Amazingly, Willy had already completed the translated draft for his English manuscript.

On another morning during January 2012, Willy came into our study and stood near me. His expression appeared very serious as he watched me. When I looked up, without hesitation, he quietly spoke words entrusting me with the responsibility of completing the work of his English manuscript. Lastly, he expressed, "You already know. You are in it." Remaining standing where he was, he continued looking at me with sad eyes, no trace of his usual winsome smile evident on his face. Little did I know in those moments what my husband, my beloved Schat and Sumatran Warrior was actually referring to; and what his words would mean to our family two short months later.

At time of this writing, it has been almost four years since my husband went to Heaven's Rest. The fact that thousands have already read his story in Indonesia helps comfort me as I face each new day. In the brokenness of missing and longing for the man I have loved and lived life with for forty-two years, I nevertheless find beautiful joy in knowing that the Indonesian version of his words has been reaching many souls.

For me, at very young age, to have met this gentle loving man, who exuded kindness and vibrant youthful energy like gushing waters; was indeed the greatest privilege. From that day so long ago, he became my Endless Love.

Today, I live in the full realization of why God allowed it. Having experienced the countless days and nights, alongside the man, first introduced to me as "Amrull," and who then became "*Schat*" (my love) to me, I find it difficult to refer to him as "Abdul Wadud Karim Amrullah" or even "Willy Amrull." To me, he has been so indescribably much more.

Above all, it has been a tremendous honor to be his wife for more than four decades and to live out all the adventurous highs and saddest disappointing lows with him. We have done so with our hands tightly clasped together, and never letting go of the very center of our marriage, Jesus Christ our Lord and Savior. For our family, this memoir is a gift from their father and grandfather, a legacy left to them that they too can pursue and honor.

In the course of those last few weeks through hospice care at home and especially during the final nights, my husband and I, together stepped with each passing moment "through the valley of the shadow of death." We did this *as one* in the same way we faced life, never letting go of each other. With each step taken together through life's passages, we understood our path would eventually reach the place where one of us would ultimately step into eternity first and the presence of our God.

In those quiet nights sitting by his bedside, yet still walking with my beloved husband through the valley, we both knew that at one point we would have to release each other and continue walking separately – but would do so always joined with God, whom we have loved deeply and obediently followed. During the early part of his last hours, I knew I must be brave enough to release my Beloved from what was here on earth, to step into the presence of Almighty God.

Today, because of the coming resurrection and its promise, I can continue this journey until my days on earth are also finished. How eagerly I look forward to the moment when I see my Soul Mate, my SUMATRAN WARRIOR again, reunited with him and stand before God's Holy Throne.

My husband's spirit was to give of himself by freely bestowing compassion and time to the people he loved much because of the grace, mercy and love, which God had shown him.

Because of Willy's own intimate relationship with his Lord, he never sought sensationalism or fame, but simply desired one thing. He only hoped to reach and touch the Minangkabau people with God's purest love and Truth. My SUMATRAN WARRIOR was *a true leader who led with his heart* – no matter what the price.

My prayer is that after glimpsing into the life of this precious man, who loved others deeply with the love of Christ, you too may be inspired to do the same. In returning to West Sumatra to be with his people, even if for a short time, he never brought grandiose ideas. He never sought recognition about his life or identity. He simply went, desiring for the Minangkabau of West Sumatra to set aside all earthly hindrances, to discover an intimately personal relationship with God through Christ, and truly be the Minangkabau (*Winning People*) triumphant in fullest victory.

May your having read this memoir of the SUMATRAN WARRIOR lead you also to love and reach out; especially to those who so often seem staunch and furthest away. As they await your coming, go in God's peace, strength, and above all His LOVE.

Vera Ellen Amrull                                        January 2016

## A HERO IS...

Committed to excellence ~ no matter what the price
Dreams beautiful dreams ~ than goes for it
Does what he must do
Is decisive ~ even though they know there's a real risk
Is determined ~ Heroes have critics –
"A HERO, BE ONE, FIND ONE"

Robert Schuller

# LIFE JOURNEY GLIMPSES

## PHOTO COLLECTION

*Author's Father, Dr. H. Karim Amrullah ~ Young Minangkabau Leader*

*Dr. H. Karim Amrullah at later age during Japanese occupation of Indonesia*

*Author (2ⁿᵈ left) after arrival new beginnings in America*

*Author – "Willy Amrull" changed his name with friends
as farm workers in Penryn, California – 1950*

*Author (2ⁿᵈ from right) made lifelong friendships extending through the years*

*Author (left) with IMI organizers Al Roza (middle) and Albert van den Berg (right)*

*Willy and Vera before going to Indonesia in 1977*

*Refereeing Soccer Games – favorite sport*

*Vera with Rehana and Sutan ~ living in Bali – 1979*

*Family Christmas outing at Bali Beach Hotel 1979*

*Always love for a game of Tennis in Bali – 1979*

*Introduction as Bali Branch Manager by Pacto Tours and*
*Travel with owner Dr. Hasyim Ning – 1977*

*"Willy Amrullah" at Orient East Travel Seminar in Canada*

*Willy with Hermand Jonas "Hermie" close friend, they began life together in US*

*Willy and Vera with members of the first Discipleship*
*teaching team in Padang, West Sumatra –1996*

*Teaching in West Sumatra villages – Author (1ˢᵗ right) 1996*

*Visiting author's family in Sungai Batang village and birth place – 1996*

*A panoramic view of Danau (Lake) Maninjau where as a young boy*
*"Wadud" climbed the sloping hillsides with his childhood friends*

*The Sungai Batang village rice field where "Wadud" and
young friends played soccer before planting of ground*

*Pastor Willy Amrull preparing Discipleship lessons at Batang
Lembang house in Padang, West Sumatra – 1996*

*Pastor Willy Amrull with the ministry's first SETIA Seminary graduates. His last trip to his beloved West Sumatra in 2007*

*Pastor Willy his wife Vera and daughter Rehana with Ministry Team 2007*

*Re-united with "youth days" best friend Murad*
*Aidit in Menteng, Indonesia – 2006*

*Savoring the moment with Vera – always lots of love and laughter together – 2008*

*Author A.W.K. Amrullah (Pastor Willy Amrull) in his beloved
place of birth – "Ranah Minang" West Sumatra, Indonesia*

It is our profound hope that you have enjoyed reading the courageous life journey detailed within these pages.

If reading *SUMATRAN WARRIOR* has inspired or encouraged you, and would like to share your thoughts with us, please e-mail to: sumatranwarrior@gmail.com

We will attempt replying to your communication soonest.